Ess

Essential Firepower

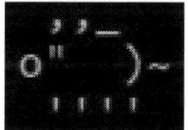

Alex Tatistcheff

Essential Firepower   Copyright © 2019 by Alex Tatistcheff

First published in May 2019

Technical Reviewers:
Michael Culp
Steve Franzluebbers
John Gay
Marshall Lewis
Thomas Marsh
Paritala Ravikant Rao

Cover Design:
Anna Tatistcheff

All rights reserved. No part of this work may be reproduced or transmitted by any means or in any form, electronic or mechanical, including photocopying, recording, or by information storage or retrieval system, carrier pigeon or sled dog or any other method without the prior written permission of the copyright holder.

This book is 100% based on my experience in using, teaching and supporting Snort, Sourcefire 3D and Firepower deployments over the past 14 years. The opinions expressed here are just that – opinions. They may work for you and they may not. There is no representation or warranty with regard to completeness, suitability for any particular purpose or accuracy. In short, there are plenty of errors and omissions in this book. The steps and strategies depicted here are not applicable or suitable for every situation.

Written on a Samsung Chromebook Plus,and a $50 Dell 1090 PC from Goodwill running Ubuntu 18 with LibreOffice Writer.

Cover illustration licensed through DvargShop via CreativeMarket.com

ISBN: 9781798502044

Acknowledgements

This is the third Firepower book I've contributed to and the first one I've written completely by myelf. Creating a book is a significant task and not one that can be accomplished in a vacuum. I want to thank my wife Shelly for allowing me to stay sequestered in my office for hours without a single complaint. Thanks to all the other Sourcefire and Cisco consultants, instructors and engineers who have always been ready and willing to share their experiences or expertise. To my technical reviewers who agreed to work on the book just for a little credit and a free copy. To Todd Lammle who I've worked together with on two other books.   I met him while I was teaching a Sourcefire class in 2013 and he had a wild idea that we should write a book. That was the SSFIPS Study Guide, I never would have started down this path if it weren't for him. And finally, thanks to God and my Lord Jesus Christ without whom I literally couldn't do anything.

About the Author

Alex Tatistcheff was introduced to the Sourcefire 3D System as an Information Security Consultant for Idaho Power Company in 2005. For three years he learned what it's like to configure and operate Sourcefire's Snort-based Next Generation Intrusion Protection System (NGIPS). In 2008 he was hired by Sourcefire, where he worked as a Sr. Security Instructor and Professional Services Consultant until the Cisco acquisition in October, 2013. He is currently a Security Technical Leader for Cisco's Security Services organization.

Alex is also a co-author of two books: "*SSFIPS Securing Cisco Networks with Sourcefire Intrusion Prevention System Study Guide: Exam 500-285*" by Sybex and "*Cisco Firepower 6.x with Firepower Threat Defense*" by Amazon.

Brief Contents

Chapter 1 - Introduction..1

Chapter 2 - Definitions and Versions..9

Chapter 3 - FMC Configuration..17

Chapter 4 - Updates, Tasks, Platform Settings.........................28

Chapter 5 - System Health..45

Chapter 6 - Objects..54

Chapter 7 - Network Discovery Policy..68

Chapter 8 - Intrusion Policy..82

Chapter 9 - Network Analysis Policy...116

Chapter 10 - Malware & File Policy..133

Chapter 11 - Prefilter Policy..147

Chapter 12 - SSL and Identity Policy...153

Chapter 13 - DNS Policy...161

Chapter 14 - Access Control Policy...170

Chapter 15 - Miscellaneous Tips and Tricks............................192

Appendix A - Preprocessor Generator IDs...............................224

Appendix B - Talos Intrusion Policy Criteria...........................227

Appendix C - Security Intelligence Categories..........................228

Contents

Chapter 1 - Introduction 1

Pontification 1
How To Use This Book 2
        BP - This is a specific recommendation 2
Policy Progression 3
What is a "Best Practice"? 4
Design Principles 5
Fresh Security is Best 7
Aren't New Rules Risky? 7

Chapter 2 - Definitions and Versions 9

Definitions 9
Software Version Considerations 12
        BP1 - Don't get too far behind new Firepower releases 14
        BP2 - Read the release notes! 14
Software Bugs 15
        BP3 - Be careful deploying "dot zero" software versions 16

Chapter 3 - FMC Configuration 17

Audit Logging 17
        BP4 - Send your audit log to an external log host 18
Login Banner 18
        BP5 - Configure an FMC login banner 19
Database 19
    Circular Logging 20
    It's all about the hardware 20
    Connection Events 22
        BP6 - Review your FMC database settings 23

Email Notification..23
  BP7 - Configure an SMTP mail relay...................................23
Time Synchronization...23
  BP8 - Configure FMC NTP time sync....................................24
Alerts..24
  BP9 - Configure Alert destinations..25
Domains..25
  BP10 - Think long and hard before you create leaf domains, then think again..27

Chapter 4 - Updates, Tasks, Platform Settings.........................28

Updates..28
 The Snort Rule Update (SRU)..29
  BP11 - Configure daily SRU updates....................................31
 Geolocation Updates..31
  BP12 - Configure weekly geolocation updates...................32
 Vulnerability Database...32
  BP13 - Schedule regular VDB updates................................33
 Maintenance Updates/Patches..33
  BP14 - Schedule regular download of updates/patches.......33
Tasks..33
 Software Downloads..34
 Backups...35
  BP15 - Perform regular backups..37
  BP16 - Backup to a remote storage device........................37
Platform Settings...38
  BP17 - Deploy Platform Settings policy..............................39
 Time Synchronization..39
  BP18 - Have a good time synchronization strategy............42
 Banner..42
  BP19 - Configure a device login banner.............................43
 Other Settings...43
  BP20 - Evaluate other Platform Settings as needed...........44

Chapter 5 - System Health..45

Health Overview..45
  BP21 - Your health status should normally be green!.........47

Health Policy..47
    CPU Usage..48
        BP22 - Don't enable the CPU Health alert, it's disabled for a reason..49
    Interface Status...49
        BP23 - Disable the Interface Status health alert unless your system is passive..51
Blacklist...51
        BP24 - Health Blacklist is a good way to manage temporary health issues...53

Chapter 6 - Objects..54

Network..54
        BP25 - Ensure you have network objects created that contain your internal "protected" address space...................55
        BP26 - Create network objects containing any public address space you own that will be visible to your devices. 55
Interface...55
        BP27 - Give some thought to your Interface Security Zones and assign interfaces as appropriate.................................56
Variable Sets..56
        BP28 - Assign your internal address space and any public IP space you own to the $HOME_NET variable.....................61
        BP29 - leave the $EXTERNAL_NET variable at it's default value of "any"...61
Security Intelligence..63
    Talos Feeds..63
        BP30 - Consider shortening the default Security Intelligence feed update interval..65
    Custom SI Feeds...65
        BP31 - Don't forget to add your own custom Security Intelligence feeds..67

Chapter 7 - Network Discovery Policy...................................68

Discovery Networks..68
        BP32 - Configure Network Discovery to create host records for your protected networks...70
Users...70

Advanced Settings..71
    Event Logging Settings...72
        BP33 - Disable noisy Network Discovery events................76
    Indications of Compromise...76
        BP34 - consider tuning Indications of Compromise to reduce false positive IOCs...81

Chapter 8 - Intrusion Policy..82

Policy Information...82
        BP35 – Make your policy Description descriptive...............83
    Drop when inline...83
        BP36 - Upon initial deployment of an inline or routed device, leave the "Drop when inline" checkbox unchecked............83
        BP37 - Don't deploy Intrusion policies with "Drop when inline" enabled on passive devices......................................85
    Commit and Discard...85
        BP38 - When you edit an Intrusion policy, whether you make changes or not, always click either the Commit Changes or Discard Changes button when you are finished..................86
Policy Layers..86
    How Layers Work..87
    Danger Will Robinson - Danger!..90
        BP39 - Avoid using Shared Layers in your Intrusion policy - you'll thank me later...91
Base Policies..91
        BP40 - Consider a hierarchical policy model if you have multiple Intrusion policies..93
Rule Set Selection...93
        BP41 - Start with the Balanced Security and Connectivity Intrusion policy..95
Intrusion Rules...95
    Rule Layers..96
    Searching Rules..99
    The Generator ID (GID)...102
    The Snort ID (SID)...103
    Changing Rule States..105
    Other Rule Properties..106
        BP42 - Never suppress a rule that is set to Drop and Generate in the Intrusion policy......................................107

Firepower Recommended Rules..107
    BP43 - If you don't have good host data, don't use Firepower Recommendations..108
    BP44 - If you do run Firepower Recommendations, schedule a task to update recommendations periodically................109
    BP45 - If you use Firepower Recommendations, consider disabling preprocessor rules (GID 100 and higher)..........110
Finding Preprocessor Events..110
Enabling Firepower Recommendations....................................110
Modifying, Updating or Removing Recommendations................112
A Final Word on Recommendations..112
    BP46 - The Balanced Security and Connectivity rule set from Talos provides a great balance of security and performance, it is probably all you need..113
Advanced Settings..113
    BP47 - Leave the Sensitive Data Detection setting disabled. 114
    BP48 - Don't be afraid to disable the Global Rule Threshold. 115

Chapter 9 - Network Analysis Policy..................................116

History..116
Finding It...117
Pre What?..119
    BP49 - When editing the Network Analysis policy, if you don't know what a setting is for - leave it alone!..............120
Preprocessor Run-Down..120
    Inline Mode...121
        BP50 - Enable NAP Inline Mode for inline type deployments 122
    HTTP Configuration...122
        BP51 - HTTP preprocessor settings can have a significant performance impact don't change them without clear justification...124
    SCADA Preprocessors..124
        BP52 - If you know what SCADA means then consider the SCADA preprocessors, if you don't, leave them disabled..125
    Inline Normalization..125
        BP53 - If your devices are inline then use inline policy

settings..126
　Pre-ack and Post-ack..127
　IP Defragmentation and TCP Stream.......................................129
　Portscan Detection..130
　　　BP54 - Leave the Portscan preprocessor disabled............132

Chapter 10 - Malware & File Policy.....................................133

Overview..133
Advanced Settings..135
　　　BP55 - You can't override the Threat Grid malicious threat score in Malware & File policy...137
　　　BP56 - Consider your archive file inspection settings in the Malware & FIle policy..137
Malware & File Rule Options...137
　Rule Action...138
　Blocking Files..139
　Uploading Files to Threat Grid..140
　　140
　　　BP57 - Ensure your device can communicate to Threat Grid if using file Dynamic Analysis...141
　Store Files...141
　　　BP58 - Consider the "why" when storing files in the Malware & File policy, avoid storing Unknown file types unless you have a good reason..142
　File Types and Categories..142
　　　BP59 - Understand the possible privacy ramifications of Dynamic Analysis for document type files........................143

Chapter 11 - Prefilter Policy...147

The Default Prefilter Policy..147
Customizing the Prefilter Policy...148
　　　BP60 - Don't use Prefilter Fastpath rules for tiny flows....151

Chapter 12 - SSL and Identity Policy..................................153

SSL Policy..153
　　　BP61 - SSL decryption is fraught with peril, proceed only if you have a clear business need..155

Identity Policy......158
Authoritative Users......158
 BP62 - Identity policy requires coordination/setup of external authentication mechanisms, make sure you understand them if this is a requirement......160

Chapter 13 - DNS Policy......161

Overview......161
 BP63 - use the DNS Security Intelligence drop actions only on devices which can actually drop......164
To Sinkhole or Not to Sinkhole......164
Enter the DNS Sinkhole!......167
 BP64 - Try out the sinkhole, you may like it......169

Chapter 14 - Access Control Policy......170

Overview......171
Parent/Child Policies......172
 BP65 - Consider using a Parent/Master Access Control policy, especially for Security Intelligence and Advanced settings......175
Security Intelligence Settings......176
 BP66 - Use the Block action for enabled Security Intelligence categories when inline......179
 BP67 - Use the Monitor-only action for Security Intelligence when in passive mode......179
Logging......179
Advanced Settings......181
 Network Analysis and Intrusion Policies......181
  BP68 - Ensure your Default Network Analysis Policy setting matches your Intrusion policy......182
 Intelligent Application Bypass Settings......182
  BP69 - Consider Intelligent Application Bypass to automatically bypass large flows......186
Rules......186
 Rules and Hierarchy......187
 Rules and Actions......189
  BP70 - Don't forget to enable logging on any Block rules. 190

Chapter 15 - Miscellaneous Tips and Tricks............................192

    Moving from IDS to IPS Mode...193
    Tap Mode..198
    High Volume Event Logging..199
        Versions Prior to 6.3..202
        Version 6.3 and Later..203
    Trust/Fastpath/Bypass..205
    Admin Preferences..207
    Hit Counts...209
    Reduce Annoying Pop-up Notifications...215
    Minimizing Network Impact...217
        Intelligent Application Bypass (IAB).......................................217
        Automatic Application Bypass (AAB).....................................217
        Packet Performance Monitoring (PPM)..................................219
        Snort Busy/Down..222
        Take Aways...223

Appendix A - Preprocessor Generator IDs................................224

Appendix B - Talos Intrusion Policy Criteria...........................227

Appendix C - Security Intelligence Categories........................228

Chapter 1 - Introduction

Pontification

My goal in setting out on this project is to write down some of my thoughts regarding what I think is important when it comes to configuring and using Cisco's Firepower product. I have a somewhat unique perspective on the product having used it as a customer back in the Sourcefire days starting in 2005. Then after using the product - the 3D System - for three years I went to work for Sourcefire and for the next five years taught classes on the 3D System, Snort, Rule Writing and FireAMP (the endpoint malware product). After Sourcefire's acquisition by Cisco Systems I moved into the Advanced Services organization working with customers in a post sale role as a Security Consultant, Solution Architect and Technical Leader.

Throughout the years in my various roles I have always prioritized practicality in everything I do. Whether it's teaching classes or helping customers set up their system for the first time, I've always placed a priority on what works today and also what is maintainable down the road.

If you talk with me very long on the subject of network security you'll find that one of my guiding principles is "complexity is the enemy of security." I believe that network communications are complex enough by themselves. Throw in the random attacker or the latest malware threat and things can get interesting very fast. What you don't want is a security solution that is so complex you never quite know if you've gotten it right.

One thing the Sourcefire 3D System or Firepower has never been accused of is being overly simplified. In fact, just the opposite is true. We like to say there are a lot of knobs in this system and most people should probably leave the majority of these knobs alone!

How To Use This Book

I did not set out to create the definitive Firepower Bible with every setting and detail you could imagine. You will also not find multiple designs for high-availability, clustering or various network topologies. It's important to understand that the focus of this book is on the configuration of Firepower, not system/network design. I mention this because Firepower itself is positioned as both a network and a security device. If desired, customers can use it as simply a layer 3/layer 4 firewall and enable none of the "threat" features. Conversely, you can insert it into your network as an inline or passive security device and perform no networking functions at all. This book will be focused much more on Firepower's security or threat features and not so much on networking.

The goal is for you to be able to move through the configuration of your system as you progress through the book. A major challenge with Firepower is knowing which settings are important and which ones can be left alone. By following the practices recommended here you should be able to hit the high points or the "low hanging fruit" and give your system a good check-up. Of course, if your Firepower system is new, you can also use this book as a guide through the initial configuration of your policies and settings.

To make it as easy as possible to pull out the key points you'll see the letters "BP" (Best Practice) indented and shaded with a short description of my recommendation. These will be scattered throughout the book and will also appear in the Table of Contents.

They look like this:

> |BP - This is a specific recommendation.

If there is a menu item or a screen element you can click on, it will be shown in **bold print**. This is how the Firepower online help is written as well. Hopefully this will make navigating to that item easier.

I will move through the various configurations and policies and highlight some of the settings or design principles that I consider to be most important. To be sure, I'm not the sole authority on Firepower. There are some very smart folks at Cisco who know much more about the internal workings and configurations of the system than I do. However, like the Oracle in The Matrix, I'd like to think I know – enough.

Policy Progression

The chapters in this book will move through the Firepower settings and policies in a logical progression. This is because many of the policies build on, use or refer to other policies and settings.

The "mother of all policies" is the Access Control policy, it sits at the center as the central traffic cop bringing other policies and objects into play. Access Control policy is what I would call, the last piece of the puzzle. If you try and start with this policy you'll find yourself constantly stopping to go and create or configure the other policies and objects it depends on. That is why it is one of the last chapters in this book. Once all the other pieces are in place we can finally move to Access Control.

Of course, you can read the book in any order you like. However, especially if you are configuring a new system, you will find that following the chapters in order will work the best.

The diagram below shows how some of these policies are related.

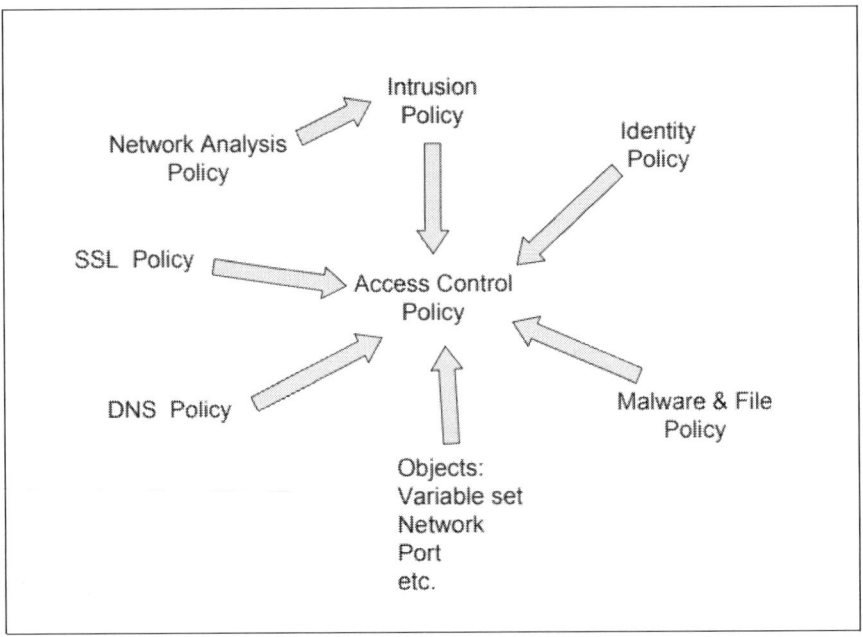

As the chapters progress we will move from the outside of the diagram to the inside, culminating at Access Control policy.

What is a "Best Practice"?

The term Best Practice means different things to different people. Here is what I think when I hear this term. If you start with a blank slate or in our case a Firepower system with default settings, there are certain policy and configuration changes that most deployments would benefit from. When I use the term Best Practices here I'm referring to configuring the system in such a way that you will achieve a good balance of connectivity and security which is appropriate for most organizations.

Think of it like the classic 80/20 rule or the Pareto principle. The way it applies here is that once you expend a certain amount of effort you are 80% of the way towards the ultimately tuned NGFW system. At this point, you can either call it good and spend your time on other pursuits or you can continue pushing past the 80% mark. The downside is that your return on investment will drop rapidly as you tweak the more esoteric detection settings.

This book is designed to get you to that 80% mark. Following the

Pareto principle, I could continue with additional thoughts and advice on configuration but the size of the book would balloon several times and the material would not be appropriate for most readers.

Finally, this is not a one-size-fits-all book. You should *consider* the practices and advice you read here but if it doesn't line up with your goals, policies or priorities then feel free to make different choices. Best practices are somewhat subjective, there are some that everyone would agree on but they are still somebody's opinion.

I wrote this book because of the constant requests I've seen over the years for a best practice guide for Firepower. These best practices are mine and mine alone. No one else should get the blame for any of my recommendations. That being said, I do not have a corner on the market. I want to know if there is something not quite right with some of my recommendations. To that end, I have created an email account just for feedback. Amazon reviews are fine and I welcome them. However, if you have a specific bone to pick or just want to share something you think I've overlooked please use the email below for your feedback. If it's a really good suggestion I may give you a credit in the next edition! (Unless nobody but my family buys this book)

Send feedback to: **firepower@pobox.com**

The information I have to share also does not apply only to a particular version of Firepower. While it's true that there are some feature differences between the various major releases, this information will apply equally to any of the Firepower versions of the past few years - say version 6.1 or later. If a particular feature is mentioned with a specific software requirement this will be noted.

Design Principles

As I mentioned, the focus of this book is not on system design. The assumption is that you already have a design and possibly the system is already in production - or at least on its way there. However, just a quick word to start off on designing a good Firepower system. If complexity really is the enemy of security, then my advice is to go with a design that has been proven to be effective and reliable. In computer networking we like to go with the fast, new, sexy design with the multi-gigabit links, cross connected, clustered, highly available, scalable, add in all your own adjectives. Surely there is nothing wrong with that. However, remember the knobs I discussed earlier? The Next Generation Firewall (NGFW) is a pretty complex beast on its own, adding additional layers of "coolness" can also add to the system complexity.

Here's a quick example. When designing a redundant system with Firepower there are several options from least to most complex.

- Stand-alone devices with transparent inline sets
- High Availability (HA) pair in active/passive mode
- Cluster

Each of these options has its own specific use-cases. For example, if you're dealing with asymmetric routing (packets from the same connection taking different paths) then your only option is the cluster. If your network has dual redundant active/standby paths and you need a firewall solution then High Availability (HA) is a good choice. These networks typically have a primary and standby path and HA is a tried and true solution which provides session state synchronization between the firewalls.

Say you already have the firewall function covered by another device but you need Firepower's inspection and threat defense features. On a redundant path network you can use two stand-alone devices configured with transparent inline sets. There is no routing and no state replication but for NGIPS features this is not as critical as it would be for a firewall. Plus, you can use bypass network modules which will allow packets to pass in case of a device failure.

There's a saying, "if all you have is a hammer, everything looks like a nail." That holds true for these designs as well. A cluster may have been the ideal solution for a previous situation. However, If you don't need the advanced features, you may be better served with a simpler solution. I suppose you could even call this a derivative of Occam's Razor. You may need to Google that but it generally follows the principle of the simplest solution is probably the right one. Make sure you're implementing a design that makes sense both now and in the future.

Fresh Security is Best

One of the primary advantages of Firepower are the resources and ecosystem available from Cisco and especially Talos. If you're not familiar with Talos this is Cisco's security research division. Talos consists of hundreds of security professionals whose only job is research, rule writing, malware disassembly, etc. Add to this the huge amount of telemetry which Cisco's worldwide sensors provide and you have a tremendous amount of security intelligence available.

This intelligence comes to Firepower in the form of Snort rules which are updated at least twice weekly on Tuesdays and Thursdays. There is also Security Intelligence in the form of IP, URL and DNS blacklists. These are updated constantly giving customers protection within minutes of an IP address, URL or host being classified as evil. For protection from malware files, there is the Advanced Malware Protection (AMP) cloud which provides SHA-256 lookups as well as file sandbox analysis, machine learning and other "big data" techniques to identify malicious files.

I know this sounds like a Cisco marketing blog but there is a point. Just like in conventional warfare, in cyberspace the value of intelligence decreases with time. The faster you can act to stop a new threat the better protected you will be. Snort rules are released twice a week, however if you only deploy policies to your devices once a month you may be missing the most effective time window for new rules.

Aren't New Rules Risky?

I run across customers all the time who want to "vet" new Snort rules for some time before allowing them to drop traffic. This stems from the fear that a new rule will come from Talos and start dropping legitimate traffic resulting in business impact.

I get it, your job could be on the line if you administer a security solution that brings down the entire business. However, we know that security is not black or white, there's often no right or wrong answer. We have to balance the risk of a new rule impacting legitimate traffic with the increased security gained by implementing rules when they're still fresh. There will always be tension between security and connectivity. Most of the people reading this book don't have the authority to decide where this balance lies. However, we should be able to understand and articulate the risks associated with these security policies to management.

Here are some considerations I like to share with my customers:

- Consider how likely it is that a new Snort rule will actually cause a business impact. In my experience it is very rare that a Talos Snort rule will drop legitimate business traffic. It's much more likely that a poor system design (Occam's Razor again) will cause an unexpected outage.
- By delaying deployment of new rules you are not taking full advantage of all that Talos intelligence and research - which by-the-way you are paying for!
- The majority of customers I have dealt with configure their systems to automatically download and deploy new Snort rules after they are released. Generally, this is done with an automated daily job that runs late at night. The point is - you are not alone - there is plenty of precedent to deploy new rules as soon as they are available.
- If you still opt to implement a process to set rule states to alert for some period before allowing them to drop traffic that is perfectly fine. As I mentioned, it is a business decision. However, you have to commit the resources to maintain this process. I run across installations all the time where they started out this way but somewhere along the line the process became broken and now it's been 5 months (or more) since Snort rules have been updated.

The bottom line is, do what makes sense in your situation. We have plenty of FUD (Fear Uncertainty and Doubt) in the security industry already. Honestly, it's easy to fall back on that crutch if you're a security professional. The perception is that we have the secret knowledge of encryption protocols, vulnerabilities, exploits, etc. For example, everyone is sure that hackers can see all their online communications and no public WiFi access point is safe. Trying to convince them that SSL/TLS actually works pretty well is the hard part. Movies have trained us that it only takes a security geek about 10 seconds on a keyboard to bypass any encryption or access codes. But we know better. As long as your business leaders have a good understanding of the pros and cons of keeping rules up-to-date then they can provide the appropriate guidance.

Chapter 2 - Definitions and Versions

Definitions

Let's talk about definitions so we're on the same page. This is something I often do when first engaging with customers. Not all the terms are immediately apparent so it's always helpful to set a foundation up front. Here are some terms in no particular order.

Firepower - the overarching name for Cisco's entire family of NGFW/NGIPS products. You really can't just say Firepower without some kind of additional qualification. We used to have different terms for all the various features and technologies in this system but now it's pretty much all Firepower.

ASA with FirePOWER Services - this is an ASA 5500x appliance which is running the venerable ASA software and also has a Firepower module running along side. The Firepower module - also known as the sfr module - uses a SSD for storage and runs in a virtual machine using some of the ASA CPUs. This was Cisco's first major integration of Sourcefire technology into their ASA line. Virtually any ASA 5500x model with the appropriate SSD can run this software.

Firepower Threat Defense (FTD) - this is the "converged" ASA and Firepower code now running in a single operating system. We still have two personalities, the ASA "Lina" code and the Sourcefire "Snort" code but they are much more tightly coupled than in the ASA with FirePOWER Services sfr module. FTD is the future for Cisco's security appliances. It can run on all ASA 5500x platforms (except the 5585x) as well as the new FP2100, FP4100, FP9300 appliances. It also is available in a virtual version that can run on VMware, KVM,

Microsoft Azure, Amazon AWS and probably other places I have missed.

Classic Firepower - while this isn't really an official term I use it to refer to the hardware that Cisco inherited from Sourcefire. This includes the 7000 and 8000 series devices. The FP8350 being the real workhorse of this line. It's a very solid performer with thousands of installations worldwide. It went end-of-sale in June, 2019, but these will be around for several years to come because they (mostly) just work. These devices don't run any of the ASA "Lina" code, they are strictly Snort based. They can be deployed with routed interfaces as a NGFW as well as a NGIPS with inline or passive interfaces. The the vast majority are deployed as inline (bump in the wire) NGIPS appliances.

Appliance - this is a discrete physical or virtual host, it could be a Firepower Management Center, a Firepower 4100, a Firepower VM, or a classic device like an 8350.

Device - this is an appliance that performs NGIPS or NGFW inspection. While all devices are appliances not all appliances are devices. These used to be called sensors back in the Sourcefire days prior to version 5 of the 3D System. I guess once they became more than just inline or passive sensors and could have firewall/router roles the term device seemed more appropriate.

Chassis - while I don't use this term much on its own, devices like the FP4100 and FP9300 do have a web interface called the Firepower Chassis Manager. You could say that the 4100 and 9300 appliances are considered chassis which contain security modules. The 4100 contains one security module and the 9300 can host up to three.

Firepower Management Center (FMC) - this is an appliance that serves as the manager for all of your devices. It's basically a big Linux database server on a virtual or Cisco Universal Computing System (UCS) platform. The FMC doesn't do any detection itself, it serves to store and deploy policies to the devices as well as collect events for storage and analysis.

Sensor - technically we don't have sensors anymore in Firepower. These are now called devices.

Firepower eXtensible Operating System (FXOS) - it's a cool name for the operating system that runs on the FP4100 and FP9300 chassis. This is where the FCM lives. This operating system manages the interfaces and logical devices on the chassis. The FP2100 also runs FXOS but it's read-only and pretty much hidden from the user completely.

Firepower Chassis Manager (FCM) - the chassis manager is a web front-end for FXOS that is specific to the FP4100 and FP9300 devices. This manager is used to manage interface configurations, software images and logical devices. Just between you and me I'm hoping it goes away someday. One more thing to maintain if you ask me.

Logical Device - this is an application instance on a FP4100 or FP9300. Prior to Firepower 6.3 you were limited to a single logical device per 4100 or per module in the 9300. With version 6.3 comes multi-instance so you can have several (FTD) logical devices on a single 4100 or 9300 security module. Logical devices can run the Adaptive Security Appliance (ASA) or Firepower Threat Defense (FTD) software.

Firepower Device Manager (FDM) - also known as, "Sir not appearing in this picture." This is a web-based manager that runs locally and be used to manage a stand-alone Firepower device. It runs on the low to midrange FTD platforms and is designed for onesy twosy installations where there is no FMC. I know nothing about this so it will not be covered at all in this book.

Talos - Talos is the name for Cisco's security research team. It was formed when Cisco's various security teams and the Sourcefire VRT joined forces. Talos provides the security research behind Firepower including creating Security Intelligence feeds and writing Snort rules.

FireSIGHT – this was a marketing term that was inherited from Sourcefire. Initially, it referred to the system's ability to passively detect host data and build a database on the FMC. After the acquisition the meaning was broadened a bit but was always a bit nebulous. It was dropped with the release of version 6.

Sourcefire, Inc. – the company founded by Martin (Marty) Roesch in 2001 to create a commercial security product based on his open source Snort software. Cisco acquired Sourcefire in July, 2013 for $2.7 billion. (It is never spelled with a capital "F")

Inline – for the purpose of this book, inline means a device is deployed in such a way that it can block traffic. Sometimes, I will need to specify whether a device is able to block vs. just trigger alerts. Rather than rattle off the various ways a device can be inserted into traffic flow every time I'm just going to say "inline" when the device is deployed in any of the inline, switched or routed modes.

Software Version Considerations

When you receive your shiny new Firepower appliances they will come with some version of Firepower pre-installed. In a perfect world you can just start using them right away. If you haven't noticed - we live in a less-than-perfect world.

The first thing you have to consider is what will work with what. That is, if you have an FMC running a certain version of Firepower what device versions can it manage? An important principle is that the FMC should be running the same or newer version as the devices is manages. This is universally true although you can sometimes fudge a little with the maintenance release versions if you want to. Another rule of thumb used to be you could manage devices running the current major version and one version back. That is not universal but let's talk more about versions.

Speaking of versions, what do the numbers mean?
When you see a Firepower version like 6.2.3.7 these numbers break down as follows:

- 6 - this is the major version. These change very seldom and moving to the next version here is a major product revision. Some very new and exciting features will come about when this version increments. Oh and with them can come some really nasty bugs.
- 2 - major feature release. This number represents a fairly major feature change. You will see a number of important features bundled into a software version where this number is incremented.
- 3 - feature release. This number represents a less significant feature release. In fact, for some versions this number remains at zero. For example in version 5.x we had

5.0, 5.1, 5.2, 5.3 an finally 5.4 but we never had a 5.x.1.x. Apparently there was no reason to release a version with just a few feature changes.

- 7 - maintenance release. This number is a maintenance release update. These should never contain new features, just bug fixes. Now, from time to time a minor feature has slipped into a maintenance release over the years. But this is the exception rather than the rule. Conventional wisdom dictates that with each maintenance release there SHOULD be fewer bugs than the previous one. However, that is not a universal truth as we've seen maintenance release versions pulled from time to time for introducing regression bugs. However, for the most part you can safely say there are fewer bugs as the maintenance release version increments.

So, when we say that an FMC can manage the same major version and one version previous we're talking about the first two numbers. If the version is:

6.2.x.x

This means an FMC running this software can manage a 6.2 or a 6.1 device. It cannot manage a 6.0 or a 5.4 device.

Now that's important if you buy a new 6.2 FMC and you still have some old 5.4 or (heaven forbid) 6.0 devices on your network. This has come up a lot in the past year or so because of the success and stability of the 5.4 version. It is somewhat like Windows XP, it just works and as a result nobody wanted to upgrade. Well, "nobody" is a bit of an exaggeration but it has definitely been an issue as Firepower versions continue to increment. This sometimes leaves older appliances stuck and their owners in a similar pickle.

When it comes time to refresh hardware, companies have been faced with the requirement to upgrade their 5.4 devices to a minimum of 6.1 if they want to buy some of the new hardware. For example, the Firepower 2100 devices simply will not run any version older than 6.2.1. We know that your FMC has to be the same or newer version as the devices so it also has to be 6.2.1 or higher. But if you have any 5.4 devices left on your network you're stuck. This is because they're too old to be managed by a 6.2.x FMC.

The answer of course is to upgrade the 5.4 devices. However, you end up having to do a stutter-step upgrade. This involves upgrading the FMC to 6.1, then upgrading the devices to 6.1, then upgrading the FMC to 6.2.x. At that point you can bring in your new Firepower 2100 devices and also bring all your devices up to 6.2.x.

The scenario above is just one example but it illustrates a key principle. You have to stay abreast of the new Firepower versions! This software and the entire security industry is moving so fast that you can't afford to fall behind in your upgrades. This doesn't mean you have to be on the bleeding edge but anything less than a yearly upgrade cycle will likely leave you in a difficult spot sooner or later.

Even yearly may not be enough. If you consider that new vulnerabilities in Firepower itself or it's supporting software are discovered from time-to-time you may need to upgrade more often than annually. This is especially true if any of your Firepower devices are on the network edge - directly exposed to the Internet. You can't afford to leave these devices in a vulnerable state if a new vulnerability is discovered.

> |BP1 - Don't get too far behind new Firepower releases.

How do you know what versions will work together? Two words: *release notes*. I know we don't always read the README but in this case the release notes are your best source of truth. They will clearly define what the dependencies are for various versions when it comes to upgrading and managing Firepower devices.

> |BP2 - Read the release notes!

Let me pause for a minute and mention that the discussion above is talking only about the actual Firepower software version. I haven't scratched the surface on other updates like Snort rules, Security Intelligence, Vulnerability Database Updates, geolocation, FXOS, etc. This is just the Firepower software itself! It's literally the software tip of the iceberg. Remember, if this was easy everybody would be doing it. You are a highly skilled security/network professional, you get the big bucks because you know how to deal with these intricacies.

My examples above cover some issues with specific versions and they may not apply to you. For example, the current version and one version prior rule is not set in stone. Newer 6.x versions may remain backwards compatible all the way back to 6.1. However, there are some key principles we can glean from this:

- Stay abreast of major version updates. Don't let yourself fall too far behind. Upgrade yearly at a minimum and that still may not be sufficient.
- When looking to integrate brand new device models consider carefully their minimum software version requirements. If you have gotten too far behind, you may not be able to mix new devices with your existing code version.
- Watch for new features which are important in your environment. These may be drivers to upgrade sooner than your normal cycle.
- At the risk of sounding like a nag - read the release notes! They are your best source of truth when it comes to Firepower version requirements.

Software Bugs

Nobody likes software bugs. However, when you have as much code complexity as found in Firepower, bugs are inevitable. I'm not making excuses for Cisco, we know there were some quality issues with early 6.x versions. Cisco put a lot of effort and resources into finding and fixing bugs - even putting new features on hold in early 2018 for several months while they focused on hardening the existing code. As a result of this, the number of user reported bugs took a pretty big drop. All the statistics on bugs and support cases pointed to the improved state of software quality in Firepower.

My own position on bugs is - don't let bug avoidance dictate your security strategy. If there's a major show-stopper bug in a Firepower version it will be discovered soon after its release. You don't need a "bug scrub" to tell you this. Cisco will either quickly release a maintenance update, a hotfix or will pull the version completely. My advice is - just don't be one of the early adopters - at least not in production. Give the software some time to bake before you roll it out. If it's a major version update you probably want to wait until at least the first or second maintenance release before implementing it in your environment.

> BP3 - Be careful deploying "dot zero" software versions.

Enough about bugs, let's move on to configuration!

Chapter 3 - FMC Configuration

FMC Configuration covers some noteworthy settings on the Firepower Management Center itself. These are not policies that are applied or deployed to devices and these settings don't actually impact the detection of the devices. However, they are important for compliance and logging as well as forwarding alerts and events to external systems. We will just hit some of the "low hanging fruit" settings which are commonly used and that you should probably think about.

Audit Logging

A common requirement for any business system is to keep an audit log of administrative activity. Firepower keeps its own audit log of activities performed by admins on the FMC. However, this log is actually kept on the FMC itself. Audit best practice dictates that this log should be stored somewhere external to the system actually being audited. You will find the configuration to send these events to an external system under **System → Configuration → Audit Log** as shown below.

Essential Firepower

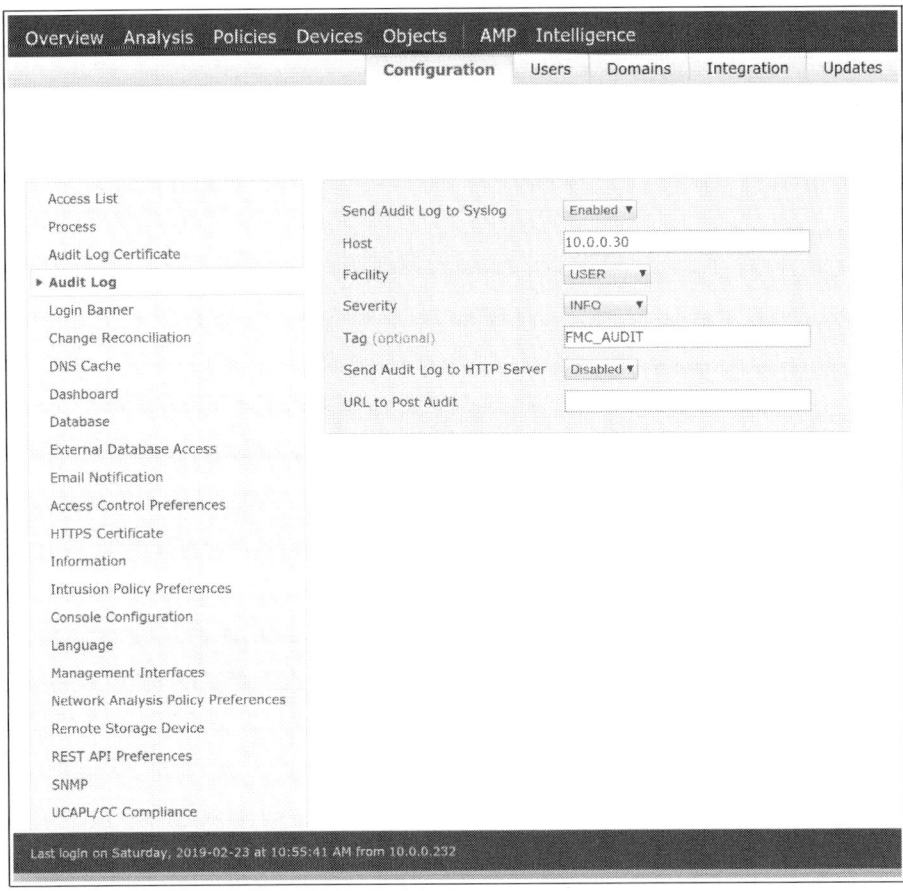

The configuration here is pretty self-explanatory. Configuring a syslog or HTTP audit destination will mirror all the events saved to the FMC Audit log (**System → Monitoring → Audit**) to an external log destination. Selecting the **Facility** and **Severity** only changes the syslog fields in the event, it does not filter or otherwise affect the events that are sent. The **Tag** will allow you to add the specified text to the syslog message making it easier to identify on the log host as an FMC audit log event.

|BP4 - Send your audit log to an external log host.

Login Banner

While we're at the **System → Configuration** page you might also check the **Login Banner**. This is text presented on the web page prior to logging into the FMC. It is also shown upon an initial SSH connection to the FMC management IP. The FMC Login Banner configuration is shown below.

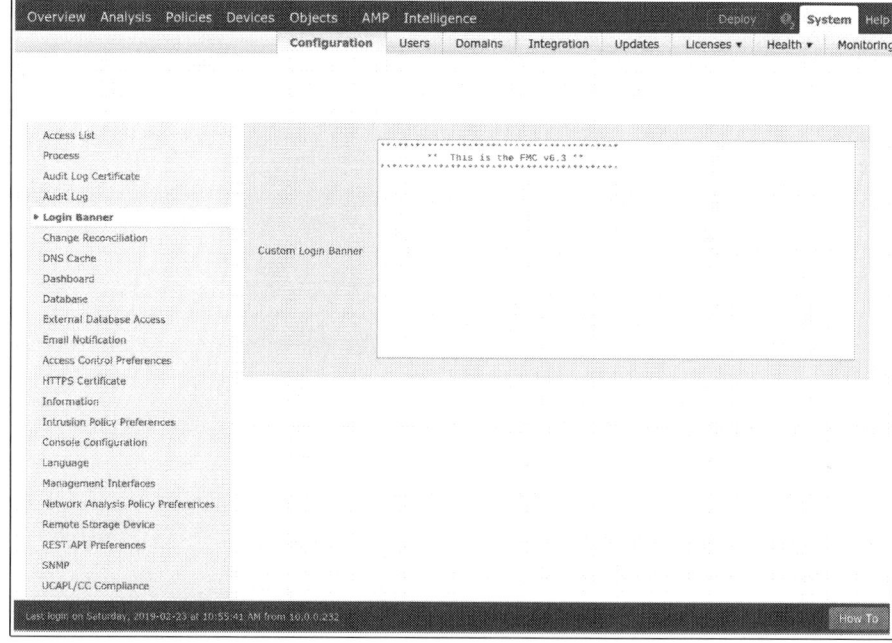

BP5 - Configure an FMC login banner.

Database

The Database settings for the FMC are an area that is often misunderstood yet one that can be quite helpful if configured properly. You'll find it under **System → Configuration → Database** - this page is shown below.

Access List	**Intrusion Event Database**	
Process		
Audit Log Certificate	Supported Platforms	Firepower Management Center
Audit Log	Maximum Intrusion Events	1000000
Login Banner		
Change Reconciliation	**Discovery Event Database**	
DNS Cache	Supported Platforms	Firepower Management Center
Dashboard	Maximum Discovery Events (0 = do not store)	1000000
▶ Database		
External Database Access	**Connection Database**	
Email Notification	Supported Platforms	Firepower Management Center
Access Control Preferences	Maximum Connection Events (0 = do not store)	3000000
HTTPS Certificate		
Information	Maximum Security Intelligence Events	1000000
Intrusion Policy Preferences		
Console Configuration	**Connection Summary Database**	
Language	Supported Platforms	Firepower Management Center
Management Interfaces	Maximum Connection Summaries (0 = do not store)	2000000
Network Analysis Policy Preferences		
Remote Storage Device	**Correlation & White List Event Database**	
REST API Preferences	Supported Platforms	Firepower Management Center
SNMP	Maximum Correlation & White List Events	1000000
UCAPL/CC Compliance		

Circular Logging

The first thing to understand is that the event databases on the FMC use circular logging. That is, they maintain the last n number of events. When the number of events in a database reaches the maximum configured, a chunk of those events is purged to make room for more. The result is that the number of events stays somewhere around the values configured here. In actuality, the FMC allows the database to grow beyond this number slightly before it prunes. The result is that once you've reached the database limit, you can count on having at least the number of events shown here at any given time.

It's all about the hardware

The second key to this puzzle is that the maximum numbers you can configure here vary depending on the FMC model. This is a product of the storage and event processing capability of the particular FMC hardware. This information can be found in the help (**Help → Online**).

While we're on the subject of Help, let me say that the online help included with Firepower is quite good. This legacy goes back to the Sourcefire days and as a user of the system I was always impressed at

3 - FMC Configuration

the completeness and usability of the information provided. This is one product where you would do well to use the help function often and mine as much information as you can there. You'll find that virtually all of the information found in the Configuration Guide can be found in the Online Help as well.

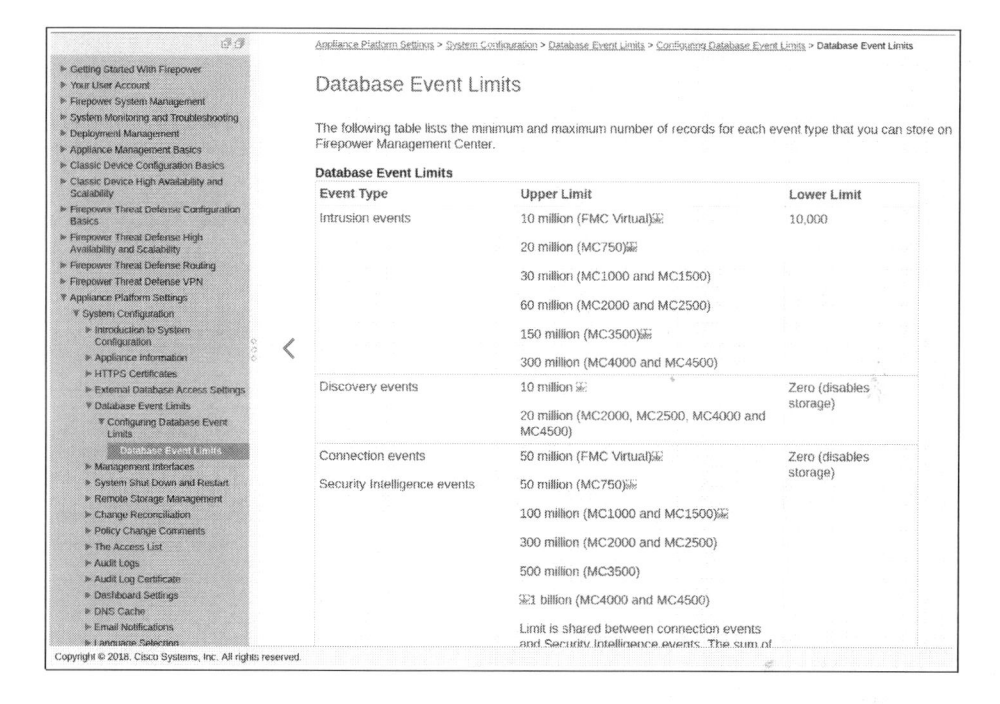

Database Event Limits

The following table lists the minimum and maximum number of records for each event type that you can store on Firepower Management Center.

Database Event Limits

Event Type	Upper Limit	Lower Limit
Intrusion events	10 million (FMC Virtual)	10,000
	20 million (MC750)	
	30 million (MC1000 and MC1500)	
	60 million (MC2000 and MC2500)	
	150 million (MC3500)	
	300 million (MC4000 and MC4500)	
Discovery events	10 million	Zero (disables storage)
	20 million (MC2000, MC2500, MC4000 and MC4500)	
Connection events	50 million (FMC Virtual)	Zero (disables storage)
Security Intelligence events	50 million (MC750)	
	100 million (MC1000 and MC1500)	
	300 million (MC2000 and MC2500)	
	500 million (MC3500)	
	1 billion (MC4000 and MC4500)	

Limit is shared between connection events and Security Intelligence events. The sum of...

In the screenshot above you can see that Intrusion events have a much different upper limit as the model of FMC changes.

Let's take Intrusion events as an example. The default setting regardless of the FMC model is 1 million events. Honestly, that is probably enough for just about anyone regardless of the FMC model. Intrusion events are not something you should normally be seeing thousands of per day. Nevertheless, on a FS4000 or 4500 you can increase this up to 300 million if desired.

That's all fine and good but the thing to keep in mind is that just because you can store 300 million Intrusion events it doesn't mean you can *query* that many events. Trying to load an event view or run a report on that many events is not likely to succeed as the query will timeout before it completes. But if you do want decades of intrusion event history then increasing the storage capacity of this database might be warranted.

Although, I want to be very clear that configuring anything approaching the maximum for this database is almost certainly a bad idea.

Connection Events

The real reason for increasing the size of any database is to provide more history. The place where this comes up the most often is with Connection events. Many times, there is a need or desire to log all the connections passing through your devices. The Connection database, like the Intrusion database, defaults to a pretty low number out of the box. The 1 million connection event default is often only a few hours worth of events on small to medium deployments and may only be a few minutes for a large deployment. Because of this, increasing the size of the connection database is a common practice.

The issue with increasing this database however is that even at the absolute maximum setting of 1 billion events on a FMC 4000/4500 this still may not provide the connection history needed. Factor in the event rate that the FMC is capable of (20,000 events/sec on the largest models) and you run into some real issues trying to keep any decent history for all connections in an enterprise environment. Also remember that a query of several hundred million events will likely timeout, yet in a large environment this may only be a few hours worth of events.

We will discuss options for offloading these high volume events later in this book but for now here are the main things to keep in mind when you are looking at these database numbers:

- Your FMC model has specific limits on how many events it can store - know what these are.
- Pushing a database to its maximum limits is not generally a good idea unless you (and the entire FMC admin staff) clearly understand the query and performance ramifications. Even if you do understand these limitations I still would not recommend exceeding 50% of the max on the Connection database.
- Don't be afraid to bump these limits up if you have to. That FS4500 cost somebody a pretty penny. You don't need to hamstring the system by keeping the original default database limits.

|BP6 - Review your FMC database settings.

Email Notification

Further down on the **System → Configuration** page you will find the **Email Notification** settings. Nearly every customer I've ever worked with has configured this setting to allow the FMC to send email notifications for various events or conditions. Because of that, it should probably be on your short list as well. The settings are self-explanatory and you can even generate a test email to verify your mail relay is happy with FMC's configuration. The configuration dialog is shown below.

Mail Relay Host	
Port Number	
Encryption Method	TLS ▼
From Address	
Use Authentication	✓
Username	
Password	Saved. Click to change.

[Test Mail Server Settings]

|BP7 - Configure an SMTP mail relay.

Time Synchronization

While the default Platform settings will ensure the device time is synchronized with the FMC, you still need to ensure the FMC is using an accurate external time source. You'll find that under **System → Configuration → Time Synchronization**.

Essential Firepower

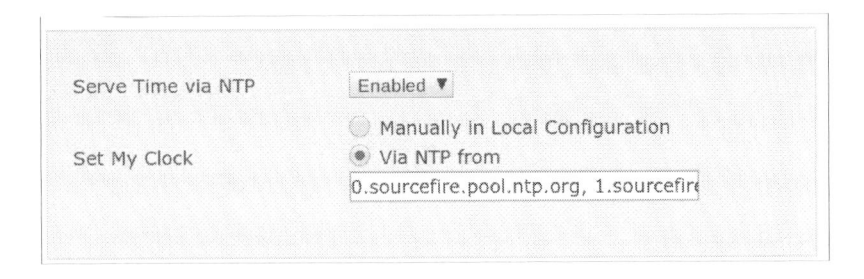

Serve Time via NTP	Enabled ▼
Set My Clock	○ Manually in Local Configuration ● Via NTP from `0.sourcefire.pool.ntp.org, 1.sourcefire`

Simply make sure you have good time server(s) entered here. Of course, if you are using host names instead of IP addresses these must be resolvable by the DNS server(s) you entered for the FMC's management network connection.

|BP8 - Configure FMC NTP time sync.

Alerts

Alerts is a pretty broad term but here I'm referring to pre-configured alert destinations. These are used by policies, impact alerts, health, etc. When you want the FMC to generate an email, SNMP trap or syslog message you will configure the specific alert address or destination here. Say you want all of your intrusion events forwarded to a syslog host. The first thing you'll need is an alert specifying the host and other syslog specific parameters. Then you can configure the system to send intrusion event alerts to that syslog host. It's the same if you want an email sent in response to a Correlation event. The Correlation policy would be configured to use an email alert you had already setup which specified the email address and the from address.

To set up alerts for use by the system go to **Policies → Actions → Alerts**. Add one or more alerts here for use in your various policies. When setting up these alerts my recommendation is to name the alert for the destination not the intended use. For instance if you create an alert to email a notification for a health monitor you might be tempted to name it "Health Notification". However, when you come back later or if someone else sees that notification it makes it difficult to determine who the recipient is. Plus, you might want to send different types of notifications to this same email address. Sending intrusion events to the Health Notification email address doesn't make a lot of sense. Consider alert names like:

- Email SOC
- Email Bob
- Splunk Syslog

These are friendlier and their function is immediately apparent to anyone coming after you. Some example alerts are shown below.

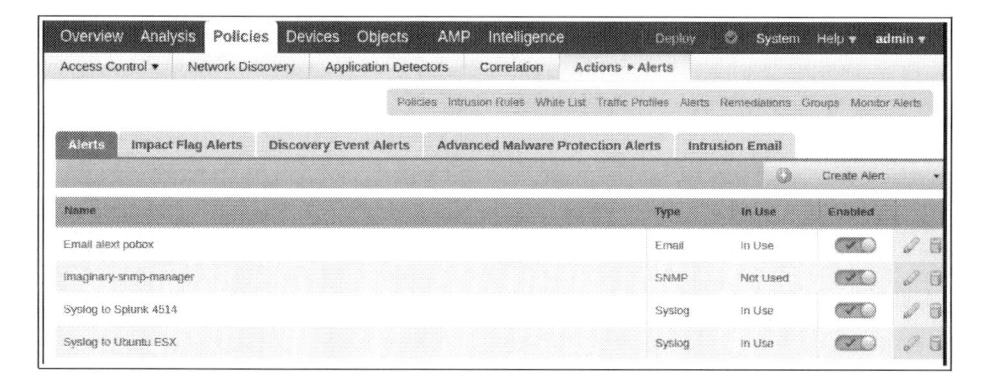

Name	Type	In Use	Enabled
Email alert pobox	Email	In Use	
imaginary-snmp-manager	SNMP	Not Used	
Syslog to Splunk 4514	Syslog	In Use	
Syslog to Ubuntu ESX	Syslog	In Use	

Creating these alerts is pretty self-explanatory. Note that you can only configure one destination email/IP for each alert. Lastly, keep in mind that for an email alert to work you must have a mail relay configured under **System → Configuration**.

|BP9 - Configure Alert destinations.

Domains

The concept of domains is fairly broad in the world of information technology. Microsoft Active Directory has them, there's the Domain Naming System (DNS), Wikipedia defines domains as "a taxonomic subdivision larger than a kingdom." Umm, ok whatever.

In the world of Firepower, management domains are a way to divide up your devices. Why would you want to do that? The main use-case for creating domains is to provide autonomous management of one or more devices.

In a large, diverse organization you may need to split off management of some of your devices. By using domains you can give selected administrators complete control over a subset of the devices registered to the FMC. They can only see their own devices, network map, policies, etc. These admins can't see any information about the other devices registered to the FMC - they can't even tell how many other devices there are.

Domains are ideal if you are a Managed Service Provider (MSP) and you have several different customers. You can give each customer control over their own assets but keep them from seeing or knowing about any of your other customers.

Firepower domains offer specific benefits for those who need them, but if you don't need these specific benefits - AVOID THEM. Or to be more accurate, be very, very sure you need them before you go down this path. I say this because undoing a domain configuration can be quite messy. Imagine every molecule in your body exploding at the speed of light - I'm talking bad. If you really need this kind of segmentation then go right ahead but realize that your objects, policies, in fact all of your configurations will likely become more difficult. If you still want to proceed then navigate to **System → Domains** as shown below and proceed.

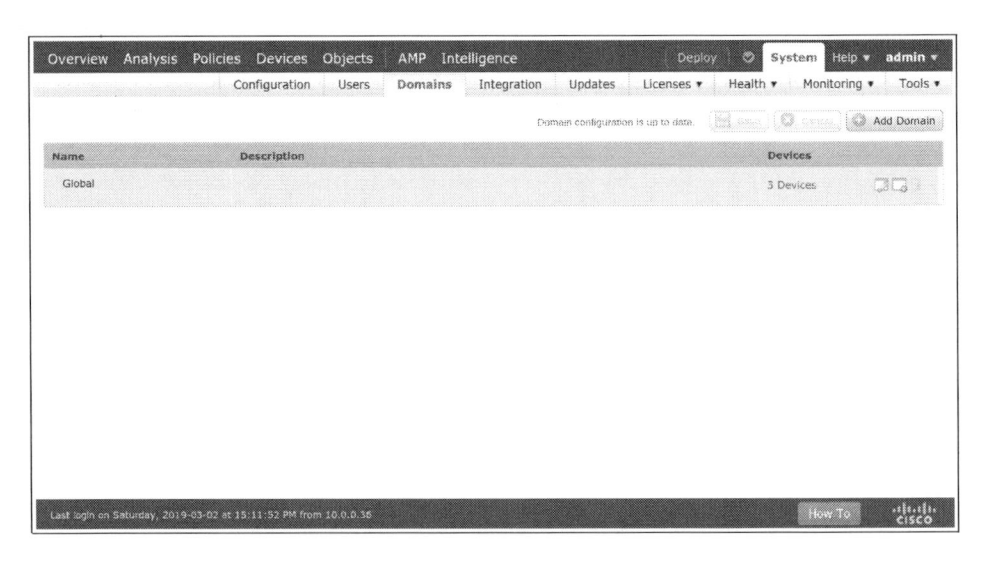

Keep in mind that once you start creating leaf domains (subdomains) only these leaf domains can contain devices. This means it makes no sense to create only one so you will create at least two leaves and start distributing your devices between them. If you're up for it then go ahead but don't say I didn't warn you!

BP10 - Think long and hard before you create leaf domains, then think again.

Chapter 4 - Updates, Tasks, Platform Settings

In this chapter we will discuss configuring your software and rule updates, platform settings and selected device settings. This isn't the most exciting material but Firepower isn't just about detection policies. Neglecting updates or not having a backup can come back to bite you.

Updates

One of the first things I check when doing a system assessment is the currently deployed version of software, Snort rules and the vulnerability database.

For a quick overview of the system software versions check out the Summary dashboard. On the FMC, navigate to **Overview → Dashboards → Summary Dashboard**. Then click the **Status** tab.

You'll see a widget called **Software Versions** which shows the currently installed version and optionally the latest version available for download. I say "optionally" because this Latest version is the newest version the last time the FMC checked the Cisco site. If you have not configured regular updates this Latest version may not be correct. An example of this widget is shown below.

Product Updates

Type	Current	Latest
Geolocation Update		
Local Geolocation Update	2019-02-04-002	2019-02-04-002
Rule Update		
Local Rule Update	2019-02-13-001-vrt	2019-02-13-001-vrt
Software		
1 Management Center	6.3.0	6.3.0
1 Device	6.2.3	6.2.3.10
1 Device	6.2.3.6	6.2.3.10
1 Device	6.3.0	6.3.0
VDB		
1 Management Center	308	309

If your currently installed version of Security Rule Update (SRU), Software or Vulnerability Database (VDB) is not the latest one you will see it is highlighted in red.

Running updated software, rule and VDB versions is often a good indication of how well maintained the system is. When I get my first look at a customer FMC, one if the initial screens I look at this the Product Updates widget above. This tells me quite a bit about how well the system is being maintained. Lots of red here means there are likely some issues we need to address.

We already discussed software versions in Chapter 2. Keeping Snort rules up-to-date is critical to the system's primary purpose. Keeping the vulnerability database updated is not as critical but allowing this to lapse will degrade the system's effectiveness over time. If the software versions are not the latest that doesn't necessarily mean the system is neglected. There are plenty of operational and organizational variables that might dictate upgrading only once or twice a year.

The Snort Rule Update (SRU)

Snort rules can arguably be called the core of the Firepower system. These are the rules used in the system's Snort-based deep packet inspection capability. They can have several sources such as:

- Cisco Talos
- Third-parties such as Emerging Threats
- User-created rules

Of course Cisco Talos is the primary source of rules for Firepower. Cisco recommends (and I happen to concur) that you only use Cisco provided rules with your system. There are two main reasons - performance and detection. Poorly written Snort rules can put a drain on system resources by using more than their share of CPU or producing a high number of false-positive alerts. Talos rules are tested for detection and performance across a large number of devices and traffic profiles prior to being deployed to customers. More on that in the chapter on Intrusion policy. For now, when we discuss intrusion rule updates, we're talking about rules from the Talos group within Cisco.

SRUs are normally released twice-weekly on Tuesday and Thursday. Occasionally, you will see a SRU released out-of-band for a serious vulnerability or threat. Because of the cat and mouse nature of cyber security, Snort rules are typically the most effective when they are first released. This is when the threat or vulnerability is new and most likely to be found in the wild. This means security is best served if you can get these new rules deployed to your devices quickly.

My recommendation for SRU updates is to configure your system to download and deploy new rule updates every night. This ensures you have the freshest rules deployed in a timely manner thus fulfilling the primary reason you purchased Firepower.

It should be noted that all SRUs are cumulative meaning you only have to install the latest one regardless of when you last updated your rules. Each one contains the complete Snort rule set.

You fill find the update page on your FMC under **System → Updates**, then click the **Rule Updates** tab as shown below.

4 - Updates, Tasks, Platform Settings

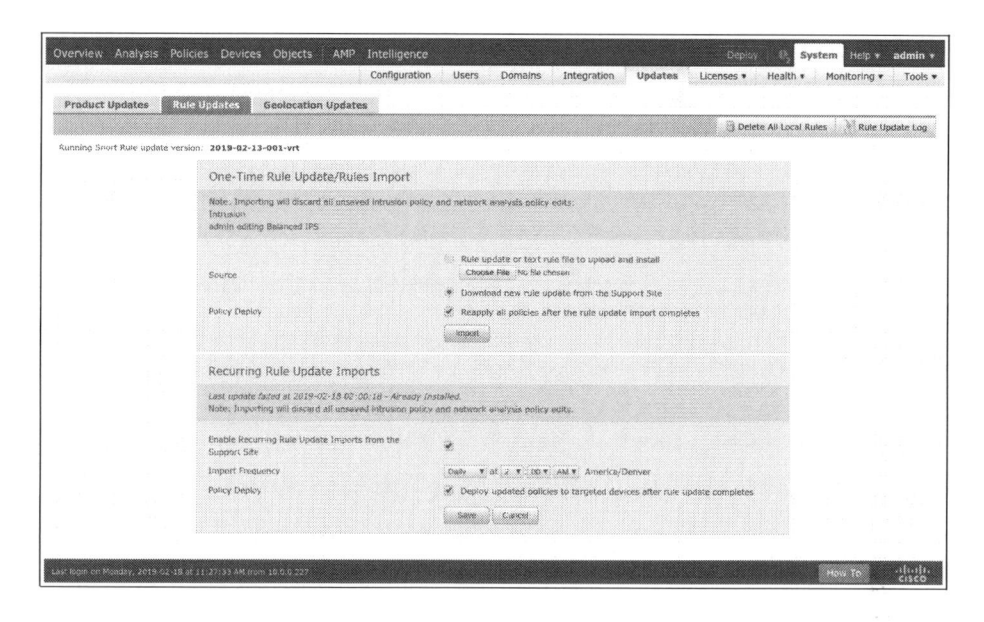

To configure daily updates:

- Select the **Download new rule updates from the Support Site** radio button
- Check the **Enable Recurring Rule Update Imports from the Support Site** box
- Select an import frequency (daily) and time
- Optionally check the **Deploy updated policies to targeted devices after rule update completes** box.

Of course, you will have to balance the benefits of deploying the most up-to-date rules against any change control requirements within your organization. Some organizations prioritize stability above security and you may find that another update schedule will be required. In my experience, the risks of deploying new Talos rules are low. I have seen significantly more issues from administrator error, misconfiguration, software bugs, etc. than I have seen from new Snort rules.

| BP11 - Configure daily SRU updates.

Geolocation Updates

Geolocation updates are pretty straightforward. This update is IP-to-country mapping database which (loosely) ties an IP addr location on the planet. This should be updated weekly, ideally pick a time when the FMC is not being used to administer the system such as the wee hours on the weekend. There's no issue with down time but FMC users could see some sluggishness in the interface if they are working during the update.

You will find this setting under **System → Updates**, then click the **Geolocation Updates** tab.

The only part of this screen that really matters is the lower portion which is shown below. Just check the box and pick a time when you want to download and install the update.

|BP12 - Configure weekly geolocation updates.

Vulnerability Database

The Vulnerability Database (VDB) is used to identify the well-know vulnerabilities from the Catalog of Vulnerabilities and Exposures (CVE). These are cross-referenced with information like the operating system and or applications where they exist as well as which Snort rules have been created to detect or stop attacks against these vulnerabilities. Periodically, Cisco releases updates to the VDB as new vulnerabilities are discovered and added to the database. The VDB also contains operating system and application fingerprint data so Firepower's passive detection can correctly identify what it sees on the network.

Like SRUs, VDB updates are cumulative and you never have to install intervening VDB versions. VDBs are simply numbered sequentially so VDB 304 is followed by VDB 305 and so on. Sometimes you'll see a number skipped because an internal version was not released but just get the latest one and you'll be happy.

I recommend checking for a new VDB every day and installing once a week.

4 - Updates, Tasks, Platform Settings

> Note: Depending on your Firepower version, installation of a VDB update on the FMC may trigger a Snort restart on your devices.

You can schedule the VDB update and installation in the task scheduler. More on that coming up in the Tasks section.

| BP13 - Schedule regular VDB updates.

Maintenance Updates/Patches

The last update I typically recommend is to download the latest Firepower maintenance release available. Like the VDB, I generally schedule a job to check daily for new software updates. Unlike the other updates however you won't be installing these automatically. By checking for updates daily you will have the latest software version already downloaded to your FMC and when it comes time to upgrade you won't need to go to the Cisco software site to find it.

> Note: By configuring these software downloads you will only get maintenance releases within your major version. When the next major release of Firepower comes out you'll need to download this one manually from the Cisco software download site.

| BP14 - Schedule regular download of updates/patches.

Tasks

Firepower has more than one way to schedule recurring tasks. We've already seen that several of the update types have their own scheduler configuration. The rest of your regularly scheduled jobs can be configured on the Tasks page. You'll find the Task Scheduler under **System → Tools → Scheduling**. Typical jobs you would configure here are:

33

Essential Firepower

- Download, push, install updates
- Backups
- Firepower Recommended Rules
- Reports
- Nmap scans

We are only going to look at the first two as best practice recommendations.

Software Downloads

To round out your regular checks for new updates you should create a task to download the latest Firepower maintenance release and VDB. From the page at **System → Tools → Scheduling**, click the **Add** button in the top right. This will bring up the New Task dialog shown below.

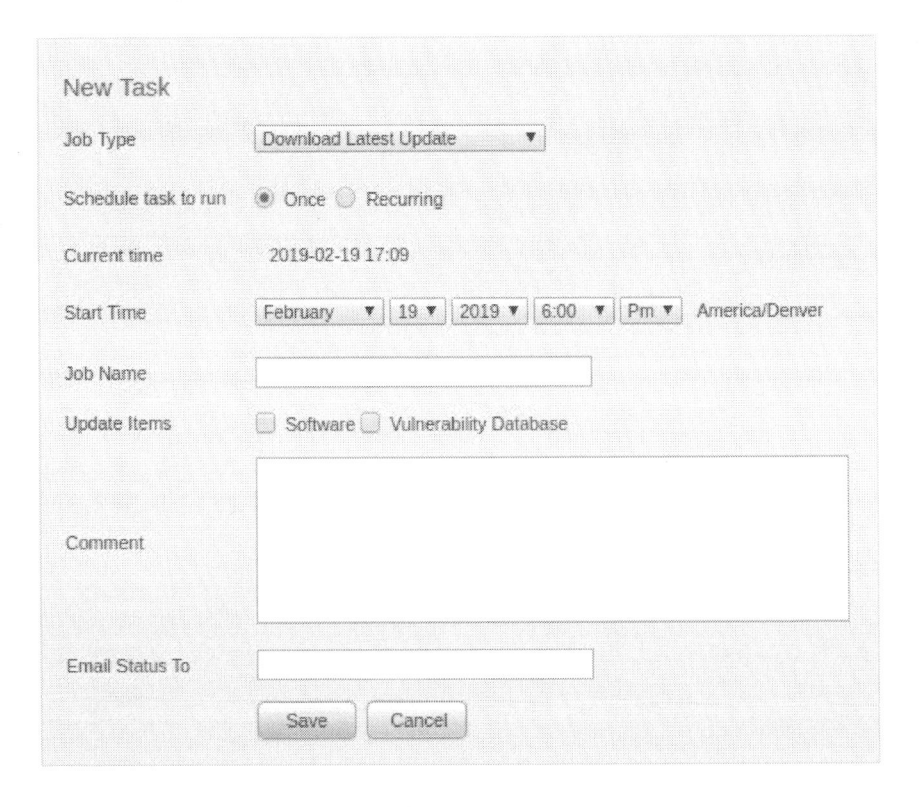

New Task

Field	Value
Job Type	Download Latest Update
Schedule task to run	● Once ○ Recurring
Current time	2019-02-19 17:09
Start Time	February 19 2019 6:00 Pm America/Denver
Job Name	
Update Items	☐ Software ☐ Vulnerability Database
Comment	
Email Status To	

[Save] [Cancel]

You will find several job types in the drop down menu. Depending on

34

the task you select, the dialog will change to collect the information for that task. For example, ff you select **Download Latest Update** you will see the dialog in the figure above.

Many of the fields in this dialog are standard for all jobs but there are also some custom selections depending on the job type. In this case we have all the normal knobs for determining how often to run, the **Job Name**, **Comment** and **Email Status To**.

Under **Update Items** you see check boxes for **Software** and **Vulnerability Database**. We're going to check both of these and then set the rest of the options to run this check daily. I usually do it late at night or early in the morning (when it's still dark). The effect is exactly the same as if you had gone to the **System → Updates** page and clicked the **Download Updates** button at the bottom. Every day, the FMC will go out to Cisco and check to see if there is a new software update or VDB. Of course, if there is no new update it will not download anything.

Backups

Another job you should schedule to run regularly is a backup. There are usually many hours of work that go into configuring the policies on the FMC. You want that work backed up in case the unthinkable happens – the loss of the FMC itself. Of course, before you can schedule a backup you have to create a backup job to run. To do that let's hop over to **System → Tools → Backup/Restore**. Click the **Firepower Management Backup** button near the top of the page to create an FMC backup job.

Create Backup

Name	
Storage Location	smb://10.0.0.201/public
Back Up Configuration	✔
Back Up Events	☐
Back Up Threat Intelligence Director	☐
Email when complete	☐
Email Address	
Copy when complete	☐

[Start Backup] [Save As New] [Cancel]

The backup dialog above will appear. Pick a name, something creative like "FMC Backup." Notice the Storage Location. If you have not setup remote storage this will show the backup path on the FMC where the backup files will be stored (/var/sf/backups).

My advice is to configure a Remote Storage location for your backups. You don't need to do it right now but please do it at some point. By using a Remote Storage location your backup is immediately copied off of the FMC, there's no second step to move the backup files to an off-box location. Notice my backup above is going directly to my SMB public share.

If you create a backup job before you configure a remote storage location, the backup files will be written to the /var/sf/backups directory. However, if you go back later and configure a remote storage location, your backups will automatically start being saved there. There is no need to return back and update your backup jobs.

> *Note: The "Copy when complete" option above is a legacy setting that was used before the Remote Storage feature was added. Using Remote Storage is now the recommended way to configure an off-box backup location.*

The important thing to backup on your FMC is the configuration. This is the configuration database with all your policies. If you use the Threat Intelligence Director feature to import STIX feeds then you should check that box as well.

I never backup events. In most installations your events are stored not only on your FMC but also on an external log management system. Because of this you don't need to bloat your backup files by backing up your events. Of course, your mileage may vary and if your organization requires you to backup the events then feel free. Just keep in mind that if you are storing millions of events on your FMC this could make your backup quite large.

> BP15 - Perform regular backups.
>
> BP16 - Backup to a remote storage device.

When you have your options selected save this backup job and return back to the task scheduler page (**System → Tools → Scheduling**).

Here you're going to create a new task (again with the **Add Task** button on the upper right). Backup will already be selected as the default job type and notice now that your FMC backup job shows in the Backup Profile drop down in the figure below.

New Task	
Job Type	Backup ▼
Schedule task to run	⦿ Once ○ Recurring
Current time	2019-02-19 17:29
Start Time	February ▼ 19 ▼ 2019 ▼ 6:00 ▼ Pm ▼ America/Denver
Job Name	
Backup Profile	FMC-config ▼
Comment	
Email Status To	
	Save Cancel

Fill in the rest of the dialog with the name and job run time parameters. Complete the **Email Status To** field if you want an email when the backup is run.

Platform Settings

Platform Settings refers to configurations that are applied at the device level. This is also called Platform policy, probably because it was called System policy in the old Sourcefire 3D System.

In terms of best practices I don't have much to say here. Most deployments will actually work just fine without customized Platform settings. That being said, I do recommend you at least configure a Platform policy and assign it to your devices as there are a few settings that most organizations will want to tweak.

There are actually two types of Platform policies you can configure.

One is for Firepower devices and one is for Threat Defense devices. Of course, you will want to create the type appropriate for your devices. At a minimum, you will want one policy for each type of device you have (Firepower or FTD). If you start to configure more detailed settings in the policy you may need to create additional policies for your various device types or locations. You will find Platform Settings under **Devices → Platform settings**. A Threat Defense Platform policy looks like the figure below.

|BP17 - Deploy Platform Settings policy

Time Synchronization

The primary setting I look at in the Platform policy is the time source. It's one of the main things that can cause real issues if it's not correct. The FMC and devices must have their time synchronized for events to be recorded properly in the FMC database.

Events are inserted into the FMC database tables with the time stamp from the device. When you query events on the FMC you are doing so for a given time window. By default this is an expanding time window that starts at the last one hour. Events can be sorted any number of ways but many of the default workflows sort by time with the newest events at the top. If the device time is not synchronized with the FMC and the other devices then the events from that device will appear in

Essential Firepower

the wrong sequence. That makes trying to correlate this activity with events from other devices difficult or impossible.

In addition, if the device time is ahead of the FMC time, the events will not even appear in the FMC event view until some time after they actually occurred. This is because time windows such as expanding or sliding show events only up to the current time. These time windows don't extend into the future since there should be no events in the database with timestamps newer than the current time.

This is why the default Health policy contains a time synchronization check and will change the device and FMC health to red if a device time diverges more than 10 seconds from the FMC clock. Note that Firepower doesn't care if the time is actually correct, just that the FMC and devices have the *same* time.

Ok so now we know why it's important. However, there's more. Time is set differently on different Firepower device models. Devices really only fall into one of two camps: 1) 4100/9300 devices, 2) everybody else.

4100/9300 Devices

The Firepower 4100 and 9300 appliances are the only devices which use the Firepower Chassis Manager (FCM). The FCM (not to be confused with the FMC) is a web user interface using the chassis management connection on the device. The FCM has its own Platform Settings and it's there that you should configure an NTP server. Ideally, this is the same time source used by your FMC but that's not a requirement - any decent NTP source should return the same time. If you are managing 4100 or 9300 devices then the time setting in your Platform policy is ignored. It doesn't matter what you set here as the time will always be set by the NTP source specified on the FCM.

On the FMC, if you clock on the Time Synchronization option in the Platform Settings you'll see the screen below.

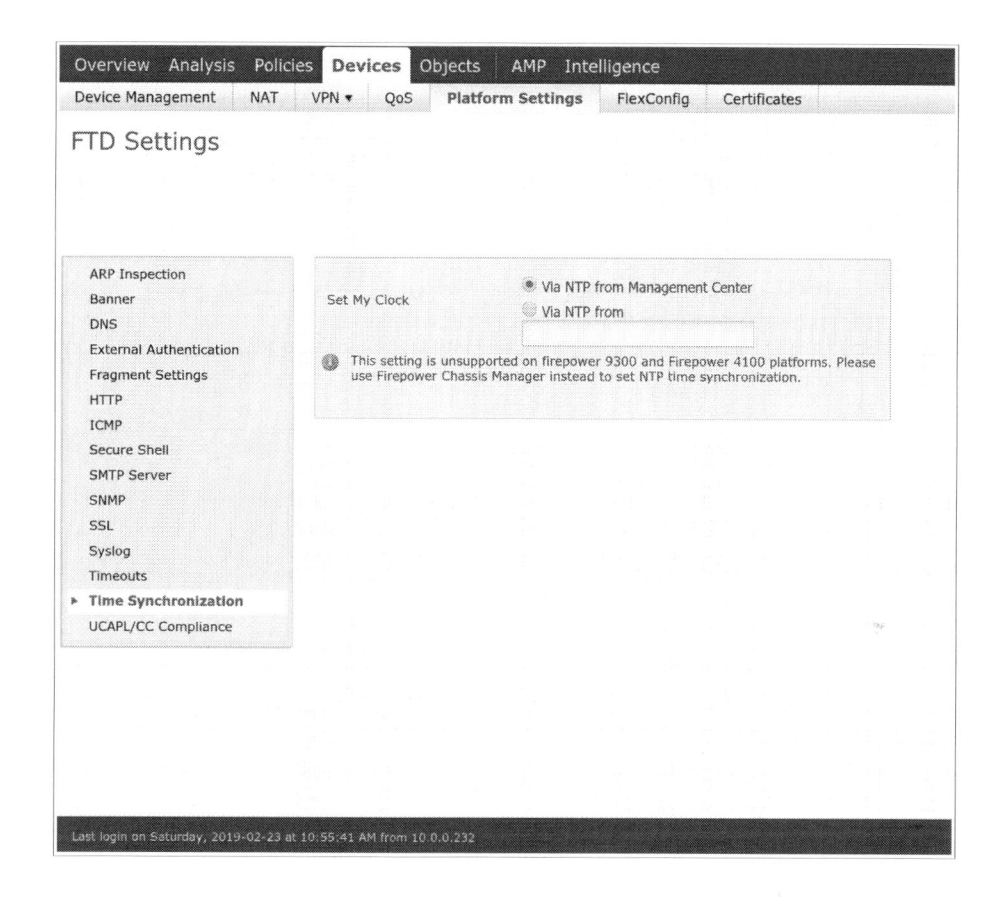

4 - Updates, Tasks, Platform Settings

[Screenshot of FTD Settings page showing Platform Settings tab with left navigation menu (ARP Inspection, Banner, DNS, External Authentication, Fragment Settings, HTTP, ICMP, Secure Shell, SMTP Server, SNMP, SSL, Syslog, Timeouts, Time Synchronization, UCAPL/CC Compliance) and Set My Clock options: Via NTP from Management Center, Via NTP from. Note: This setting is unsupported on firepower 9300 and Firepower 4100 platforms. Please use Firepower Chassis Manager instead to set NTP time synchronization.]

If we zoom up on the **Set My Clock** area of the screen there are two options for setting the time as shown below.

- Via NTP from Management Center
- Via NTP from <some NTP source>

[Zoomed screenshot of Set My Clock area showing the same two radio button options and the unsupported note.]

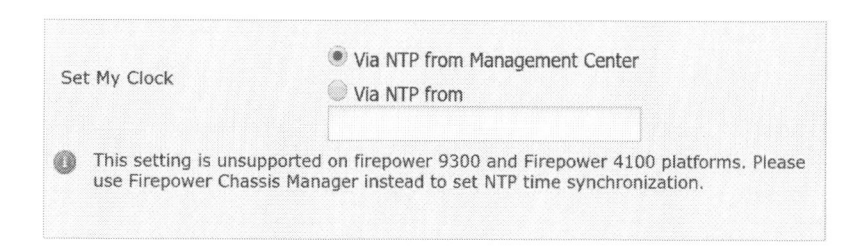

However, reading the information note below the radio buttons we see that this setting is unsupported (unused) for the 9300 and 4100 platforms. As stated above, for these devices it doesn't matter what you set because it will be ignored.

41

All Other Devices

For every other device except the 4100/9300 this setting is used. By default, the time will be synchronized from the FMC to the device via the management tunnel. This uses the NTP protocol but the traffic is tunneled over the 8305/tcp management connection. This means there's no need to ensure that the NTP port (123/udp) is open between the device and the FMC.

Leaving this to the default setting is probably the easiest and most reliable method to ensure the FMC and device stay in sync. You can opt to enter an IP address here for an NTP server but honestly there's very little reason to do so. It requires ensuring the device can access the NTP server and if it's the same one the FMC is using - what's the point?

>BP18 - Have a good time synchronization strategy

Banner

I will mention the Banner setting not because it impacts anything about how Firepower works but because it's a very commonly configured item. Nearly every organization has a blurb that you place on all your critical systems warning folks about whether there is any expectation of privacy and also notifying unauthorized hoodlums to stay away. The Banner settings are shown in the figure below.

4 - Updates, Tasks, Platform Settings

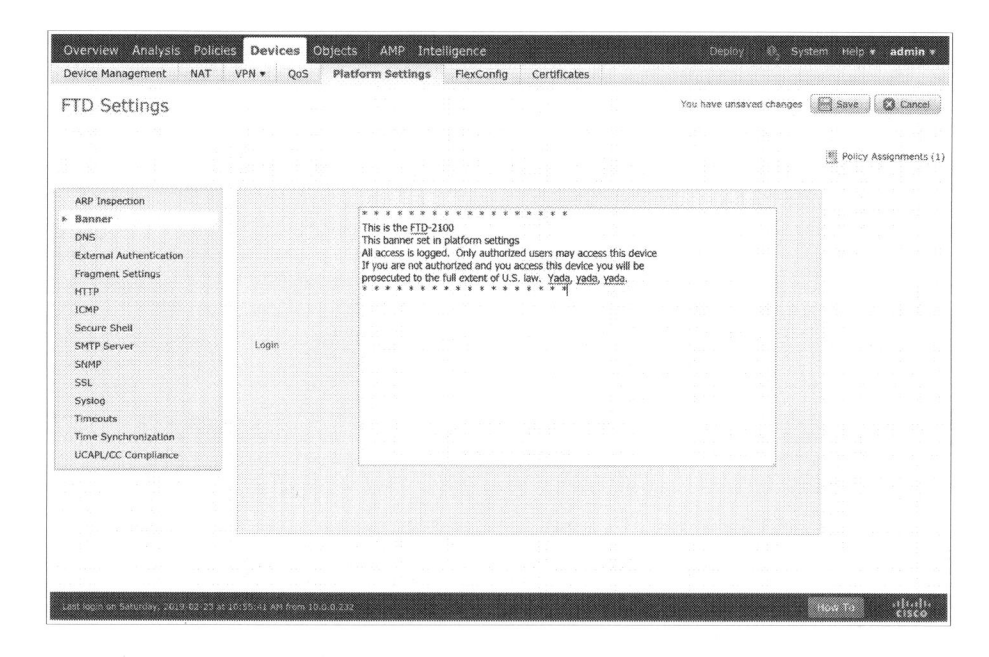

The banner you set here will appear on the initial web page in the case of the classic 7000/8000 Firepower devices as well as upon an SSH initial connection for all devices.

|BP19 - Configure a device login banner.

Other Settings

The rest of the Platform Settings don't fall in my 80/20 criteria. This is is mostly because they don't impact the actual detection of the system. Most are configured for compliance or audit purposes and have to do with things like logging, timeouts, etc.

There are a couple I will mention because you may want to ensure they're set according to your own local system use policies.

ICMP

If your system is deployed as an edge Firewall you may want to look at the ICMP settings. By default FTD will respond to ICMP Echo Requests (ping) on the data interfaces. If these are facing the Internet this may not be ideal. You may want to be more selective on how your device responds (or doesn't respond) to these packets.

43

DNS

In FTD 6.3 and later you can create FQDN objects and use these in your Access Control rules. Doing so requires some additional configuration of DNS settings on your device so it can lookup the IP addresses for these FQDN objects. This is an example of a Platform Setting that can cause a device not to work correctly if it's not properly configured.

Logging

If you have a requirement for ASA-style firewall logs from your devices then you will have to visit the Syslog section of the Platform policy. There you will find seven tabs where you can configure the type of syslog messages, their destination, the interface they will be sent from, etc.

> BP20 - Evaluate other Platform Settings as needed.

Chapter 5 - System Health

The question of health monitoring comes up quite often during initial Firepower deployments. Sysadmins are used to configuring things like SNMP alerting for their various Windows and Linux hosts. Because of this, a common question is how to configure this health monitoring for Firepower.

Health Overview

Before I dive into the policy, I want to discuss the overall operation of the health system in Firepower. The Health policy contains a number of checks. These checks are run periodically on all the appliances and return a status. Each check can return a Normal, Warning, Critical or Recovered status. By default, these checks run every 5 minutes and events are recorded in the FMC Health Database. The Health Status Indicator, located on the right side of the top menu bar shows the status of the most unhealthy appliance in your entire deployment.

In the figure below, the health status indicator is a green circle with a check inside.

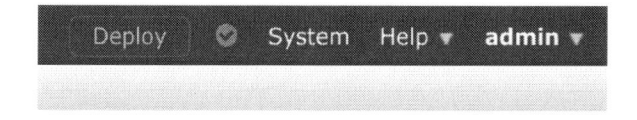

The table below, taken from the Firepower online help, shows each of the health status indicators along with their description.

Essential Firepower

Health Status Indicator

Status Level	Status Icon	Status Color in Pie Chart	Description
Error		Black	Indicates that at least one health monitoring module has failed on the appliance and has not been successfully re-run since the failure occurred. Contact your technical support representative to obtain an update to the health monitoring module.
Critical		Red	Indicates that the critical limits have been exceeded for at least one health module on the appliance and the problem has not been corrected.
Warning		Yellow	Indicates that warning limits have been exceeded for at least one health module on the appliance and the problem has not been corrected.
Normal		Green	Indicates that all health modules on the appliance are running within the limits configured in the health policy applied to the appliance.
Recovered		Green	Indicates that all health modules on the appliance are running within the limits configured in the health policy applied to the appliance, including modules that were in a Critical or Warning state.
Disabled		Blue	Indicates that an appliance is disabled or blacklisted, that the appliance does not have a health policy applied to it, or that the appliance is currently unreachable.

I can't count the number of times I've arrived at a customer or viewed their FMC over a WebEx and seen the Health Status Indicator is red. My first question is, "Why is your health red?" The answer is almost always, "Oh, it's always like that." (Alex mutes the phone and breathes out a long sigh)

Why is this a problem? Well, you may have some tiny ongoing issue on a single device that is generating a critical health alert. This means your FMC Health Status Indicator will turn red. The problem is when you become accustomed to this and start ignoring the red health status. In this case, if you have another device that has a real health situation it is now masked behind the constantly red status indicator.

This situation has been improved a bit in recent Firepower versions by the addition of a tiny subscript number next to the health status icon. This tells you how many devices are at the displayed health status (if it's not green). However, my advice is not to depend on your memory of what this little number was last time you checked. Not to mention that you still don't know for sure if one of your critical health alerts needs immediate attention.

The best practice here is to keep up with your Health Status Indicator. It should be green. If it's not, find out why and deal with it. Some options are:

- Fix the health issue
- Adjust the Health policy - maybe the threshold is too high or the check is unwarranted
- Blacklist the health check on the device - for temporarily dealing with a specific issue
- Blacklist the entire device - maybe the device is in maintenance, offline or in the process of being configured

|BP21 - Your health status should normally be green!

Health Policy

One thing I find myself repeating often is that these Firepower appliances are - just that - appliances. They are based on customized versions of Linux and for some such as the 4100/9300 the Firepower eXtensible Operating System (FXOS) is very different from anything most folks have dealt with. Because of this, Cisco does not recommend or support installing any type of 3rd party monitoring agent on these devices. Chances are the underlying libraries needed are not there and even if you get such an agent to work you are monitoring processes and interfaces which are atypical.

The system does include a health monitoring component which can send alerts via email, syslog or SNMP if desired. This monitoring is controlled by the Health policy.

You'll find Health policy under **System →Health → Policy**. The system ships with a default Health policy. This policy contains a number of health checks that can be performed. Some of these apply only to specific types or models of appliances, some apply only to the FMC. Here is my advice - use the default Health policy for all of your appliances. You don't need to worry about only having FMC checks enabled on the FMC or customizing the policy to your specific device types. If a particular check doesn't apply to a given appliance it simply won't run there.

There are two specific checks in the Health policy which I see come up more than any other. These are CPU Usage and Interface Status.

CPU Usage

The key to remember about the CPU Usage check is that it is disabled by default. My recommendation - leave it that way. However, I see customers enable this health check all the time so let's look at how this works.

As I mentioned already, Health checks run every 5 minutes on the target system. This time can be increased but it can't be shortened. Most folks leave it at the default. The CPU Usage check (shown below) will alert if any of the CPUs have exceeded the threshold over this 5 minute period. The built-in thresholds in this health check are:

- 80% Warning
- 90% Critical

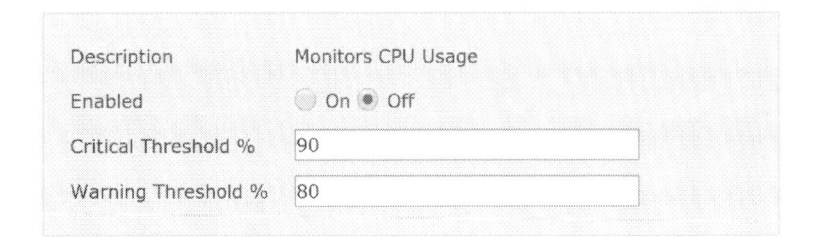

Description	Monitors CPU Usage
Enabled	○ On ● Off
Critical Threshold %	90
Warning Threshold %	80

Now, on the surface it sounds like a good idea to be alerted when the CPU usage on your system is high. However, there are a number of caveats to this reasoning on Firepower.

The main issue I have with high CPU alerts on Firepower is that they are not actionable. The way Snort processes traffic is that specific flows will be "pinned" to a single CPU core. For the lifetime of any given flow it will always be processed through a single core. For the majority of flows this lifetime is measured in seconds or less. However, for some flows such as backups, media streams, replication traffic, etc. these flows can last minutes or hours. Not only can these be long lived they also can move quite a large amount of data. In Firepower we call these "elephant flows."

A high-speed elephant flow will commonly cause a specific CPU to spike at 80% or more for the life of the flow. If you have the CPU Usage health check enabled that means you get a health alert. Now we have ways to tune out these flows, some of which we'll talk about later. If you are tuning these flows (adding rules to bypass inspection on these known elephant flow senders/receivers) then your CPU spikes will be reduced or even eliminated. However, this is a "best practice" guide which is aimed at giving you a good starting configuration.

In the interest of getting a good night's sleep and only providing actionable health alerts, my advice is to leave this check disabled in your Health policy. If you want to enable it just for a few days to verify you don't have a high CPU issue across all of your processors that's fine. Just keep in mind that you will likely get some elephant flows causing spikes from time to time regardless.

There is one other consideration if you decide to enable this check. It can cause your health event database usage to increase dramatically. The reason is that you will start getting a health event for every CPU every 5 minutes. Health events are generated for enabled health checks even if the condition is green for that check. This means if you have large devices such as 8350/4100/9300 you can have upwards of 40 CPU cores in use for Snort. That's an additional 40+ health events per device every 5 minutes. Because the health database uses circular logging like the other event databases, this can greatly reduce the overall health check history available on the FMC.

> BP22 - Don't enable the CPU Health alert, it's disabled for a reason.

Interface Status

The other health check I deal with the most is Interface Status. This health check is enabled in the Default health policy. The check has no threshold, it's just on or off as shown below.

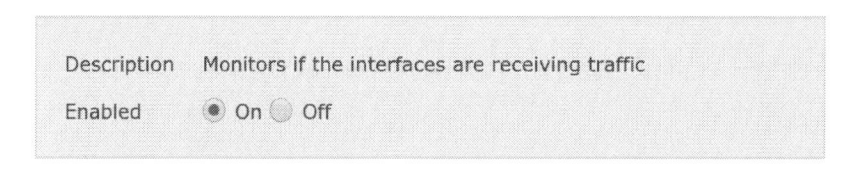

Description	Monitors if the interfaces are receiving traffic
Enabled	● On ○ Off

Notice the description for this check, "Monitors if the interfaces are receiving traffic." What this means is this check will trigger a critical health status if no packets were seen on the interface over the health check period (5 minutes by default). Now this can be a very useful check but it really only applies to a specific interface configuration.

If we look at some of the ways you can deploy Firepower we have interface modes like:

- Passive
- Routed
- Inline

There are other interface types such as Bridged Virtual Interfaces (BVI) but these are similar to routed or inline since they pass traffic through the device.

At first you might say it's important to have this check enabled in any mode where traffic passes through the device. You want to know if traffic stops passing right? Sure, you want to know if your inline/routed interfaces stop passing traffic. I mean people are going to stop getting their YouTube streams right? Yes, I definitely agree that knowing that these inline interfaces are not receiving traffic is important. However, I am going to recommend that you disable this health check on this type of interface.

My reason for this recommendation is that you will not receive an immediate alert that the interface went down. Remember, health checks only run every 5 minutes. This means it may take up to 5 minutes to get your alert syslog or email that the interface(s) are down. Is that fast enough? No way! Your help desk phones are already ringing off the hook long before you get the health alert.

Virtually every customer I've talked to already has some other more real-time method for being alerted that a critical data path is down in their environment. This alert is much better for this type of situation than the Interface Status health alert on Firepower. The bottom line, it's probably worthless on inline/routed interfaces.

Another reason why I recommend disabling this is that often times we deploy our devices in High Availability (HA) mode. This means one of the devices is passing traffic while the other is on standby. If this health check is enabled, your standby device may begin generating these health alerts for the inactive interface(s). Since the check isn't that useful even for the active device - disable it.

The interface type where this health check shines is passive. The reason is if a passive interface on your Firepower device stops receiving traffic from the Gigamon or the switch span port nobody else on the network knows (or cares) but you. Even though you care, if you don't have this health check enabled it may take you some time to discover that a particular interface hasn't generated any alerts in some time. With this check enabled you will be notified within minutes if someone pulls out a cable or disables the switch span port connected to your device.

> BP23 - Disable the Interface Status health alert unless your system is passive.

Blacklist

There is an often overlooked tool you can use to help keep your Health Status Indicator green - the Health Blacklist. This feature can be used to temporarily silence a health alert for a specific device. The health check will continue to run and you can find the status by drilling into the Health Monitor for that specific device. However, it will not change the overall health status of the system. You will find the Blacklist feature under **System → Health → Blacklist** as shown below.

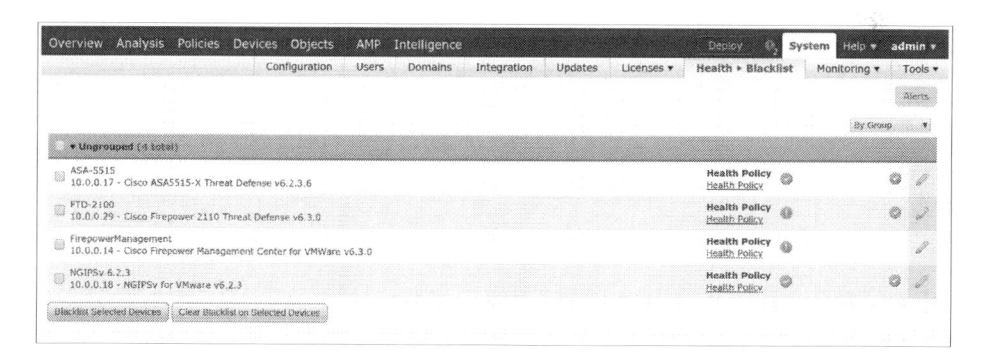

There are two ways to implement the Health Blacklist, at the health check or at the device.

The most surgical way to silence a health alert is to blacklist the specific check on the device. Say you have a disk status issue on one of your devices. While you are troubleshooting this with TAC you can blacklist that specific issue only for the single device.

51

Essential Firepower

From the **System → Health → Blacklist** screen, click the pencil to the right of the device you want to blacklist. In the example below the **Disk Status** health check will be blacklisted.

```
Overview   Analysis   Policies   Devices   Objects
                                         Configuration

Editing Health Blacklist for: FTD-2100

         ☐ AMP for Endpoints Status
         ☐ AMP for Firepower Status
         ☐ Appliance Heartbeat
         ☐ Automatic Application Bypass Status
         ☐ Backlog Status
         ☐ Card Reset
         ☐ Cluster/Failover Status
         ☐ CPU Usage
         ☑ Disk Status
         ☐ Disk Usage
         ☐ FMC HA Status
         ☐ Hardware Alarms
         ☐ Health Monitor Process
         ☐ Host Limit
         ☐ Inline Link Mismatch Alarms
         ☐ Interface Status
         ☐ Intrusion and File Event Rate
Modules
         ☐ Link State Propagation
```

Once there, select the health check you want to blacklist then scroll down and hit the **Save** button at the bottom. After the blacklist is saved you will see a Back button at the bottom. Clicking that will return you to the main blacklist page. Now you will see (Partially Blacklisted) showing next to your device. This is shown in the figure below.

52

5 - System Health

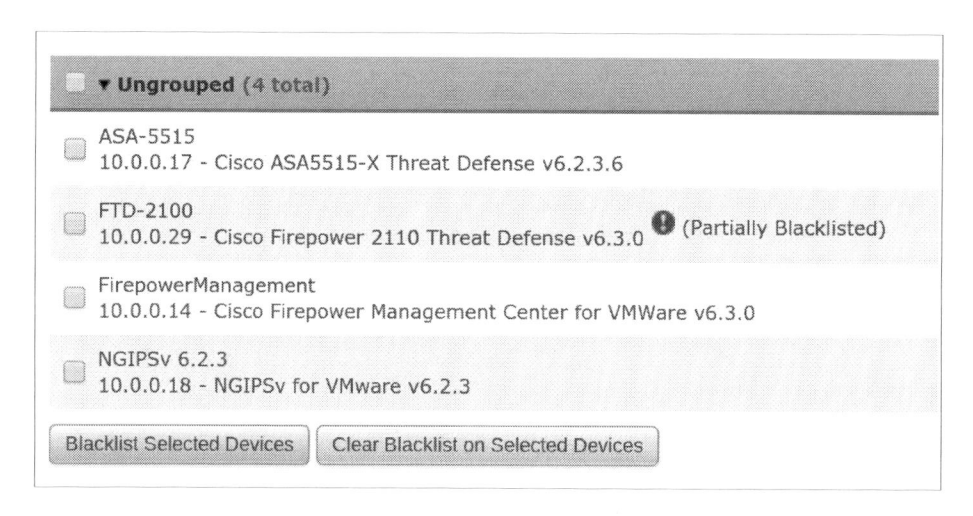

▼ **Ungrouped** (4 total)	
☐ ASA-5515 10.0.0.17 - Cisco ASA5515-X Threat Defense v6.2.3.6	
☐ FTD-2100 10.0.0.29 - Cisco Firepower 2110 Threat Defense v6.3.0 ● (Partially Blacklisted)	
☐ FirepowerManagement 10.0.0.14 - Cisco Firepower Management Center for VMWare v6.3.0	
☐ NGIPSv 6.2.3 10.0.0.18 - NGIPSv for VMware v6.2.3	
[Blacklist Selected Devices] [Clear Blacklist on Selected Devices]	

The second way to implement this is to blacklist the entire device. Again, the health checks will continue to run and you can see their status under **System → Health → Health Monitor**. However, the overall health of the device will revert to green. You can blacklist an entire device by checking the box next to the device and clicking the **Blacklist Selected Devices** button.

Regardless of the type of blacklist you implement, don't forget to come back later and remove this after you get the issue fixed.

The blacklist feature is intended to be a temporary measure. If this is more of a long term change, consider creating a custom Health policy with the particular check disabled for the device(s) in question.

> BP24 - Health Blacklist is a good way to manage temporary health issues.

Chapter 6 - Objects

As we move to Objects we're now getting into the types of settings that can have a direct impact on Firepower's detection capabilities. While there are a myriad of different types of objects, I will focus on the ones that I consider some of the key factors to ensuring your devices are inspecting like they should be. You'll find Objects on your FMC under **Objects → Object Management** as shown below.

Network

Network objects are a straightforward concept. They are basically friendly names for IP address ranges you can use in your policies, searches, reports, etc. My advice here centers around creating the proper object(s) to define your "protected" network. We will go into this concept in more depth when we discuss Variable Sets.

For now, I will make this simple. You will need to define your internal network(s) in other places within Firepower. Because of that, you should make sure you have network objects or object groups created for these ranges. For something as simple as my home network I can just use the **IPv4-Private-10.0.0.0-8** object that ships with

Firepower. In many cases, you can use the **IPv4-Private-All-RFC1918** group which contains the three standard private range objects.

Keep in mind that when it comes to private address space there is really no risk if you include ranges that are not in use on your network. Plus, you might find that there are hosts on your network you weren't aware of. For example, I've had customers insist they don't use the 192.168.0.0/16 range but later find hosts somewhere on their network using those IPs.

> BP25 - Ensure you have network objects created that contain your internal "protected" address space.

Another network range you may want to create is any public IP address space owned by your organization. This really means public address space that your devices will have visibility to. Often times, we deploy Firepower to protect DMZ hosts. Those hosts may be using public IP addresses. As with the private IP space above, we will include these public ranges in other parts of Firepower so we need to make sure they're defined here first.

> BP26 - Create network objects containing any public address space you own that will be visible to your devices.

Interface

When it comes to Interface objects, my primary recommendation is simply to give these some thought. These objects were created to make policies simpler. Specifically Security Zone objects were created so you could create a single Access Control rule which would apply to multiple devices. The idea is that if you have multiple devices and each has an "Inside" and an "Outside" interface, you can create Security Zones that apply across all of these. By putting all of the outside interfaces in a security group and all of the inside interfaces in another group you can create a single rule that would apply equally regardless of where it is deployed. This rule will also work regardless of the network ranges of the outside and inside networks. This saves having to create specific rules for each device or include each device's network ranges in your Access Control rules. An example of some Interface objects is shown below.

Essential Firepower

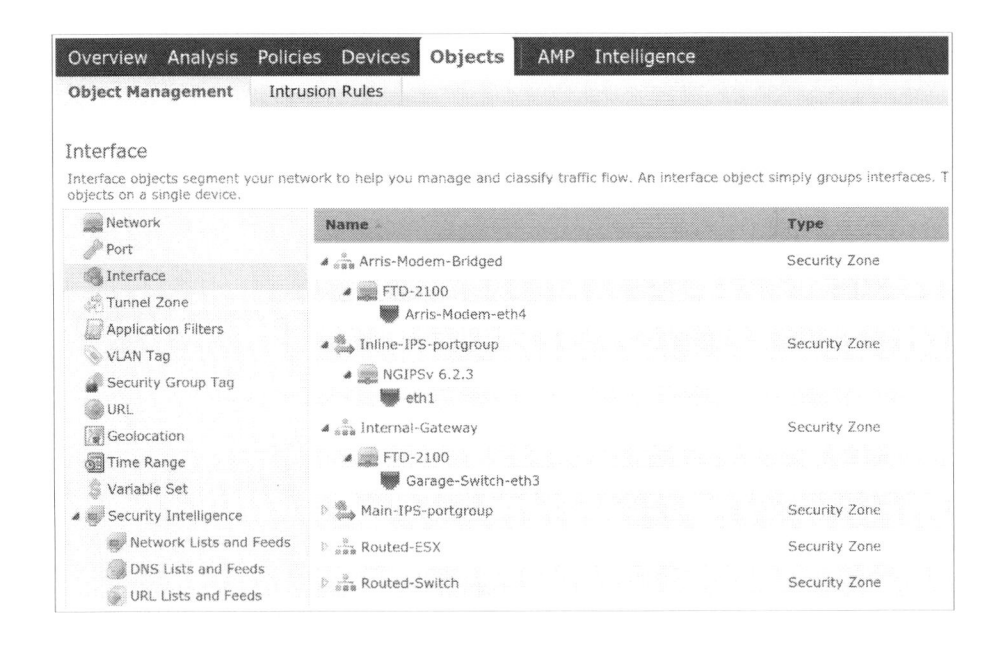

[Screenshot of Firepower Object Management interface showing Interface objects including Arris-Modem-Bridged, FTD-2100, Inline-IPS-portgroup, NGIPSv 6.2.3, Internal-Gateway, Main-IPS-portgroup, Routed-ESX, and Routed-Switch, all of type Security Zone.]

> BP27 - Give some thought to your Interface Security Zones and assign interfaces as appropriate.

Variable Sets

Variable sets are perhaps one of the least understood aspects of Firepower. They are also one of the easiest ways to mis-configure the system and introduce unintentional blind spots. This means it's something you should definitely pay attention to!

Variables are used in Snort rules to define IP address and port ranges. They help to make Snort more efficient by limiting deep packet inspection to only include the traffic a particular rule was designed to inspect.

As an example, consider an external attack conducted against one of your web servers. The attack will originate from a client and will target a server.

6 - Objects

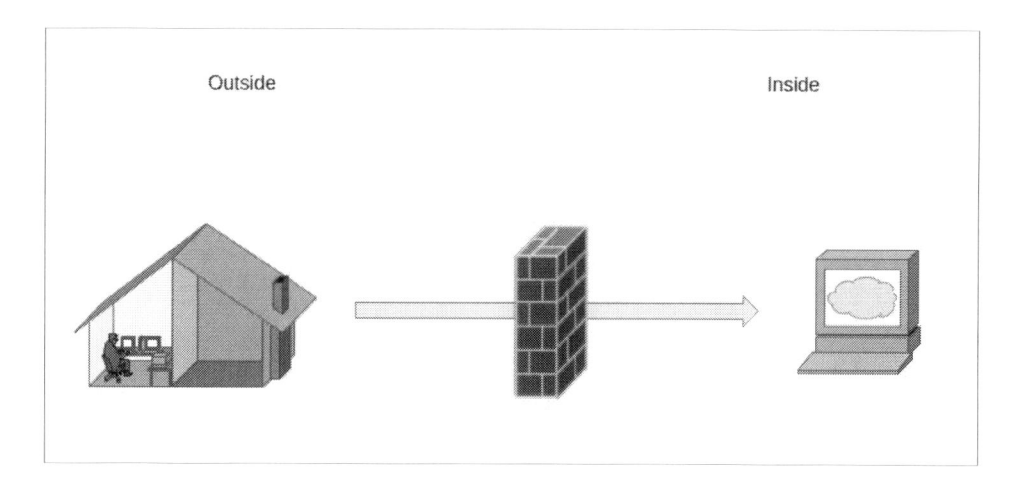

Your Firepower device will use Snort rules to inspect the traffic received by your web server to detect and stop the attack.

Snort rules each contain a rule header. This rule header identifies things like the protocol, source and destination IP address and ports that will be inspected by the rule. The purpose of the header is to limit the scope of Snort's inspection. This way a rule that is written to look for a specific web-based attack initiated against a server doesn't waste system resources inspecting server responses.

A typical rule header for a rule inspecting web server traffic might look like this:

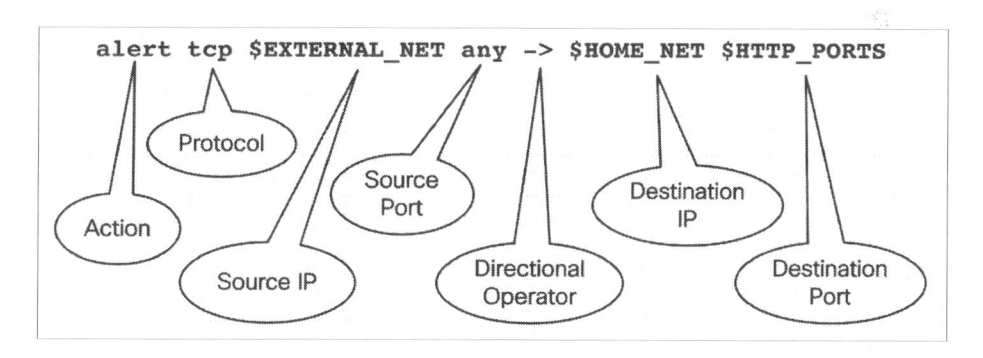

```
alert tcp $EXTERNAL_NET any -> $HOME_NET $HTTP_PORTS
```

- Action
- Protocol
- Source IP
- Source Port
- Directional Operator
- Destination IP
- Destination Port

The header fields containing the source and destination IP addresses are called variables. These variables are part of the Firepower Variable Set. The two most important variables are $HOME_NET and $EXTERNAL_NET. The names are somewhat self-explanatory, here is how they are defined:

57

- $HOME_NET = the protected network
- $EXTERNAL_NET = the unprotected network

Using the $HOME_NET and $EXTERNAL_NET variables you can now see that Snort rules designed to detect web server attacks will limit their inspection to just traffic which is destined for our web servers. Now, we are just talking about a subset of Snort rules - those designed to detect and stop attacks against web servers. Rules written for other types of attacks would have their own specific rule headers.

It's important to note that we have a *protected* and an *unprotected* network range. **There is no such thing as a *trusted* network range.** The term "zero trust" has been used a lot lately. The concept is basically that we don't assume anything is good and only grant trust explicitly not as the default. Can a network be both untrusted and protected at the same time? Let's find out.

Before we go further let's imagine another type of attack. Say someone inside your organization inadvertently runs a malware executable. Part of the malware behavior is to spread to other systems such as one of your servers. To get to the server, the traffic must pass through your Firepower device. Here we have $HOME_NET and $EXTERNAL_NET at work again. However in this case it looks like the diagram below.

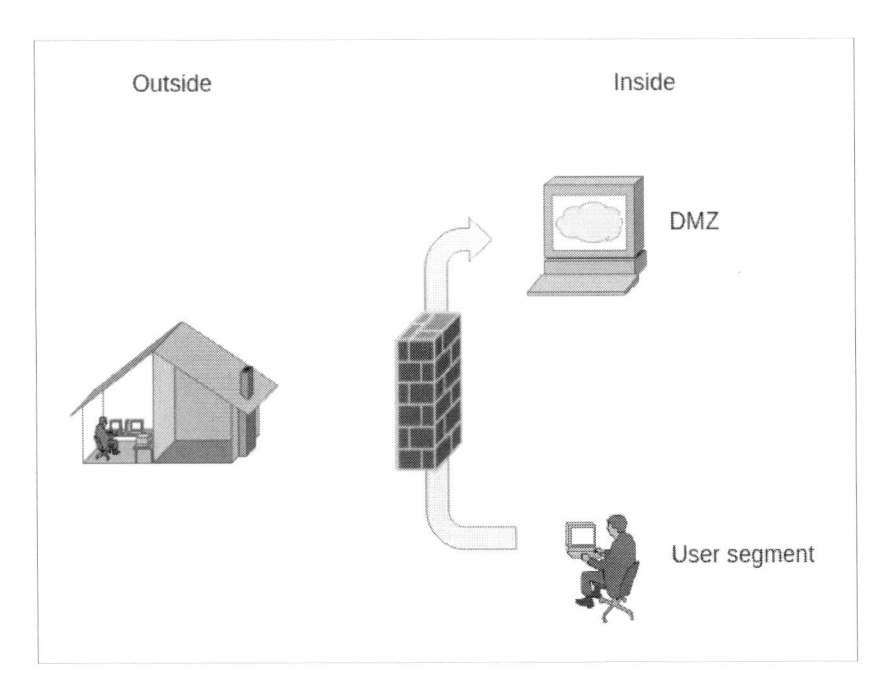

Both the source and the target of the attack are in your protected network. Although there is a security device (NGFW or NGIPS) between the user and server segments. Unlike the previous attacks there isn't a clear "us" and "them" we can use in our rule header. It's really us attacking us.

Ok, now that we know how headers are constructed and how basic attacks might work what values should we use for the two most important variables $HOME_NET and $EXTERNAL_NET? Let's expand our definition of what is protected and what is trusted. I tried saying this with words but it is much easier to explain with a diagram.

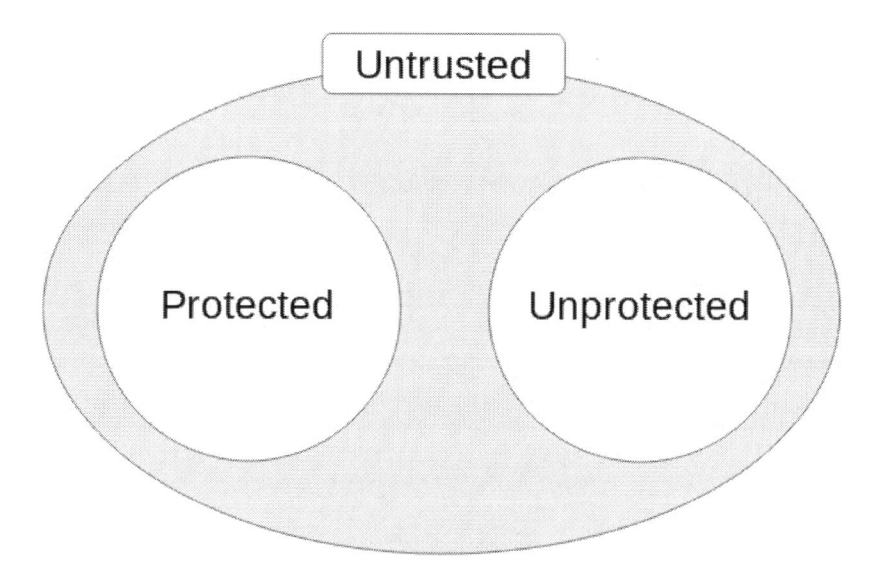

Key takeaways from the graphic above.

The Protected circle is your hosts, the ones your Firepower system is supposed to protect. The Unprotected circle consists of all the hosts everywhere that your Firepower system doesn't protect. Both of these groups are Untrusted.

> Note: The diagram is not to scale. If we took the size of the Protected and Unprotected networks into account the Protected circle would be more like a fly speck.

I want to flesh out our definitions of protection and trust because I think it makes it easier to zero in on what $HOME_NET and $EXTERNAL_NET should contain. Here's what I recommend. $HOME_NET should be your protected network. My recommendation for most organizations is to start with the IPv4-Private-All-RFC1918 network object group, then add any public IP space you own. You should already have network objects created for this space.

Substituting the variables in our protection and trust diagram looks like this:

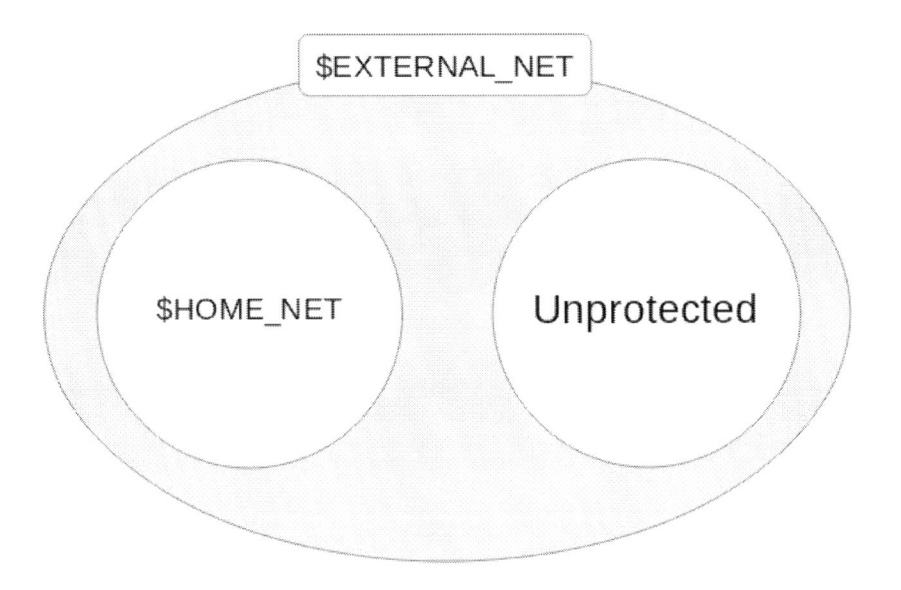

$EXTERNAL_NET

$HOME_NET   Unprotected

Continuing the logic above, since $EXTERNAL_NET includes all hosts you should assign it the default value of "any". This basically means - **everybody is untrusted**. As we saw in the malware example above, we can't afford to trust our internal hosts because they might turn on us. Associating $HOME_NET with some level of trust is a common misconception and one I've tried hard to correct. You don't have to trust the home network in order to protect it. Because of this, the fact that $HOME_NET ranges are within $EXTERNAL_NET is not a problem.

Using these values works for both external and internal attacks. In this case, the source IP range of $EXTERNAL_NET applies to all traffic because it is set to the default value of "any". Likewise, the protected network is always within $HOME_NET.

> BP28 - Assign your internal address space and any public IP space you own to the $HOME_NET variable
>
> BP29 - leave the $EXTERNAL_NET variable at it's default value of "any"

To assign your internal network ranges to the $HOME_NET variable you can just edit the Default-Set. Firepower will not let you delete the Default-Set but you are free to customize it. Clicking on **Variable Set** on the left shows the existing sets. The example below has the Default-Set and another customized Variable Set named Wide-Open.

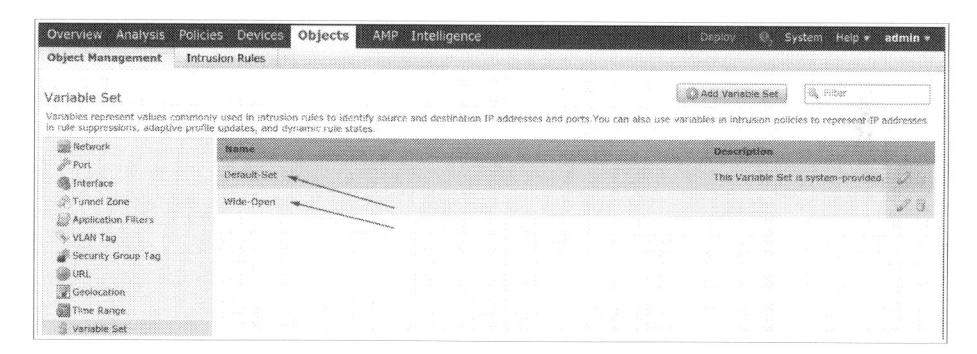

Once you click the pencil icon by the **Default-Set** you will see the dialog below.

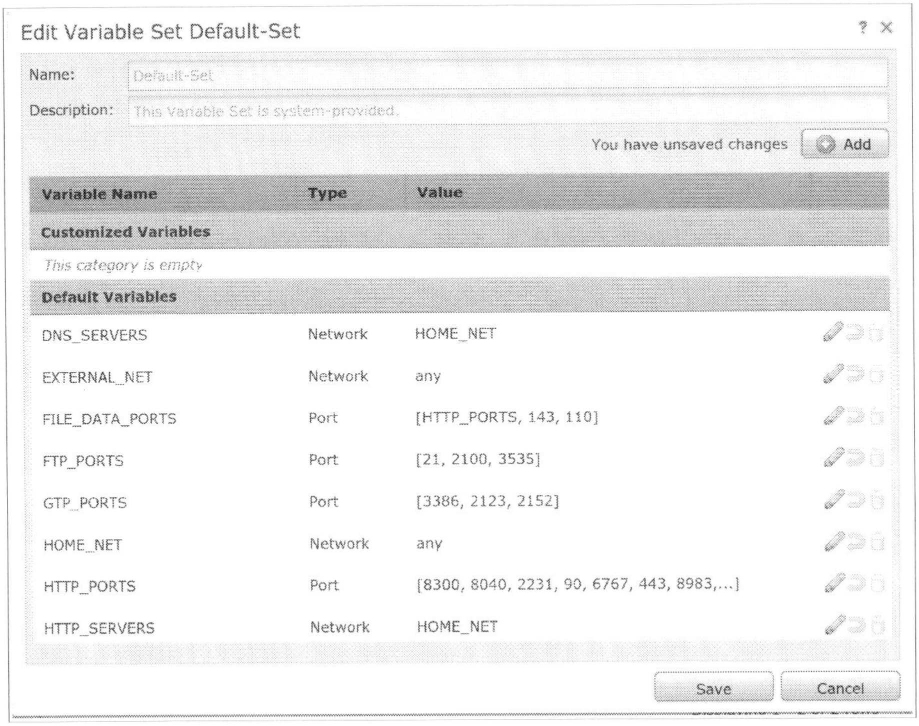
Edit Variable Set Default-Set
Name: Default-Set
Description: This Variable Set is system-provided.
You have unsaved changes
Add
Variable Name
Type
Value
Customized Variables
This category is empty
Default Variables
DNS_SERVERS Network HOME_NET
EXTERNAL_NET Network any
FILE_DATA_PORTS Port [HTTP_PORTS, 143, 110]
FTP_PORTS Port [21, 2100, 3535]
GTP_PORTS Port [3386, 2123, 2152]
HOME_NET Network any
HTTP_PORTS Port [8300, 8040, 2231, 90, 6767, 443, 8983,...]
HTTP_SERVERS Network HOME_NET
Save
Cancel

From here, just click the pencil next to HOME_NET and select the network object(s) that represent your protected address space. Add these objects to the Included Networks column as shown below.

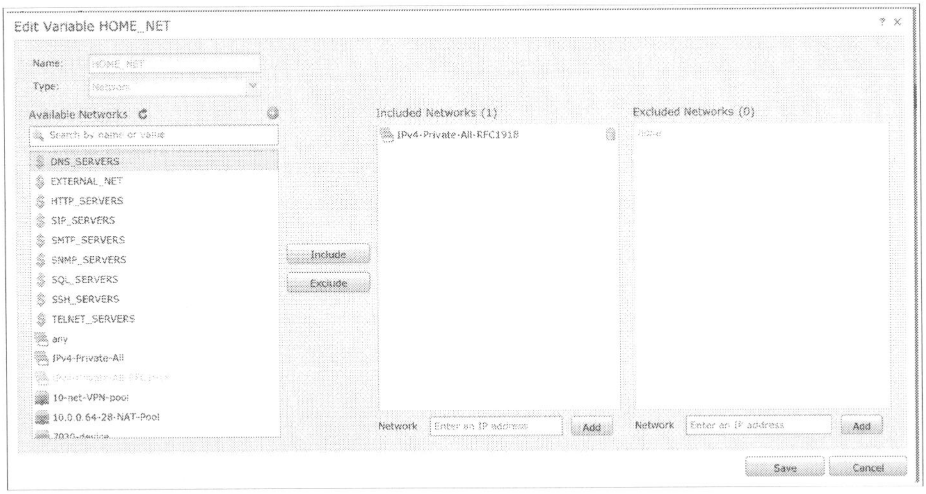
Edit Variable HOME_NET
Name:
Type:
Available Networks
Included Networks (1)
Excluded Networks (0)
IPv4-Private-All-RFC1918
DNS_SERVERS
EXTERNAL_NET
HTTP_SERVERS
SIP_SERVERS
SMTP_SERVERS
SNMP_SERVERS
SQL_SERVERS
SSH_SERVERS
TELNET_SERVERS
any
IPv4-Private-All
10-net-VPN-pool
10.0.0.64-28-NAT-Pool
Include
Exclude
Network
Add
Save
Cancel

Save your new Default-Set and stop there. Remember, we're leaving $EXTERNAL_NET at it's default value.

Once you have defined $HOME_NET and $EXTERNAL_NET you really don't need to go any further. If you look at the other variables you'll quickly see that **every other IP variable defaults to $HOME_NET**. So there's no need to keep customizing your other IP variables.

You can continue to tweak variables from here if you like. However, please keep in mind that adding additional variable sets or tweaking other variables can easily start to introduce blind spots into your detection.

I would be remiss if I did not mention one last thing. You may have heard that you should exclude $HOME_NET from $EXTERNAL_NET. This is ok in some circumstances but it can lead to false-negatives (missed detection) in others. I think this comes from a misconception about the meaning of trusted, untrusted, protected and unprotected. There is nothing wrong with including $HOME_NET in the $EXTERNAL_NET range. In fact, if you want to detect attacks within your own network it is usually a requirement! That's all I'm going to say about variable sets. I hope I haven't been too confusing.

Security Intelligence

When you think Security Intelligence - think blacklists. I'm including Security Intelligence (SI) objects in the Essential Firepower list because I think it is a powerful feature that everyone should take full advantage of. SI contains three types of blacklists:

- IP address
- URL
- DNS

We will look at how to use these in the Access Control policy chapter. In this chapter we will go over the configurations for the SI feeds.

Talos Feeds

The primary source of SI information is Talos, this is delivered to your FMC in the form of feeds. A feed is basically the FMC periodically reaching out and pulling down the latest SI information via HTTPS. The default interval for these updates is every two hours. However,

Essential Firepower

the information at Talos is updated constantly so you can get more up-to-date intelligence by decreasing this default interval.

I'm a fan of making the update interval as short as the system will allow. It doesn't generate any appreciable traffic because the lists are quite small, and it makes your system able to react faster to the rapidly changing threat landscape. That means bad IP entries will be blocked faster and it also means that good IP entries will be unblocked faster as well.

I mentioned that there are three types of SI data but there are actually only two Talos feeds. One for IP information and one that combines URL and DNS information.

You will find the feed configurations under **Objects → Security Intelligence** as shown below. Clicking **Network Lists and Feeds** brings up the list of IP feeds as shown below. The example below has some custom lists as well so yours will be different.

Clicking the edit pencil for the **Cisco-Intelligence-Feed** shows the feed update settings. This brings up the dialog shown below.

6 - Objects

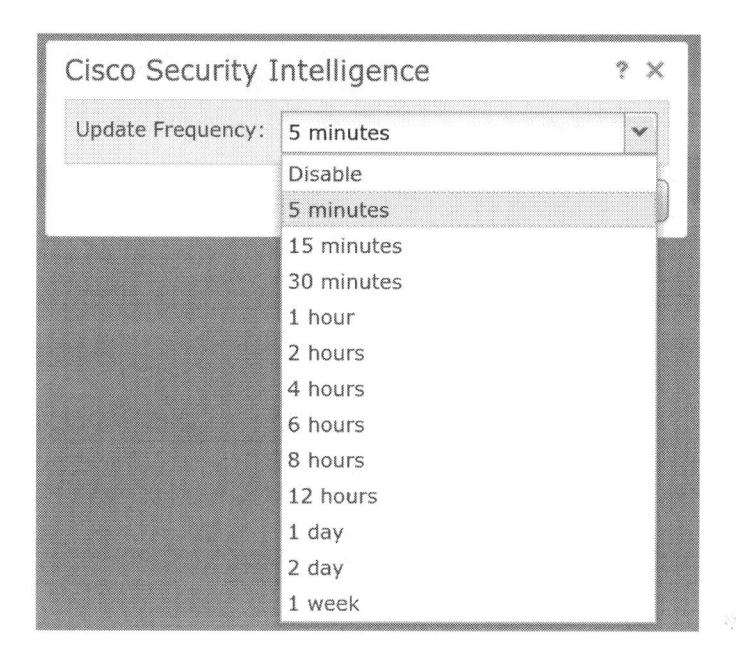

Cisco Security Intelligence	? ×
Update Frequency:	5 minutes ▼

Disable
5 minutes
15 minutes
30 minutes
1 hour
2 hours
4 hours
6 hours
8 hours
12 hours
1 day
2 day
1 week

As you can see, there are quite a few intervals you can select. The default here is 2 hours but you can set the IP feed **Update Frequency** to be as often as every 5 minutes. My advice is to go with the shortest time available for the most agile protection.

You can do the same thing for the **Cisco-DNS-and-URL-Intelligence-Feed**. You will find it under the **DNS Lists and Feeds** section. You'll see a similar dialog however the smallest update window for this feed is 30 minutes.

> BP30 - Consider shortening the default Security Intelligence feed update interval

Custom SI Feeds

In addition to the feeds available from Cisco, you can also add your own SI lists and feeds. Lists are static by nature so they don't lend themselves to rapid deployment or agility. However, feeds are another story. By using a custom feed you can implement your own blacklists quickly and efficiently and without the need to deploy policies.

They work just like the Talos feed except you point the source to your own HTTP/HTTPS server. These are really simple to setup and I

65

Essential Firepower

highly recommend you use them if you have any kind of customized blacklist you want to implement.

Like the Cisco feeds there are three types, IP and DNS and URL. However, while Cisco combines the URL and DNS lists into a single feed, with custom feeds there is one for each of the three types. To create a custom feed make sure you select the feed type in the left column and then click the **Add <feed_type> Lists and Feeds** button (shown below) at the top of the page.

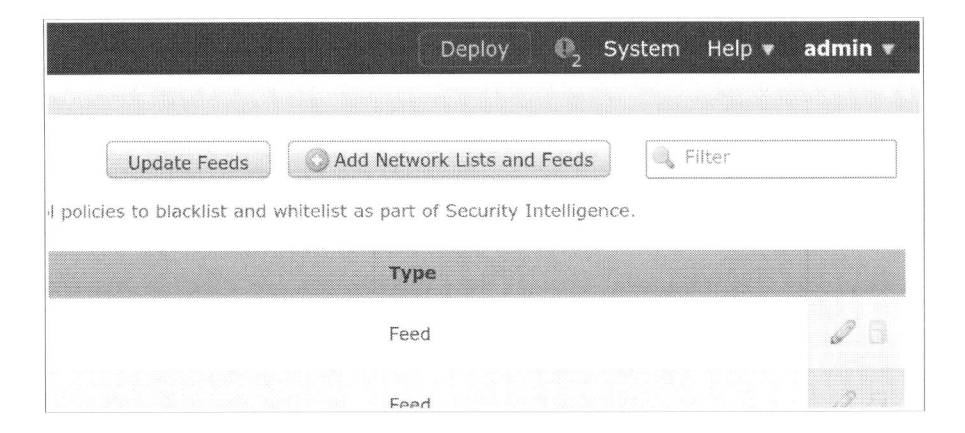

This will give you a dialog like the one below.

Give your feed a **Name** and under the **Type** drop-down select Feed.

6 - Objects

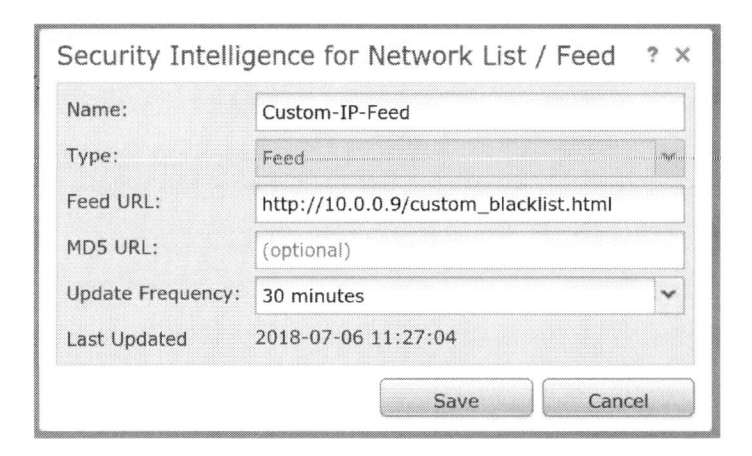

Security Intelligence for Network List / Feed	? ×
Name:	Custom-IP-Feed
Type:	Feed
Feed URL:	http://10.0.0.9/custom_blacklist.html
MD5 URL:	(optional)
Update Frequency:	30 minutes
Last Updated	2018-07-06 11:27:04

Save   Cancel

Fill in your feed information. The shortest frequency you can select for a custom feed is currently 30 minutes.

Save your feed and then add it to the **Security Intelligence** tab in your Access Control policy. More on this in the Access Control chapter!

> BP31 - Don't forget to add your own custom Security Intelligence feeds

67

Chapter 7 - Network Discovery Policy

With Network Discovery policy we are finally getting to the detection policies that will control how our devices inspect traffic. This policy controls the network scope that will be used to populate your host database. This is the database of hosts and associated information that is maintained on your FMC. This database is built primarily by using passive detection and observing traffic as it passes by or through your devices. We have to customize this policy to ensure that we are only creating host records for hosts we want to protect. Once we configure this policy with one or more IP address blocks, the FMC will begin to create host records for every IP address it discovers within these ranges.

There are also some additional Advanced Settings to think about as well so let's get started!

Discovery Networks

Navigate to **Policies → Network Discovery** and you will find yourself looking at the **Networks** tab shown below.

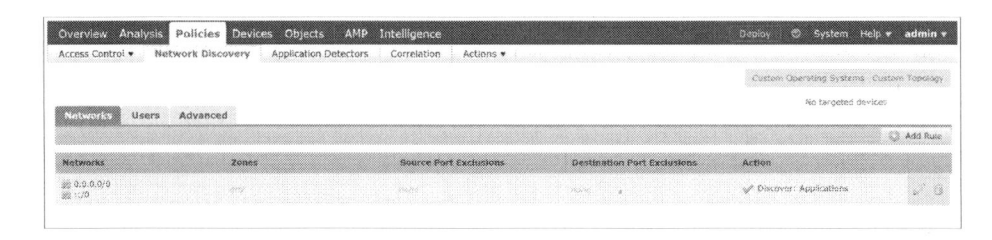

If this is a new FMC, you will probably have a single rule for the

0.0.0.0/0 network showing. This rule allows for application discovery but does not have the **Hosts** or **Users** options checked. It means the system won't create any host database entries by default. The figure below shows the default rule, it contains the entire IPv4 and IPv6 ranges. However, notice that the **Hosts** and **Users** options are not checked.

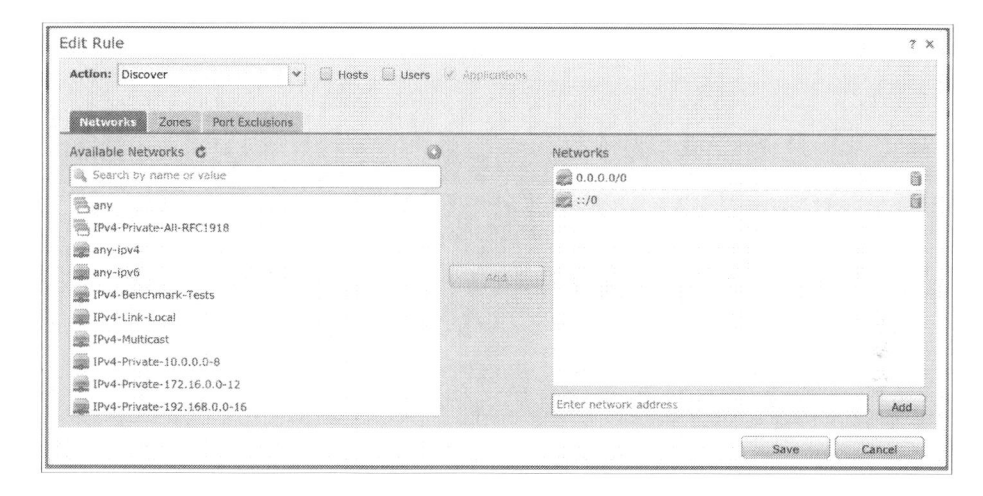

Before we go on let me explain what we're going to do. We need to configure the FMC to discover hosts and users on your internal (protected) network. To do that we're going to use the Network Objects we already setup. It's the same set of objects we configured as the $HOME_NET variable - remember? We're going to set up a single discovery rule to create host entries for these protected network ranges.

The first thing to do is either edit the default rule(s) or delete and create a new one(s). If you edit the rule you'll see something like the figure above.

Here are the changes to make here:

- Check the **Hosts** and **Users** boxes at the top
- Delete everything from the **Networks** column
- Add the network object(s) you configured for your protected network from the **Available Networks** to the **Networks** columns.
- **Save** the rule
- That's it!

Don't worry about the **Zones** or **Port Exclusions** tabs. You will probably never need them.

You just configured Firepower to create host entries in it's database for all of your internal hosts.

> BP32 - Configure Network Discovery to create host records for your protected networks

If you're in a real rush to get moving you can stop here. However, for a better understanding of what Network Discovery does and how to make it work for you - read on.

Users

The Users tab allows you to control which clear-text protocols Firepower will use to associate users with IP addresses. It does this by peeking into the login and the server response to determine the user name of an attempted login. This information is then added to the host record and also generates a User event. You'll find these user events on the FMC under **Analysis → Users**. These are not what we call "authoritative" users meaning you can't use this identity information in your Access Control rules. However, it does provide additional context around some of the security events.

Clicking on the **Users** tab brings you to the page shown below.

7 - Network Discovery Policy

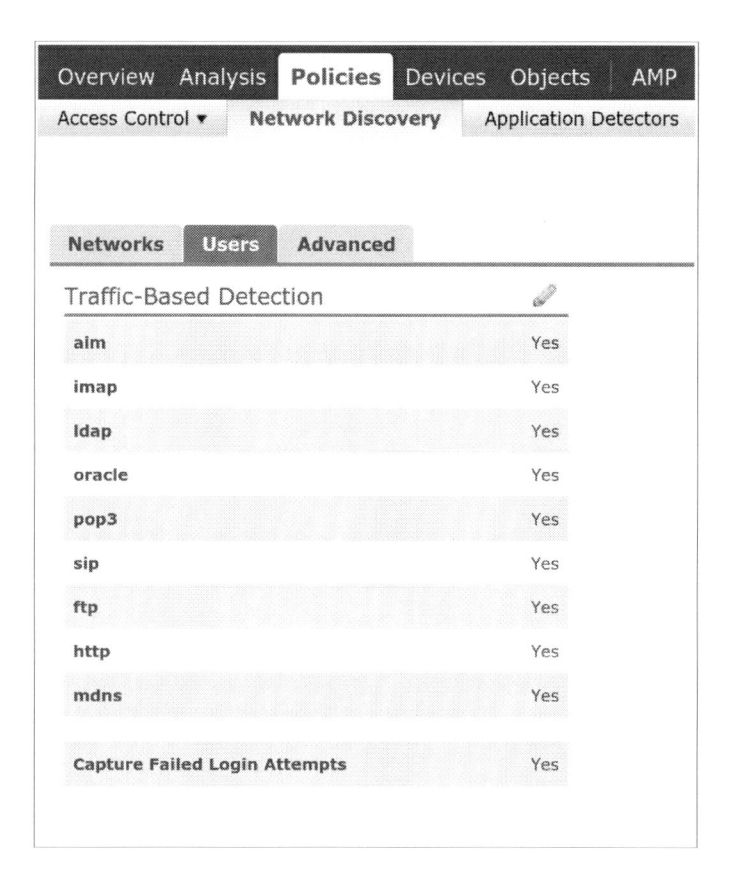

Traffic-Based Detection	
aim	Yes
imap	Yes
ldap	Yes
oracle	Yes
pop3	Yes
sip	Yes
ftp	Yes
http	Yes
mdns	Yes
Capture Failed Login Attempts	Yes

By default, Firepower will examine all the protocols listed and will also associate the user name with the host IP even for failed login attempts. If you find that there are certain protocols that are generating unhelpful or incorrect user events you can disable detection for those protocols here.

Advanced Settings

The **Advanced** tab has several groups of Network Discovery settings you can tweak as shown below.

Essential Firepower

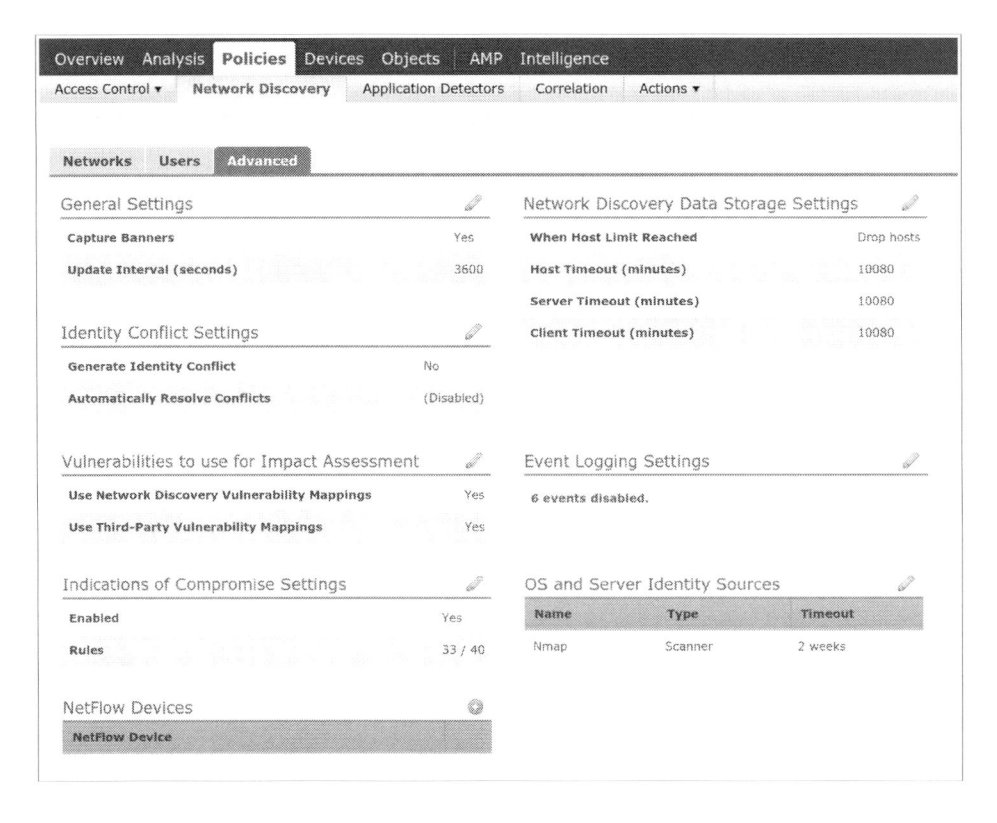

Most of these are best left at their defaults. However, there are some that bear some extra scrutiny.

Event Logging Settings

The first area to look at is **Event Logging Settings**. This controls the type of activity logged to your FMC as Discovery Events. If you are like most folks you didn't even know you were logging Discovery Events. These events record what I call "normal" activities on the network. These are events like:

- New Host
- New TCP Port
- New Network Protocol
- New Transport Protocol
- New UDP port
- New Client
- New OS
- New TCP port
- and many more...

These are triggered by Firepower's discovery process. Of course, for a newly deployed system there is a flurry of this type of events as the FMC builds out information in the database for all the hosts on the network. After that, anytime a new host is discovered and or traffic is seen by the devices, events are generated as the discovery database is updated.

There are also other events that get generated over the normal course of the day. You'll see events like:

- DHCP: IP Address Changed
- UDP Server Information Update
- MAC Information Change
- Additional MAC Detected for Host
- TCP Server Confidence Update
- UDP Server Confidence Update
- and more...

These are a bit more obscure and their meaning. In addition, the usefulness of these events is not as clear. What exactly is "TCP Server Confidence Update" and why should I care? You will also find that events like the ones above along are some of the most ubiquitous.

To see the Discovery Event view go to **Analysis → Hosts → Discovery Events**. There you can see for yourself what events are being recorded. There are actually 33 different Discovery events in all. The figure below shows some Discovery events.

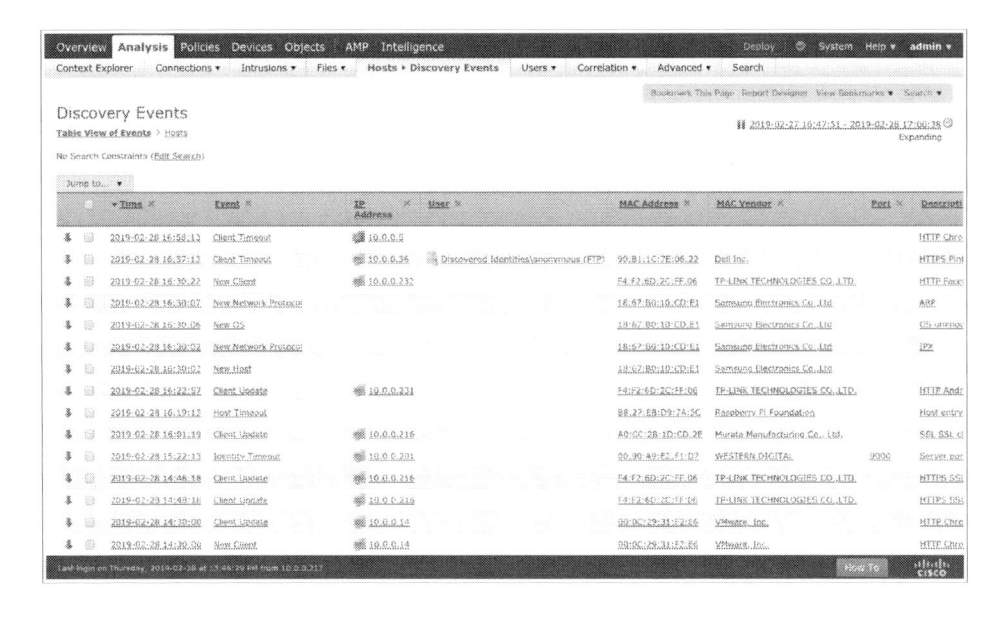

How would you use Discovery Events?

Since you probably didn't even know you had Discovery Events you might ask, "what are they for?" Well, by themselves they are not much use actually. You will rarely if ever find interesting evil activity by sifting through these events.

The best use I have found is to monitor a particular type of activity on specific network segments. For example, if you have a highly sensitive network segment where any new host or host changes would be noteworthy, you can create a Correlation rule with the scope limited to that segment. The rule can then trigger and send a notification if one or more Discovery Events you select are detected within that network segment.

An example of this would be the case when a new host is discovered. This could be a rogue machine or an unauthorized change. In this case you can create a Correlation rule to trigger on the New Host event. Another possibility is the New TCP Port event. This means there is a new service listening that hasn't been seen previously.

Correlation rules provide an effective mechanism for alerting on specific types of events or network activities. This feature did not make the cut for the first edition of *Essential Firepower*, but stay tuned!

There are also some fairly new Discovery Events which do actually have some security relevance. These are:

- Network Based Malware
- Network Based Retrospective
- Host IOC Set

Searching through Discovery events to find these may not be ideal but creating a Correlation rule which triggers on these can also be quite useful.

For now, the recommendation I will make is to disable the Discovery Events you don't need - especially the ones that seem to trigger the most often. I would propose two methods to do this:

1) Disable all the Discovery Events and then if/when you do decide to create a few Correlation rules you can enable the appropriate events.

2) Disable the noisiest Discovery Events. This will eliminate the majority of events and reduce the logging load on your devices and your FMC.

You can look through your events to find the noisiest ones in your environment, or you can just use the list below to start. Here are the events I consider the most numerous and least useful:

- DHCP: IP Address Changed
- UDP Server Information Update
- MAC Information Change
- Additional MAC Detected for Host
- VLAN Tag Information Update
- TCP Server Confidence Update
- UDP Server Confidence Update
- DHCP: IP Address Reassigned
- TCP Server Information Update

To disable logging for these events navigate to **Policies → Network Discovery → Advanced**. Then click the pencil by **Event Logging Settings**. In the figure below you can see that all events are enabled by default.

Essential Firepower

Network Discovery Event Logging	Host Input Event Logging
✔ New Host	✔ Add Scan Result
✔ New TCP Port	✔ Set Vulnerability Impact Qualification
✔ New Network Protocol	✔ Delete Protocol
✔ New Transport Protocol	✔ Delete Client
✔ New UDP Port	✔ Set Operating System Definition
✔ New Client	✔ Set Server Definition
✔ New OS	✔ Delete Host/Network
✔ DHCP: IP Address Changed	✔ Delete Port
✔ UDP Server Information Update	✔ Vulnerability Set Valid
✔ TCP Port Timeout	✔ Vulnerability Set Invalid
✔ UDP Port Timeout	✔ Set Host Criticality
✔ MAC Information Change	✔ Host Attribute Set Value
✔ Additional MAC Detected for Host	✔ Host Attribute Delete Value
✔ Host Type Changed to Network Device	✔ Add Host
✔ VLAN Tag Information Update	✔ Add Port

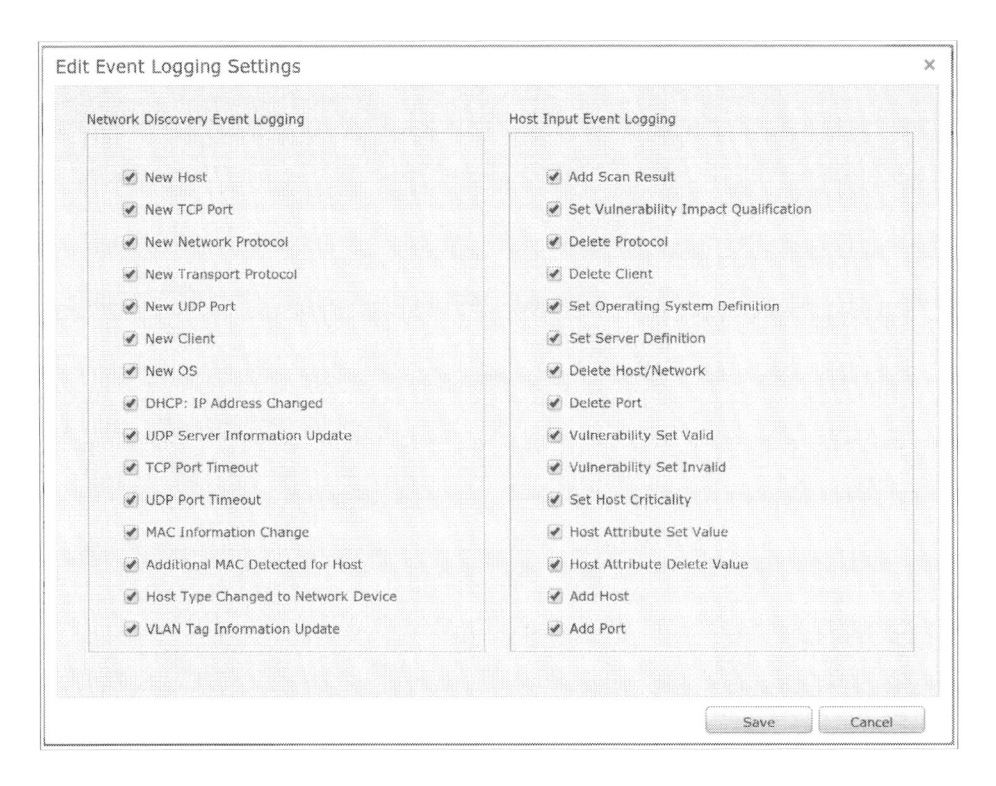

You can ignore the right column, these events are only triggered when using the Host Input API. The discovery events you saw previously (at **Analysis → Hosts → Discovery Events**) will be the ones in the left column. Here you can uncheck the events you feel like you don't need. As I mentioned earlier, you could safely uncheck all of these and it would have no negative impact on Firepower's detection capabilities.

It's important to note that you are simply turning off events here. The host database will continue to be updated as new hosts are discovered, disappear or their characteristics change. The logging here has nothing to do with what is stored in the database. All you are doing is disabling the corresponding event when the database is updated.

|BP33 - Disable noisy Network Discovery events

Indications of Compromise

Returning to **Policies → Network Discovery → Advanced** let's look at another opportunity for tuning in Discovery Policy - the **Indications of Compromise Settings**. Indications of Compromise (IOC) are one of the lesser known and understood features of Firepower. An IOC is simply a flag that is associated with a host. They are triggered when certain events are triggered.

These are not correlated events as in, "if you see this and then this..." Rather they are just a way to draw attention to specific events which may indicate that a host is compromised in some way. There are currently 40 different types of events that can trigger an IOC flag on a host. Clicking on the pencil next to **Indications of Compromise Settings** will bring up the dialog below.

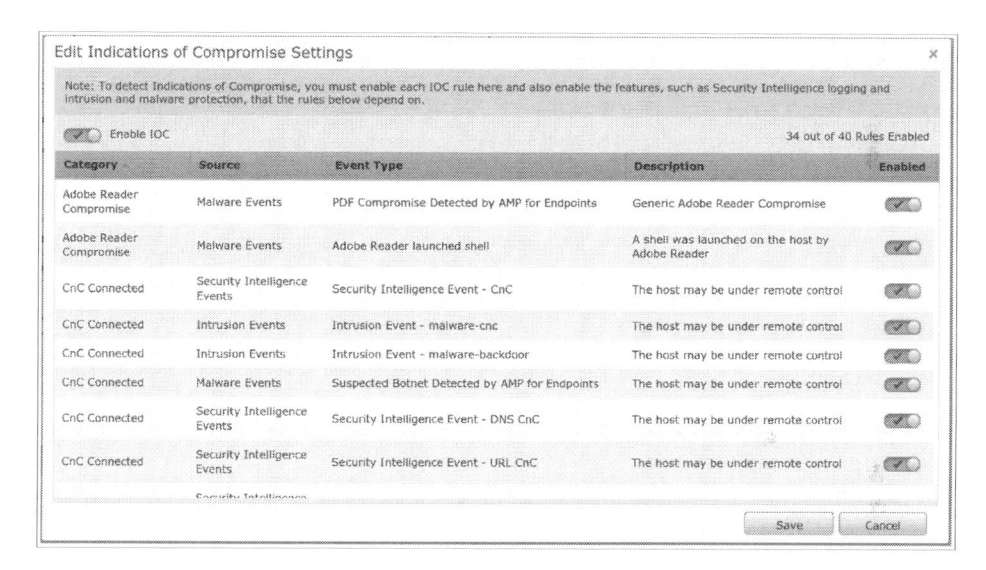

Category	Source	Event Type	Description	Enabled
Adobe Reader Compromise	Malware Events	PDF Compromise Detected by AMP for Endpoints	Generic Adobe Reader Compromise	✓
Adobe Reader Compromise	Malware Events	Adobe Reader launched shell	A shell was launched on the host by Adobe Reader	✓
CnC Connected	Security Intelligence Events	Security Intelligence Event - CnC	The host may be under remote control	✓
CnC Connected	Intrusion Events	Intrusion Event - malware-cnc	The host may be under remote control	✓
CnC Connected	Intrusion Events	Intrusion Event - malware-backdoor	The host may be under remote control	✓
CnC Connected	Malware Events	Suspected Botnet Detected by AMP for Endpoints	The host may be under remote control	✓
CnC Connected	Security Intelligence Events	Security Intelligence Event - DNS CnC	The host may be under remote control	✓
CnC Connected	Security Intelligence Events	Security Intelligence Event - URL CnC	The host may be under remote control	✓

Edit Indications of Compromise Settings

Note: To detect Indications of Compromise, you must enable each IOC rule here and also enable the features, such as Security Intelligence logging and intrusion and malware protection, that the rules below depend on.

Enable IOC — 34 out of 40 Rules Enabled

The first thing I recommend here is to honestly evaluate whether you will use this feature at all. If you don't know (or care) what an IOC is and never plan to use this feature then you should probably just flip off the **Enable IOC** switch in the upper left and disable the feature altogether. There's no shame in doing this and it will prevent you from seeing the little red computer icons in your event views. Turning the computer icon red is what tells you that the host has triggered one or more IOC flags.

When I say "little red computer icons" I'm referring to the icon you see in many event views next to an IP address for a host. There are four of them in the figure below just to the left of the IP address.

Essential Firepower

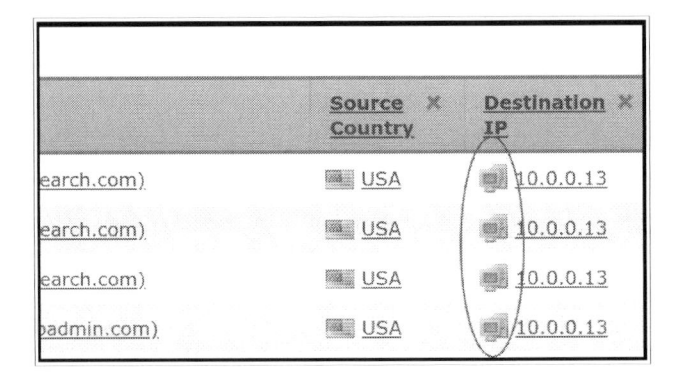

	Source Country	Destination IP
earch.com)	USA	10.0.0.13
earch.com)	USA	10.0.0.13
earch.com)	USA	10.0.0.13
admin.com)	USA	10.0.0.13

This icon can take several forms.

- **Blue** - a host which has an entry in your host database
- **Red** - a host in your database that has one or more IOC flags set
- **Grey** - a host that does not have a record in your database (it's outside the scope of your Discovery policy)

Clicking on this computer icon (if red or blue) will open a new browser window with the host record as shown below.

7 - Network Discovery Policy

Host Profile	
IP Addresses	10.0.0.217
NetBIOS Name	
Device (Hops)	ASA-5515 (1) FTD-2100 (2) NGIPSv 6.2.3 (255)
MAC Addresses (TTL)	00:50:B6:5B:C2:63 (GOOD WAY IND. CO., LTD.) (255) F4:F2:6D:2C:FF:06 (TP-LINK TECHNOLOGIES CO.,LTD.) (254)
Host Type	Host
Last Seen	2019-02-28 20:37:55
Current User	
View	Context Explorer	Connection Events	Intrusion Events	File Events	Malware Events

Indications of Compromise (1)

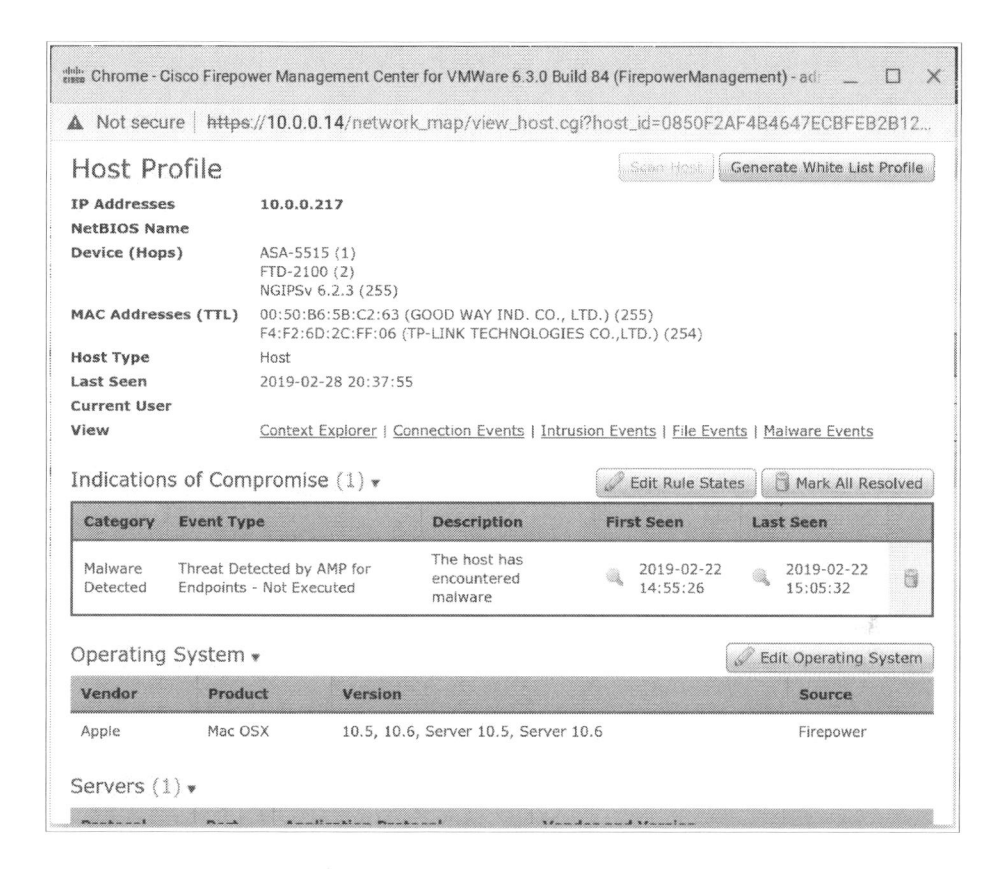

Category	Event Type	Description	First Seen	Last Seen
Malware Detected	Threat Detected by AMP for Endpoints - Not Executed	The host has encountered malware	2019-02-22 14:55:26	2019-02-22 15:05:32

Operating System

Vendor	Product	Version	Source
Apple	Mac OSX	10.5, 10.6, Server 10.5, Server 10.6	Firepower

Servers (1)

This shows all the information currently available in the host database for this IP address. If there is an IOC flag (if the computer icon was red) this will be shown prominently near the top outlined in red. In the figure above, the box under the Indications of Compromise heading is red.

Getting back to the Discovery policy. If you decide you do want to use this feature, then you will probably want to tune it. It will likely take some analysis to determine the particular IOCs you feel are the most accurate and applicable for your environment. However, I have found there are several that I generally always disable. Here are my thoughts on the various IOC categories you will find here.

- **CnC Connected** - these are a pretty good indication that the host has communicated with a CnC server. Especially if it's a workstation that only initiates outbound connections. I've seen some false positives where a CnC server attempted to initiate a connection inbound which of course, doesn't mean the destination IP is compromised.

- **Impact 1 Attack and Impact 2 Attack** - I see a lot of false positives with these. Especially the Impact 2 attacks. Rarely, if ever, do these actually mean a host is compromised.
- **Malware Download and Malware Executed** - definitely good indications to take note of.
- **Anything with a Malware Events source** - this probably came from AMP for Endpoints and are a good indication that the host encountered malware. It might not actually be compromised but it did see something bad.

The bottom line is to understand where this setting is and realize that you can tune out noisy IOCs and make this feature more valuable. Any time you can reduce noise and make your alerts more actionable it's a win.

Simply switch off the IOCs you don't like and they won't trigger on any of your hosts.

There is one other way to tune these on a per-host basis. If you look at the Host Profile figure below you'll see a button labeled **Edit Rule States**.

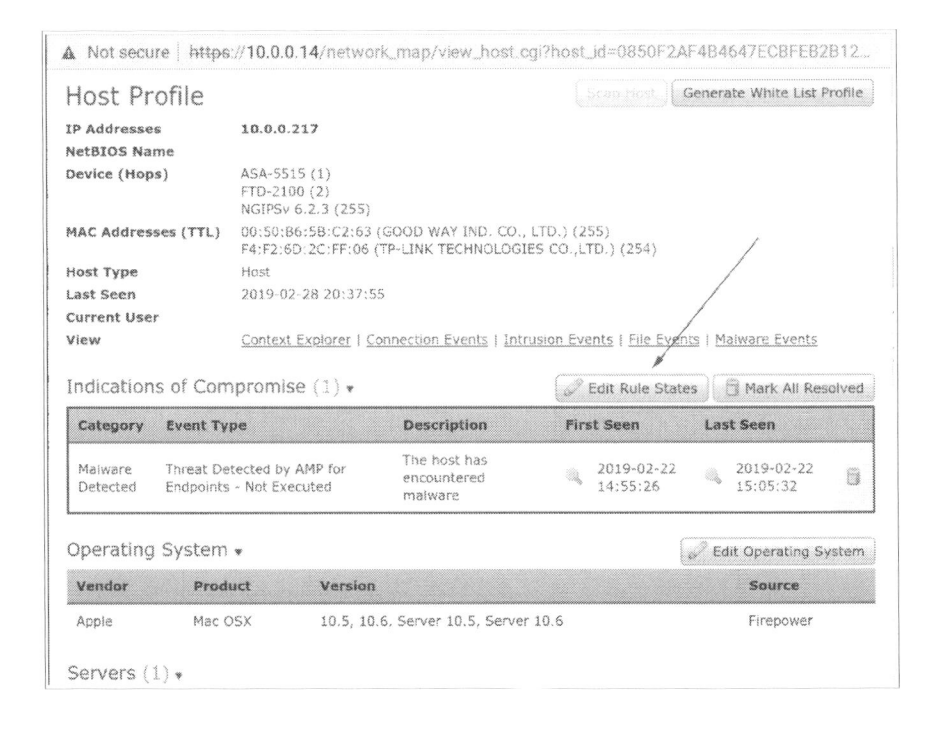

Clicking this button will allow you to enable/disable IOCs for this host only. While this is a very granular way to control IOCs, it is really not a viable method for most folks as it requires constant tweaking of individual hosts.

> BP34 - consider tuning Indications of Compromise to reduce false positive IOCs

Chapter 8 - Intrusion Policy

When you say "Intrusion policy" in Firepower, you mean Snort rules. Prior to version 5.4 the Intrusion policy contained all of the Snort configurations found in the snort.conf as well as it's associated rules files. However, as of version 5.4 and later the "Advanced" settings were relocated to the Network Analysis policy. This leaves the Intrusion policy to deal with Snort rules and just a handful of other miscellaneous settings. However, splitting the advanced settings off into a different policy did not decrease the importance of the Intrusion policy. Your Snort rule set is still a major factor in the effectiveness of your devices when it comes to deep packet inspection.

Policy Information

When you begin editing an Intrusion policy you start at the **Policy Information** screen. You will find Intrusion policy on the FMC under **Policies → Access Control → Intrusion**. Editing an existing policy will bring you to the page shown below.

Before we dive in, I want to mention something that is a pet peeve of mine. You will notice that when creating several types of policies you have an option to enter the policy name and description. My advice here is – make the description descriptive! I've watched Firepower admins constantly enter the name of the policy twice - once in the Name and once in the Description field. This doesn't benefit anyone. If you don't have any idea what to put in the Description field, just leave it blank. Repeating the name is pointless. Better yet, put in a few words describing the policy.

> BP35 – Make your policy Description descriptive

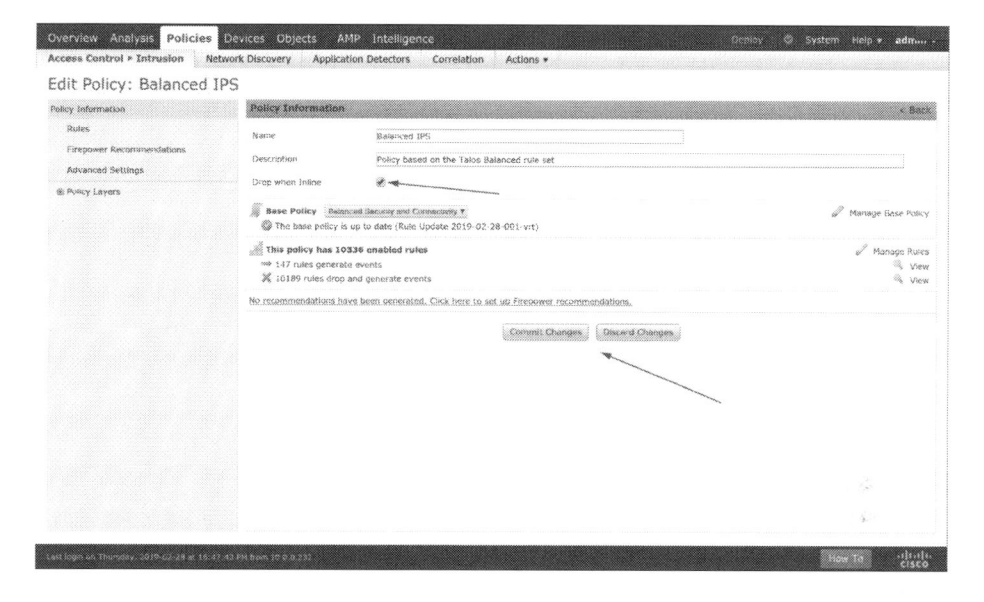

There are two items on this page worth noting, the **Drop when inline** check box and the **Commit Changes** and **Discard Changes** buttons.

Drop when inline

The **Drop when inline** setting is somewhat self-explanatory. If this is unchecked, rules will not drop traffic. Snort rules which are set to **Drop and Generate Events** will register "would have dropped" as the Inline Result. Rules set to **Generate Events** will create intrusion events with an empty Inline Result. When initially deploying an inline device you should always start with this box unchecked.

> BP36 - Upon initial deployment of an inline or routed device, leave the "Drop when inline" checkbox unchecked.

The reasons are fairly obvious. You are deploying a brand new device in your network which is designed to detect and block malicious traffic. It's important to understand what traffic it deems malicious and ensure you aren't going to impact legitimate traffic before you start blocking. After you have vetted and tuned your policy settings, you can check this box and start blocking evil with your devices.

This setting is also important if you have devices deployed in different modes with your organization. Say you have some deployed as inline devices - meaning they can actually drop offending traffic. If you also have other devices deployed passively (inspecting a copy of traffic via a tap or span port) it's important not to use the same policy on both. The inline device(s) should have the **Drop when inline** box checked in its policy while the passive device(s) should not.

The reason for this is not because of a difference in how the devices inspect traffic. It is because of the intrusion events they will generate. I mentioned the "would have dropped" (WHD) events above already. These events are generated when a rule in the **Drop and Generate Events** state matches traffic but the Intrusion policy does not have **Drop when inline** selected. The system is telling you, "I would have dropped this packet if the **Drop when inline** box was enabled for this policy." The key information here is that the packet was not dropped.

But what if you deploy a policy with **Drop when inline** enabled to a device in passive mode? Of course, it still won't drop traffic. However, the the Inline Result column for intrusion events generated by that device will indicate the packet was dropped - a black arrow. (The grey arrow indicates a "would have dropped" event.) Both are shown in the intrusion event table view snipped below.

	▼ Time ✕	Priority ✕	Impact ✕	Inline Result ✕	Source IP ✕	Source Country ✕
⬇ ☐	2019-01-31 03:09:39	high	2	⬇	185.254.120.21	LTU
⬇ ☐	2019-01-04 12:37:55	high	2	⬇	47.90.92.121	HKG

Notice the first event has a grey arrow in the **Inline Result** column while the second event has a dark arrow. If you deploy a policy with the **Drop when inline** box checked to a passive device, it will register drop events for rules that are set to **Drop and Generate Events**.

These events will mix in with the actual drop events from your inline devices and confusion will reign! This stems from the fact that your Talos base policy rule state will be set to **Drop and Generate Events** for the vast majority of enabled rules. The Talos philosophy is something like, "If a rule is worth enabling then the traffic is worth dropping."

Someone might say that you should also change the state of all your

8 - Intrusion Policy

Drop and Generate Events rules to **Generate Events** for your passive policies. It is true, that if you did that then the Inline Result column for these events would be blank instead of a grey arrow. Technically this would provide the most accurate picture of a **Generate Events** rule that triggered on a passive device.

This is an option, but because of the Talos default rule states it will require constantly editing the policy and changing rule states every time you get an SRU update – which by default is twice a week. In my book (no pun intended) that's too much work. I think it's enough to know whether a packet was dropped or not, and simply unchecking the **Drop when inline** box will accomplish this.

However, probably the biggest reason not to do this is you are manually overriding the state of the Talos rules. As we will see later in this chapter, enabling rules manually means you also take on the responsibility of disabling them when they are no longer viable.

> BP37 - Don't deploy Intrusion policies with "Drop when inline" enabled on passive devices.

Commit and Discard

When you are editing an Intrusion policy you do not have to constantly save your edits as you progress from one screen to another. All of your changes are saved in a temporary policy. You can even navigate away from the page while your editing or close the browser tab and your changes will persist. The next time you edit the policy you can continue with your changes. When you are finished, and ready to commit the changes you then press the **Commit Changes** button. If you change your mind and want to discard all the changes you've made - press the **Discard Changes** button.

This is all fine and good however I do have some advice when editing policies. It's pretty simple - don't navigate away from the policy editing screen without clicking one of these two buttons. If you do, your policy will be left in a state of limbo. It has pending changes but they have not been committed. This is indicated by an asterisk next to the policy name. The "Balanced IPS" policy in the figure below is in this limbo state. Notice the **Status** column also says "*You are currently editing this policy*".

Essential Firepower

Intrusion Policy	Drop when Inline	Status
ACME APAC APAC Intrusion Policy	Yes	Used by 1 access control policy Policy not applied on any devices
ACME Base Intrusion ** Base for all ACME policies **	Yes	No access control policies use this policy Policy not applied on any devices
Balanced IPS* Policy based on the Talos Balanced rule set	Yes	You are currently editing this policy No access control policies use this policy Policy not applied on any devices

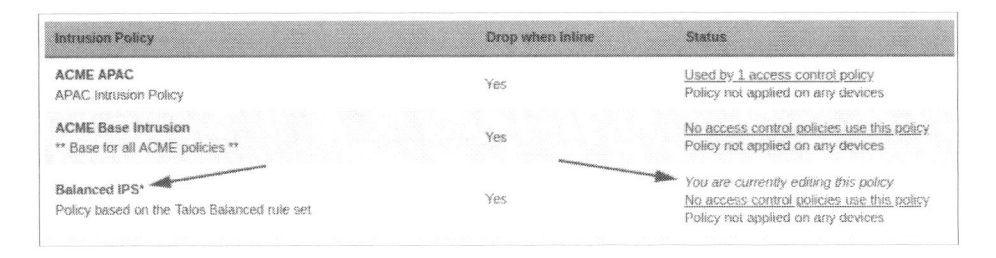

The way this usually happens is like this. Bob clicks on an Intrusion policy just to look at some settings. He doesn't change anything. However, simply editing a policy puts it into this limbo state, even if no changes have been made. Later, he might navigate away or close the browser tab. If Bob or Alice returns later and attempts to edit another policy he/she will receive the message show below.

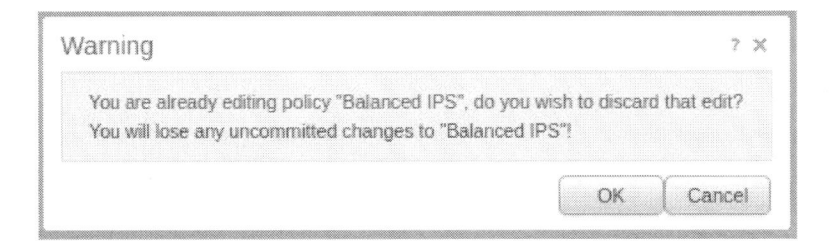

> **Warning** ? X
>
> You are already editing policy "Balanced IPS", do you wish to discard that edit? You will lose any uncommitted changes to "Balanced IPS"!
>
> OK   Cancel

Once again confusion reigns. Bob and Alice are both asking themselves: "Did I edit this policy? Did somebody else? Are these edits important?" You could use the Audit log to try and determine who was the last one editing the policy but wow, what a pain. This leads me to the recommendation below:

> BP38 - When you edit an Intrusion policy, whether you make changes or not, always click either the **Commit Changes** or **Discard Changes** button when you are finished.

Policy Layers

Intrusion policies come in layers. All policies will have at least two layers. If you add Firepower Recommendations you will have three layers. You can add additional layers as well (but be careful). This section is basically going to be a short warning about using layers.

How Layers Work

The idea behind layers is that they combine changes to rule states, suppressions, thresholds, etc. into a resulting rule set. The basic principle is that higher layers override lower layers. That is, if a particular rule is enabled in a lower layer but it is disabled in a higher layer the end state of that rule is disabled. Most of the time, higher layers inherit the majority of the rule states from lower layers. They only override a small number of rules.

The table below illustrates how layers work. It shows two layers on the left, My Changes and Talos Base. At the top the "End State" shows what the rule state will be once the layer states are all resolved. All rules will start with a rule state from the Talos base policy. The three states are:

- Disabled
- Generate Events
- Drop and Generate Events

We usually use the terms "drop" and "alert" when referring to the Drop and Generate or the Generate Events rule states.

> *Note: The rule states don't correspond 100% with the Snort rule action in the rule header. The exception is "pass" rules. There are no pass rules from Talos by default but you can create your own to tune out specific alerts. If you do create a pass rule you would enable it by setting the state to Generate Events. This activates the rule in the policy but does not change the actual Snort action to alert.*

By default, the My Changes layer will contain no changes. So, if you have a new policy, any rule states set by Talos will be the final rule end state as shown below.

Default Policy Layers

	Rule 1	Rule 2	Rule 3
End State	Drop	Disabled	Drop
My Changes Layer	<none>	<none>	<none>
Talos Base Layer	Drop	Disabled	Drop

If you wanted to override the Talos rule state for Rule 2 you could change the rule state to Alert (Generate events) and your policy would look like the one below. Notice the rule 2 state is now different.

My Changes Rule Override

	Rule 1	Rule 2	Rule 3
End State	Drop	Alert	Drop
My Changes Layer	<none>	Alert	<none>
Talos Base Layer	Drop	Disabled	Drop

If we add another layer to the policy it might look like the one below. In this case the layer was added by Firepower Recommendations but it would work the same if this was an additional custom layer.

Multiple Custom Layers

	Rule 1	Rule 2	Rule 3
End State	Drop	Alert	Disabled
My Changes Layer	<none>	Alert	<none>
Firepower Recommendations	Drop	Disabled	Disabled
Talos Base Layer	Drop	Disabled	Drop

Note that now both custom layers have the opportunity to override the Talos Base policy. However, if they disagree as in Rule 2 then the highest layer (My Changes) wins.

You may have noticed there is actually a fourth rule state. It's called <none> in the tables above but it's labeled **Inherit** in the policy management UI. It's not technically a rule state. More on that coming up.

8 - Intrusion Policy

As you already know, your policy will start out with two layers. One called My Changes and the base policy layer. This base policy is the one you selected when you created the Intrusion policy or modified it on the main **Policy Information** screen. When you click the **+** icon to the left of **Policy Layers** you see the layers in the left sidebar.

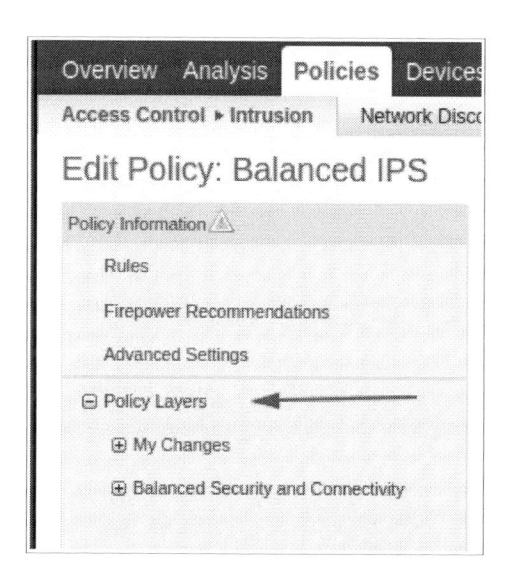

Notice in the example above you have the built-in **My Changes** layer and this policy is using the Talos **Balanced Security and Connectivity** policy as its base layer.

You can get more information by clicking on the **Policy Layers** link itself.

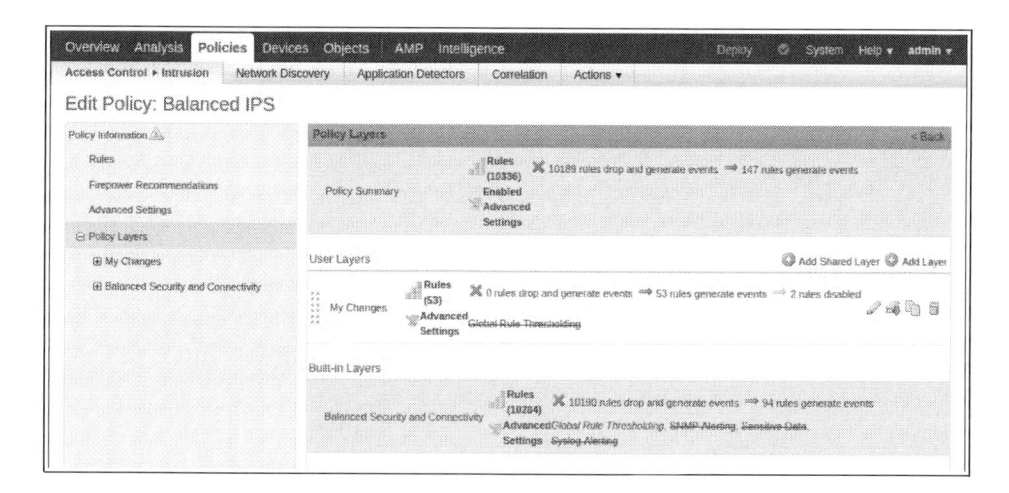

Now you can see the details of the layers on the right. We see a summary of the rules and **Advanced Settings** that are changed at each layer as well as a **Policy Summary** at the top showing the result of the changes in all the layers.

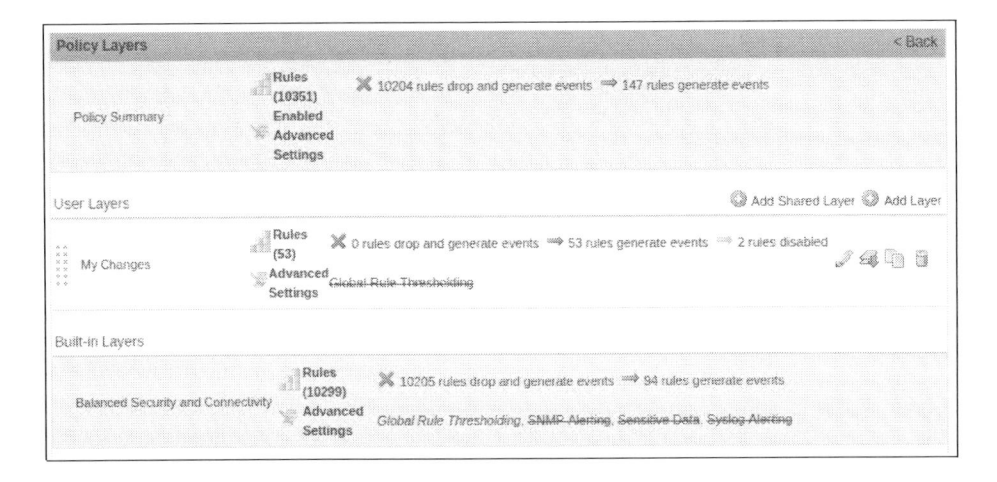

In the figure above after zooming up on the layers portion of the screen we see that the **My Changes** layer disables **Global Rule Thresholding** (signified by strike through text), sets 53 rules to generate events and 2 rules are disabled.

Using the icons on the right, you can add private and shared layers to this policy. Private layers contain settings limited to this policy however share layers can be shared across multiple policies. This sounds appealing because if you have multiple policies you can share a layer and then make changes across these policies by only changing them in the Shared Layer. There's no need to go and make the same change to multiple policies.

Danger Will Robinson - Danger!

Let me just say that using Shared Layers is almost universally a bad idea. You have to be very good at understanding your policies and you need to have the layer structure documented somewhere outside of Firepower. I would call this an advanced usage scenario and definitely not something for the majority of Firepower deployments. Now, that doesn't mean there isn't a use-case for layering but I do it in a different way which I think is much easier to understand and use -

> BP39 - Avoid using Shared Layers in your Intrusion policy - you'll thank me later.

That doesn't mean don't use layers at all. Although the vast majority of users won't need to create any beyond the defaults already there. The most common use-case I've seen for creating layers is to implement temporary changes to a policy. If you want to temporarily change some rule states you can insert a new layer and make the changes there. Later, when you are ready to remove those changes, it's simply a matter of deleting the layer. If you decide you like the changes and want to make them permanent you can then Merge the layer with the layer below it.

The Merge Layer Down button ( ) can be used to do this merging. Of course you can only merge user layers. For example, you can't merge the My Changes layer with the base Built-in layer. But there's still a better way.

Base Policies

Instead of using Shared Layers, I find that using policy base layers is a much easier concept to understand and is also easier to implement and maintain. I recommend this strategy often with customers who have several Intrusion policies within their environment.

Once you start multiplying your Intrusion policies you quickly have a problem. Unless you've done something to tie them together, each one is an island to itself. Sure, they may all be based on one of the Talos policies but other than that they are all separate.

What if you need to enable/disable a rule across all your policies? You could add a Shared Layer to each policy. Yes, that would work but now you need to know which policies are *using* that layer and which policy is *hosting* that layer. You see, you can't edit a Shared Layer in a policy that is just using it, you have to do so in the policy that is hosting it. For a single shared layer it's probably not that difficult but

I still think using the policy hierarchy I'm going to describe here is more intuitive in the long run.

This strategy involves creating a "Base" policy for your devices. So far, we've seen that every policy has to start from another policy. Most of the time this base policy is one of the system-provided Talos rule sets. However, you can also use one of your own policies for the base policy. A picture is worth a thousand words so here's what this looks like for a simple policy set:

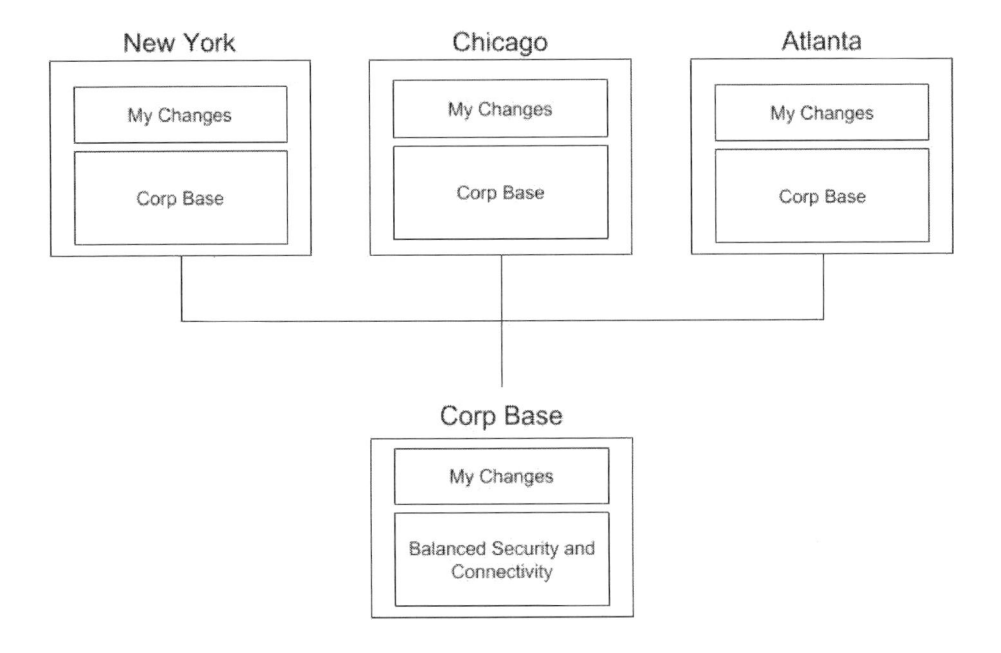

```
     New York              Chicago              Atlanta
   ┌──────────┐         ┌──────────┐         ┌──────────┐
   │My Changes│         │My Changes│         │My Changes│
   ├──────────┤         ├──────────┤         ├──────────┤
   │Corp Base │         │Corp Base │         │Corp Base │
   └─────┬────┘         └─────┬────┘         └─────┬────┘
         └────────────────────┼────────────────────┘
                              │
                          Corp Base
                     ┌──────────────────┐
                     │   My Changes     │
                     ├──────────────────┤
                     │Balanced Security │
                     │  and Connectivity│
                     └──────────────────┘
```

In the example above there is a base policy called Corp Base. This policy is using the Talos Balanced Security and Connectivity policy as its base layer. This policy serves as the base layer for the three regional policies above. The Corp Base policy is never deployed to any devices, it only serves as the base for the other policies which are deployed to their respective devices.

This design is really the best of both worlds when it comes to ease of administration and flexibility. What I mean is you get:

- The ability to make a change in one place (Corp Base) and in so doing enable/disable rules across all your policies
- The ability to make specific changes to any of the location-specific policies so you can tailor rule sets to a location as

needed

You can see that even with just a few policies there is an advantage to using this base policy design. I've seen deployments with 10+ policies where the administrator was editing all of them to make changes company-wide. This is a better way!

> BP40 - Consider a hierarchical policy model if you have multiple Intrusion policies.

Rule Set Selection

The heart of the Intrusion policy is the rule set. The FMC database contains the rules provided by the Talos group at Cisco. It may contain your own custom rules or 3rd party rules but for now we will just consider those provided by Cisco. As of this writing there are nearly 37,000 rules in total. It's important to understand that the policy does not contain the rules, rather it determines the *state* for these rules.

When it comes to selecting a rule set for your deployment, you have several choices. The following policies are available from Talos:

- No Rules Active
- Connectivity Over Security
- Balanced Security and Connectivity
- Security Over Connectivity
- Maximum Detection

These policies are referred to as System Provided Policies. It's important to note that the starting point for your own policy rule set *must* be one of the Talos policies. All policies lead back to Talos sooner or later. Here's a quick description of each.

No Rules Active
This policy is fairly self-explanatory, it leaves all rules disabled. Any rules set to drop or alert would have to be set at a layer above the base. If you want to have complete control over your rule set then start with this policy. Nothing Talos does will ever impact your rule set. I don't recommend this option.

Connectivity Over Security
The connectivity policy swings the pendulum pretty far in favor of connectivity versus security. It is a very minimal rule set which will provide only basic security. It also runs virtually no chance of impacting connectivity. The enabled rule count (drop and alert rules) runs around 500-600 rules. We're talking small! Back in the day when implementing an IPS was a compliance checkbox we saw this rule set used from time to time. But today there is a better understanding that just putting a device on the network isn't good enough, it has to actually do something. Not to mention this is an expensive solution and folks want their money's worth. I don't recommend this rule set either.

Balanced Security and Connectivity
The balanced rules set hits the sweet spot for most customers. As you may guess, this is a balance of the needs of security and connectivity. It runs a little over 10,000 rules with about 95% set to drop and 5% set to alert. Even with this many rules, we rarely see any business impact from rule false positives. The datasheet throughput numbers for each device model are also based on this rule set. This is the one I recommend for any inline deployment.

Security Over Connectivity
The security rule set (SoC) adds on the balanced rule set by enabling additional rules. These rules may have less critical Common Vulnerability Scoring System (CVSS) scores and/or they may represent threats that are a bit older. This rule set will not perform as well as the balanced rule set and will require additional tuning. The SoC rule set is fine if you have a passive device and are ok with the additional tuning. I don't typically recommend it in an inline deployment although it is being used that way in some cases. There is nothing wrong with using this set if your device is inline with traffic. Just realize that you will have more tuning to reduce noise and false positives. Right now this rule set is running about 15,000 rules with over 98% set to drop.

Maximum Detection
The max detection rule set was added by Talos a few years ago. At first it only had about 4,000 rules and was a bit of a curiosity. It caused some confusion with customers because the name made it look like, "if you want the most aggressive rule set - this is it!" For a long time it was still a little confusing because the number of enabled rules was about the same as the security rule set.

The real difference in the max detection rule set is the associated Maximum Detection Network Analysis policy. If you use this rule set with the same-named Network Analysis policy you will truly have maximum detection - and minimal performance. The settings in the Network Analysis policy are very aggressive especially when it comes to deep inspection of protocols like HTTP. In addition, Talos made a change in early May of 2019 upping the enabled rule count to a whopping 28,000 rules!

This policy really should only be used for rare situations or test environments. The performance and false positive rate are probably not going to be acceptable for most production networks.

I'm going to stop here and give my best practice advice for selecting a base rule set for your deployment.

> BP41 - Start with the Balanced Security and Connectivity Intrusion policy

That's simple and straightforward. Most deployments are going to be best served by this policy. If you want to try the Security Over Connectivity policy that's ok too but keep in mind you will have more tuning to do and reduced performance.

If you are interested in the starting criteria for enabling rules in the various Talos policies refer to Appendix B. I have not done any analysis to see how closely this criteria is followed in the actual policies. At any rate, I would expect that Talos always reserves the right to make exceptions on a per rule basis.

Intrusion Rules

Now that you know my position on the base rule set I'm going to go quickly over how you might customize the Snort rule set. But make no mistake, I am NOT recommending you do so. If you find a rule here and there you would like to enable that's fine. Please don't start going through the new rules and enabling all of them. That's why you pick a rule set and allow the experts (Talos) to do that research for you.

Here is my reasoning. By allowing Talos to do their job you are getting the best, most efficient rule set for general purpose use. Talos not only decides which rules to enable (set to alert or drop) but they also decide which rules not to enable. When their time has passed, Talos also decides which rules to disable. In so doing, the various rule sets are maintained roughly around their same numbers. Any time you decide to override a Talos rule state you are taking that responsibility on. You then must decide what rules are enabled and when it's safe to disable them. However, most customers leave off that last part - the part about disabling rules. They are great at enabling new rules but terrible about reviewing their rule set regularly and disabling those which are no longer needed. As a result the rule set grows over time. This creates more false positives and reduces system performance.

> *Note: Please remember this is an "Essentials" book. If you have a purpose-built environment such as IoT, SCADA, trading, etc. feel free to customize the rule set as needed. Hopefully, you have the staff and time resources to properly select and tune your specific rules. It's perfectly ok to pick and choose and even reject any of my advice that doesn't apply to you!*

I don't plan to go over all the mechanics of maintaining rules in the Intrusion policy but I do want to highlight some useful areas. First, to see the list of rules, click the **Rules** link on the left side of the policy edit page.

You can also expand the **Policy Layers** link on the left then expand the layers and click the **Rules** link there. You end up with almost the same view however there's a difference. Are you looking a a policy layer or are you looking at the final rule state? This is explained below.

Rule Layers

The figure below shows the rule page.

8 - Intrusion Policy

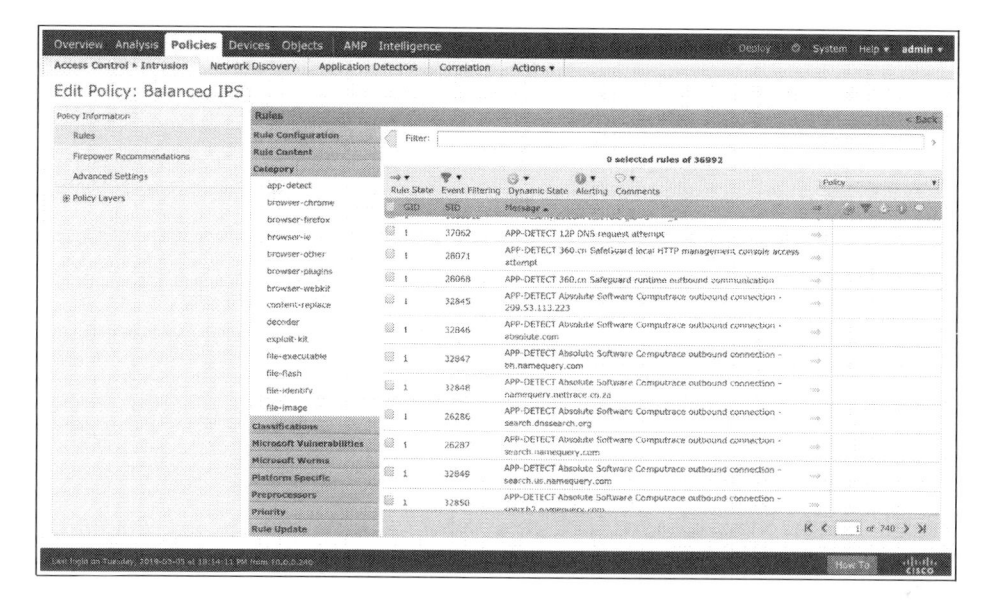

I know this figure is a bit of an eye chart on a small book page but we'll enlarge the sections as we go along. As I said, I'm not going to discuss every nuance here, just the important points.

First, it's important to know if you're looking at a layer or at the "resultant" rule set. To understand this, look at the drop-down on the right. The figure below shows the upper right corner of the screen.

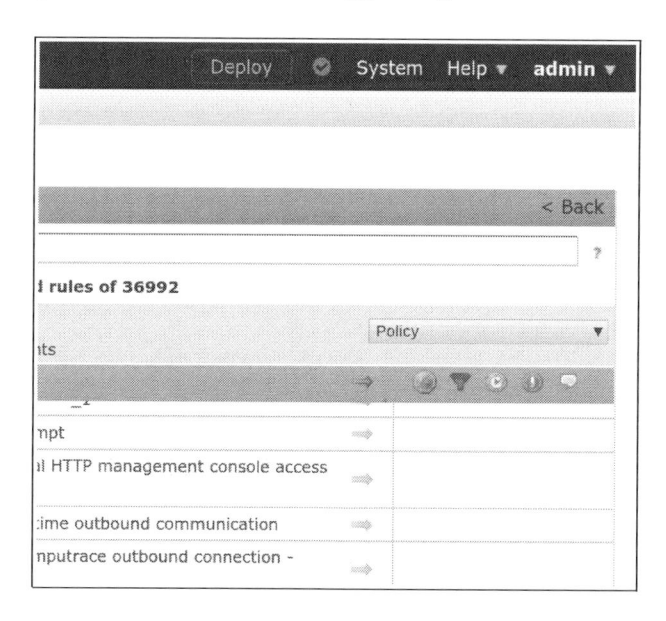

In the figure above the drop-down says "Policy". Clicking on the drop-down shows three options in my example policy, shown below, let's

97

define them.

- **Policy** - this is not a layer per se. This is the "resultant" state of the rules when the My Changes and Base Policy layers are combined. This is what I called "End State" in the layer examples earlier in the chapter. This shows the real, final state the rules will be when you deploy the policy. If a rule shows that it's enabled here you can see the final state but you can't tell which layer set this state. It could be **My Changes** or it could be the **Base Policy**. If you enable/disable rules in this view and your changes will go into the My Changes (top) layer.
- **Layer: My Changes** - this is the My Changes layer itself. This shows the same rules but the state may be different then you saw in the **Policy** above. By viewing the layer you can now see any state changes that were made specifically at this layer. In a fresh policy you won't see any rules enabled or disabled here because all the rule states are being inherited from the **Base Policy**.
- **Base Policy** - like the **My Changes** layer, selecting this shows you the rule states as set by the **Base Policy**. Rule states here are read-only. Regardless of the base policy - whether it's from Cisco or your own - you cannot change the rule states at this layer.

So the bottom line is, if you want to see *if* a rule is enabled/disabled you should use the **Policy** view. If you want to see *where* a rule is enabled/disabled you will need to drill into the specific layer and see for yourself.

Searching Rules

The rule set is large, because of this it's important to understand how to pair down this list into something manageable. There are a ton of ways to slice and dice rules by using the predefined keywords on the left. We used to call this the "rule group accordion" because of the way it slides up and down. If you click on one of the keyword categories such as **Rule Configuration** at the top you see there are quite a few predefined ways to filter the rule set. As you can see in the figure below, you can select rules by criteria such as:

- Rule state - Generate, Drop, Disabled, etc.
- Firepower Recommendation
- Threshold - Limit, Threshold, both, etc.
- Suppression - by rule, by source, by destination
- Dynamic State - by rule, by source, by destination, etc.
- Alert - SNMP, All
- Comment - set a comment filter

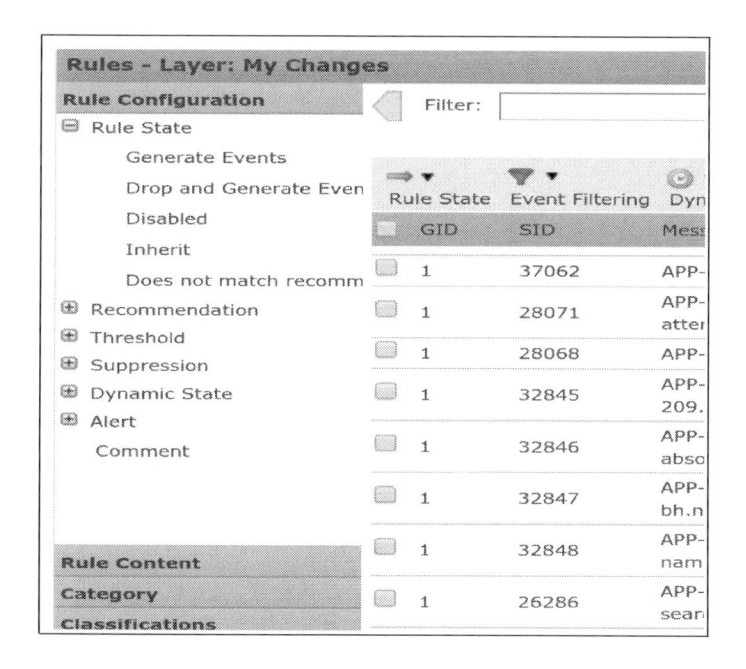

By clicking on **Generate Events** for example this will filter the list to only rules that are set to that rule state (also known as "alert"). When you click there you'll notice that the **Filter** bar at the top fills in with the search criteria. Below you can see **State: "Generate Events"** in the **Filter** bar.

This **Filter** bar is a free-form search. You could have typed this criteria in yourself if you wanted to. Using a predefined search just makes it easier. Still if you wanted to search for a particular term in the rule you could type it in and hit Enter.

If you are searching keep in mind that this is not a full-text search of the entire rule. Only select fields are searchable. For instance, you can't search for "pcre" and find all the rules using the Snort pcre keyword in the rule body.

Still it's very handy to find out something like, "how many rules have I enabled in the **My Changes** layer?" Moving down the accordion you can find a myriad of other ways to search. One that's particularly helpful is at the bottom under **Rule Update**.

Using the **Rule Update** search is a great way to answer the question, "what new rules were released yesterday?" Or, "which rules were modified in the last rule release (SRU)?"

You would do this by scrolling down the **Rule Update** list until you find the Snort Rule Update (SRU) that was released on the date you are interested in. Clicking on this will show all the new and changed rules regardless of their state. In the figure below a single SRU is selected, you can see that 18 rules were added or modified in this release.

	GID	SID	Message
	1	49254	FILE-OFFICE Microsoft Office Word styleWithEffects us attempt
	1	49253	FILE-OFFICE Microsoft Office Word styleWithEffects us attempt
	1	49289	FILE-OTHER WinRAR ACE remote code execution
	1	49290	FILE-OTHER WinRAR ACE remote code execution
	1	49294	FILE-PDF Adobe Acrobat out of bounds read atte
	1	49295	FILE-PDF Adobe Acrobat out of bounds read atte
	1	49328	MALWARE-CNC Win.Ransomware.Crytekk varian compromise outbound connection detected
	1	49327	MALWARE-CNC Win.Ransomware.Crytekk varian compromise outbound connection detected
	1	49329	MALWARE-CNC Win.Ransomware.Crytekk varian compromise outbound connection detected
	1	49330	MALWARE-CNC Win.Ransomware.Crytekk varian compromise outbound connection detected
	1	49331	MALWARE-CNC Win.Trojan.Arescrypt malicious r download attempt
	1	49332	MALWARE-CNC Win.Trojan.Arescrypt malicious r download attempt

By expanding the SRU entry (click the + icon) you'll see you have other options like which rules were changed and which rules were new. You can then combine this with the **Rule Configuration** search above to find information such as the new rules set to drop in a particular SRU.

Essential Firepower

Which leads to another key bit of information. As you click on different predefined searches your searches combine. Basically every new search is connected with an AND. Be careful as you can quickly combine a number of criteria and make your search too narrow. The result is no rule appear in your list at all.

As you can see below, there are no rules from the SRU selected which are in the Generate Events state and the malware-cnc category. Somebody got too happy clicking criteria on the left and now the result is no rules found. If you aren't careful you might forget that you've combined a number of searches together.

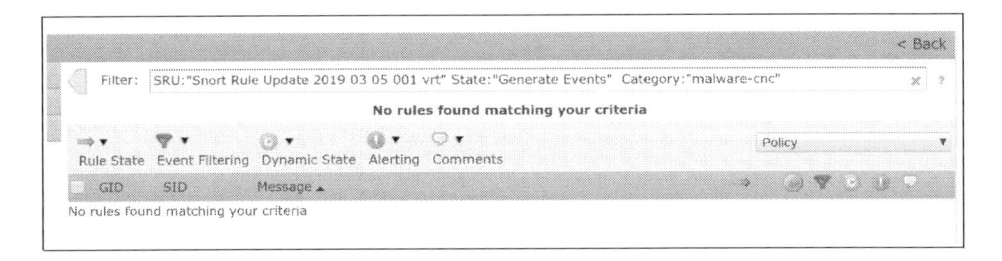

The Generator ID (GID)

To understand rules you have to understand the difference between a SID and a GID. First, each rule is assigned a GID and an SID. For example, you may see it written as 1:5388, where 1 is the GID and 5388 is the SID.

The GID is the Generator ID. The GID indicates what part of Snort can generate that event. Each Snort component has a GID assigned to it. The major GID categories are shown below.

- 1 - text-based rule. This is where the majority of the Snort rules fall. They are written using the Snort rules language and anybody can look at them and tell what they do. Well, anyone who speaks Snort!
- 3 - shared-object rule. A small number of Snort rules use object code as their detection mechanism. These are compiled and distributed without source code. You can see the rule header which is text based but you can't see what type of inspection the rule is actually doing.
- 100 and higher - these are preprocessors. Each

preprocessor is assigned one or more GIDs. Appendix A has a complete list of all the Snort GIDs and their assigned preprocessor.

The Snort ID (SID)

The SID is the Snort ID - each rule has one. This is a sequential number which Talos increments with each new rule. For GID 1 and 3 (Snort rules) they started at 100 and are nearing 37,000. However, the preprocessors start their SID numbering at 1. This means there is a 119:1 as well as a 122:1. The combination of the GID and SID is unique for each rule.

Because these rules have been getting new SIDs for over 10 years now you can tell about how old a rule is just by its SID. For example a rule with a SID in the 3,000 range is circa 2005. An easy way to see this is to look at some old rules and in the reference information you'll see the CVE which includes the year. In the rule below you can see in the reference keyword it says the CVE this rule addressed was 2005-0491.

```
alert tcp $EXTERNAL_NET any -> $HOME_NET 617 (msg:"SERVER-OTHER Arkeia backup client type 77 overflow attempt"; flow:to_server,established; content:"|00|M"; depth:2; byte_test:2,>,23,6; metadata:policy max-detect-ips drop, ruleset community; reference:bugtraq,12594; reference:cve,2005-0491; reference:nessus,17158; classtype:attempted-user; sid:3457; rev:13; gid:1; )
```

The important thing to remember here is that you can search for rules from a specific preprocessor (SID) by using the **Filter** bar. There are also predefined searches located under **Preprocessors** that will allow you to ferret out these rules. As you can see below, by expanding the **Preprocessors** section you can see all the preprocessors listed underneath.

Essential Firepower

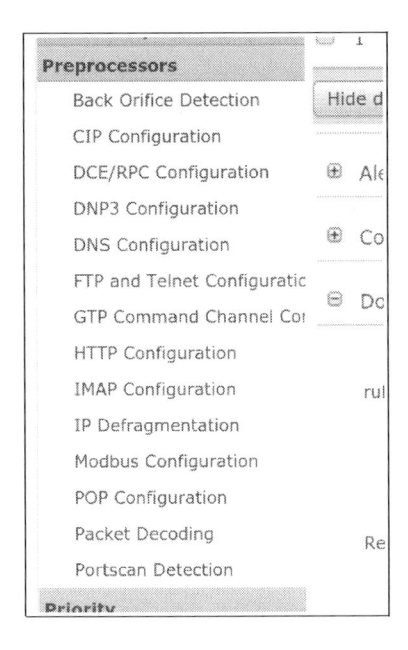

[Preprocessors menu showing: Back Orifice Detection, CIP Configuration, DCE/RPC Configuration, DNP3 Configuration, DNS Configuration, FTP and Telnet Configuration, GTP Command Channel Configuration, HTTP Configuration, IMAP Configuration, IP Defragmentation, Modbus Configuration, POP Configuration, Packet Decoding, Portscan Detection, Priority]

Clicking on one of these inserts the preprocessor GID into the **Filter** bar. In the figure below we clicked on **IP Defragmentation** and you can see that the Generator of 123 is now in the **Filter** bar. It looks like there are 11 rules for the **IP Defragmentation** preprocessor.

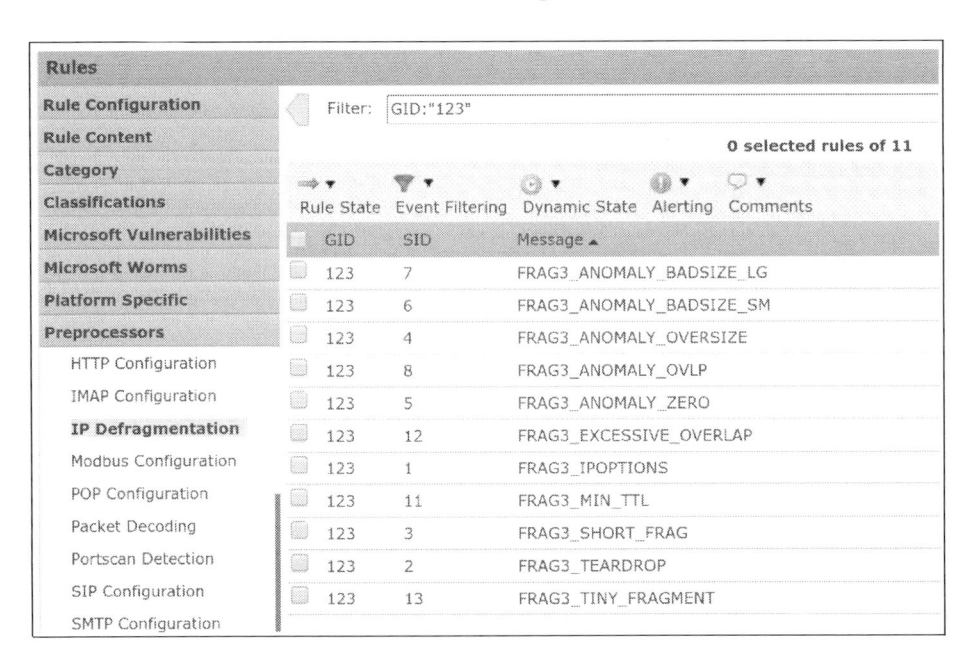

Filter: GID:"123"

0 selected rules of 11

GID	SID	Message
123	7	FRAG3_ANOMALY_BADSIZE_LG
123	6	FRAG3_ANOMALY_BADSIZE_SM
123	4	FRAG3_ANOMALY_OVERSIZE
123	8	FRAG3_ANOMALY_OVLP
123	5	FRAG3_ANOMALY_ZERO
123	12	FRAG3_EXCESSIVE_OVERLAP
123	1	FRAG3_IPOPTIONS
123	11	FRAG3_MIN_TTL
123	3	FRAG3_SHORT_FRAG
123	2	FRAG3_TEARDROP
123	13	FRAG3_TINY_FRAGMENT

Changing Rule States

The last thing I want to mention regarding rules is how to change the rule state. First, you have to remember that the layer (that drop-down on the right) is important. It will actually cause the **Rule State** options to change depending on the layer.

To change the **Rule State** you select the check box(es) by the rule(s) you want to change and then click the **Rule State** button.
If you have **Policy** selected in the layer drop-down you'll see something like the figure below.

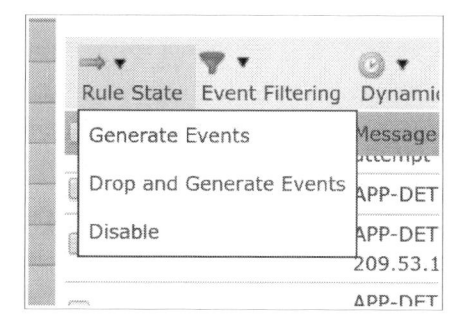

It's pretty simple, you have the three rule states. Keep in mind that you are overriding the base policy rule state with whatever you select here. This is true even if it's the same as the base policy rule state you are now taking over.

However, things change if you have the **My Changes** layer selected in the drop-down at the right. With the **My Changes** layer selected you get the options below.

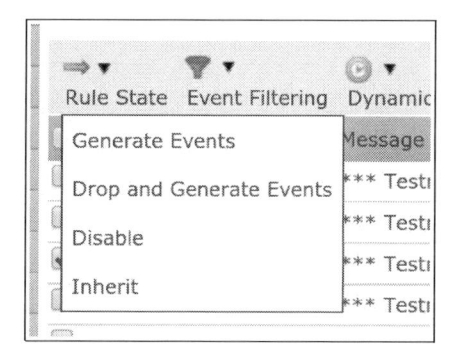

Notice in the figure above that now you now have an **Inherit** option. This can be used to revert the rule state back to whatever is set by the

Essential Firepower

base policy. This allows the base policy to decide if a rule should be enabled or not. It's the natural state for rules and one that I generally recommend.

Lastly, if you have the base policy selected in the drop-down your **Rule State** looks like this.

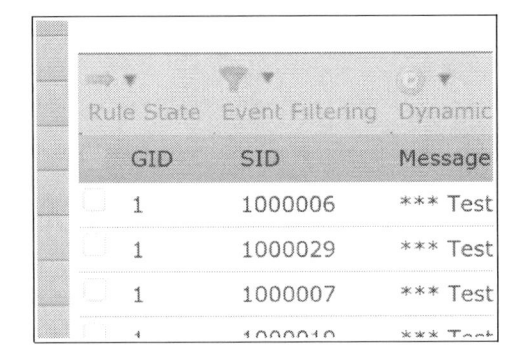

GID	SID	Message
1	1000006	*** Test
1	1000029	*** Test
1	1000007	*** Test

It's all grey and ugly, signifying that you can't make any changes at this layer regardless of who's base policy you're using.

Other Rule Properties

There are other rule properties you can set here such as **Comments**, **Dynamic State**, **Alerting** and **Event Filtering**. I'm not going to mention most of them. I do want to mention one thing because it may come up when you tune intrusion events. Notice that in your **Event Filtering** options you can filter rule alerts. Here you can add or remove thresholds and suppressions.

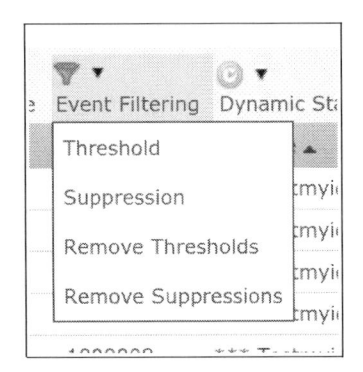

- Threshold
- Suppression
- Remove Thresholds
- Remove Suppressions

The main thing to keep in mind is that this impacts the *alerting* for the rule and not the packet processing. This is very important when it comes to drop rules and suppressions. Suppression only suppresses the alert but the rule continues to function. In short, you can suppress the output of a drop rule based on something like source or destination IP. If you do, the rule will continue to DROP TRAFFIC SILENTLY. All you've suppressed is the alert. This can be very difficult to troubleshoot!

That's important enough that I want to restate it to make sure you're clear. Event Filtering only impacts the alerting not the rule action. This means it's perfectly fine if you have a passive device but should probably be avoided like the plague for inline devices.

To suppress rules for inline devices you would use a pass rule. However, that will have to wait for the second edition, I'm not going to dive into it here.

> BP42 - Never suppress a rule that is set to Drop and Generate in the Intrusion policy

You can disable rules all day but just don't suppress a rule with the Drop and Generate Events state.

For more information on the mechanics of the rule editing interface, please take advantage of the Online help.

Firepower Recommended Rules

Firepower Recommendations are another area that is somewhat misunderstood. I say "somewhat" because I think the mechanism it uses is understood by most people but the effect is not. Let's start with a quick explanation of what Firepower Recommendations does.

Remember back when we scheduled updates? We created a job to download and install the Vulnerability Database (VDB) on a regular basis. Among other things, the VDB contains a mapping of known vulnerabilities to Snort rule(s) written to detect and/or block them. This is one component of Firepower Recommendations.

Another component is the host database. This is the database maintained on the FMC for your internal hosts. It contains information on operating systems, applications, open ports and vulnerabilities.

With the combination of the VDB and the host database all the pieces are there to automatically map Snort rules to vulnerabilities. So that's what Firepower Recommendations does. When you kick off this process, the system compiles a list of all the vulnerabilities discovered in hosts on your network. It then takes this list and cross references it with the Snort rules in the VDB. Now we have a list of all the Snort rules that apply to a given environment.

This sounds like intrusion detection Nirvana - it's the auto-tuning NGIPS/NGFW!

Here are some important keys to remember when considering whether or not to use Firepower Recommendations:

It requires good discovery data
If your devices are deployed only at the edge of your network or they only have limited visibility to your internal hosts then your host database probably doesn't have the most accurate data. The system can only record what it sees and the further away your devices are from the protected hosts the less accurate this data will be. You don't want to miss critical applications or services on your hosts. If you try and use Firepower recommendations with incomplete host data you will not get accurate recommendations. In the worst case, the system could recommend disabling rules for operating systems, protocols or applications in use on your network!

> BP43 - If you don't have good host data, don't use Firepower Recommendations

It can be useful for trimming unnecessary rules
If you need maximum efficiency from your rule set then Firepower Recommendations can help. If you leave the settings at their defaults then the system will automatically disable rules for vulnerabilities that are not found on your network. This generally reduces the enabled rules by around 10% when using the Balanced rule set. Is this reason enough to run Firepower Recommendations? Maybe.

Don't expect extra coverage
A common perception is that by running Firepower Recommendations

you will get a tailored rule set which includes enabling rules that may be specific to vulnerabilities in your environment. In my experience I have not seen this to be the case. If you start from the Balanced Talos policy, I've seen the rule set get smaller but I've never seen additional rules enabled (other than preprocessor rules which I'll discuss shortly). Sure, if you start from the No Rules Active policy you will definitely get rules enabled when you run Firepower Recommendations. However, I don't recommend this. I'm not saying that you will never see additional rules enabled, I'm sure it's happened, somewhere. I've just never seen it.

Keep it updated
If you do decide to run Firepower Recommendations then you should re-run it periodically. This way any new rules, new vulnerabilities or host changes can be considered. I would recommend doing this once a week. Don't make it a one-and-done process! You can create a scheduled job to run Firepower Recommendations just like we did for backups and software updates.

> BP44 - If you do run Firepower Recommendations, schedule a task to update recommendations periodically

Firepower Recommendations will enable some preprocessor rules
One side-effect of running Firepower Recommendations is that the process will automatically enable a number of preprocessor rules. Snort preprocessors are invaluable for normalizing traffic to remove anomalies, reassemble fragmented streams and decode complex application protocols. However, they are not useful for alerting on malicious traffic. That is why no preprocessor rules are enabled in any of the Talos system provided policies. However, Firepower Recommendations will enable a handful of these preprocessor rules which usually produce a number of alerts.

The preprocessor rules can be identified by looking for the specific Generator ID (GID) of the preprocessor. These will be 100 or higher. Rather than go through a list here my advice is to look through your intrusion events and if you see events from these preprocessors you can decide for yourself if you think they are useful. One thing to remember is that the preprocessors work just fine with or without the rules enabled. Their primary job is to process, decode and normalize traffic not to generate alerts.

BP45 - If you use Firepower Recommendations, consider disabling preprocessor rules (GID 100 and higher)

Finding Preprocessor Events

When looking for preprocessor events, pay attention to the first number following the rule message. This will be a 1 for a regular Snort rule, a 3 for a shared object rule and over 100 for a preprocessor rule. The figure below shows two intrusion alerts. The top one is a normal Snort rule. The second one is from the SMTP preprocessor (GID 124). These are found on the FMC under **Analysis → Intrusions → Events**.

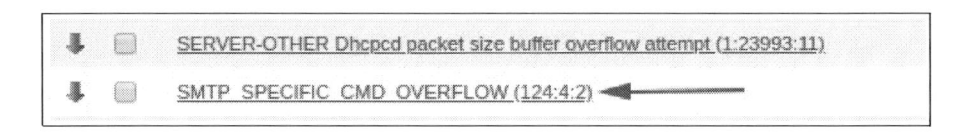

> SERVER-OTHER Dhcpcd packet size buffer overflow attempt (1:23993:11)
> SMTP_SPECIFIC_CMD_OVERFLOW (124:4:2) ◄────

Appendix A contains a list of the Snort preprocessor Generator IDs. When you are looking for the intrusion events that can be generated by a given preprocessor this is an excellent reference.

Enabling Firepower Recommendations

Ok, now that you have enough information to decide whether or not you want to enable Firepower Recommendations. Here are the steps:

1. On your Intrusion policy page you'll see **Firepower Recommendations** on the left. Click there and you will see the page shown below.

8 - Intrusion Policy

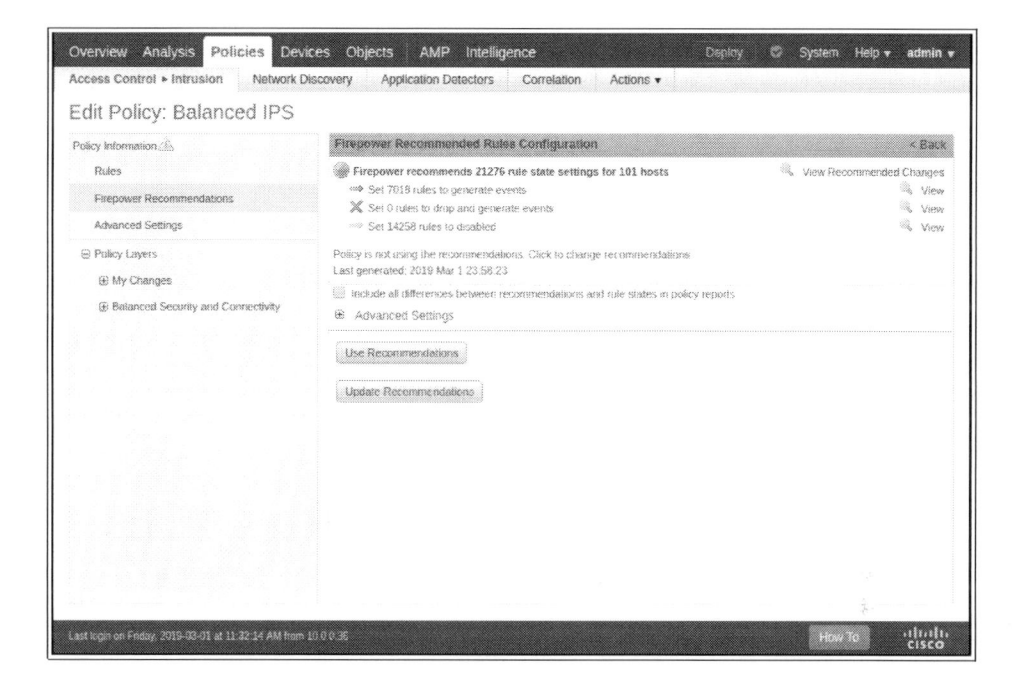

2. Simply click the **Use Recommendations** button and the process will run. After the process is complete if you expand the **Policy Layers** list on the left you will see that there is now a new layer called **Firepower Recommendations**.

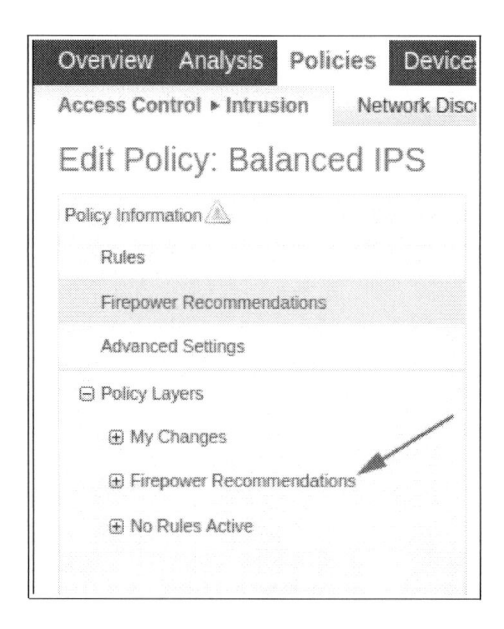

Modifying, Updating or Removing Recommendations

After adding Firepower Recommendations to a policy you will find that if you return to the recommendations section the options have changed.

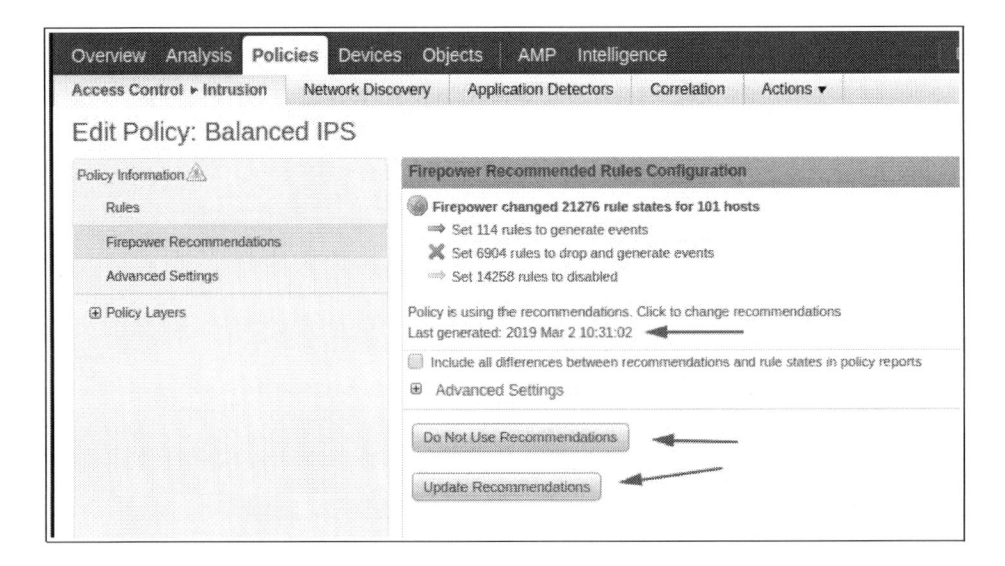

In the figure above, the page now tells you the date and time when recommendations where last generated. The buttons have also changed, you have:

- **Do Not Use Recommendations** - clicking this simply removes the Firepower Recommendations layer from your policy. This allows the base layer rule states to propagate up through the policy unmolested.
- **Update Recommendations** - this re-runs the recommendations process taking the current data in the host database and cross-referencing it with the VDB. Remember, you can schedule a regular task to do this.

If you change your mind later and decide to revert back to no recommendations, it's just a simple matter of clicking the **Do Not Use Recommendations** button to remove the recommendations layer.

A Final Word on Recommendations

One last word, you can tell from all the caveats above that I'm not a huge fan of this feature. I understand it has its benefits. My main concern is that I see examples all the time where somebody ran this process once and never ran it again. Months or years later, the original recommendations are still in use. In addition, I often see preprocessor rules generating numerous false positives and nobody understands whether they are important or how they got enabled in the first place.

The thing is, I have great confidence in the Talos rule sets. I think the Balanced Security and Connectivity rule set is a great way to provide all the protection most networks need without going overboard. It is constantly updated and pruned to make sure it remains efficient and effective. If all you do is enable that rule set I think you are doing pretty well when it comes to intrusion rules.

> BP46 - The Balanced Security and Connectivity rule set from Talos provides a great balance of security and performance, it is probably all you need.

Advanced Settings

The last area we will look at in Intrusion policy is **Advanced Settings**. There aren't many of these left since the Network Analysis policy was split-off back in version 5.4. There are only three:

- Specific Threat Detection
- Global Rule Thresholding
- External Responses

The primary one I will call a best practice applies to **Specific Threat Detection** which is the **Sensitive Data Detection** setting. This is a "poor man's Data Loss Protection" (DLP) solution. It is a preprocessor that searches for patterns of data that look like credit card numbers, email addresses, phone numbers or custom data patterns you can define.

I see this enabled from time to time but honestly, I've only seen false positives from it. The idea is that you tune the thresholds so that it only alerts for an unusual number of these items leaving your network. It's a good theory but the problem is this uses a reduced fat regex matching engine to do this work. Turns out even though it's not

Essential Firepower

full regex it's still a fairly significant performance hit to the system.

As with some of the other settings, I'm not saying never to use this preprocessor. It just requires specifc tuning and applies to limited network traffic profiles.

The bottom line is that it's almost always an albatross and you're probably better off leaving it disabled. Even if you did turn it on you still need to enable the associated rules for it to actually work. Some people leave out this little step so they end up paying the performance penalty but never enabling the alerting – ouch!

> BP47 - Leave the Sensitive Data Detection setting disabled.

Global Rule Thresholding is a default setting which prevents a new, untuned rule set from overwhelming the FMC or the analyst with events. This is enabled by default. It's worth noting just because most folks don't realize it is enabled. By default there isn't a one-to-one relationship between the number of events you are seeing and the number of times rules are triggering or blocking. The defautls are shown below.

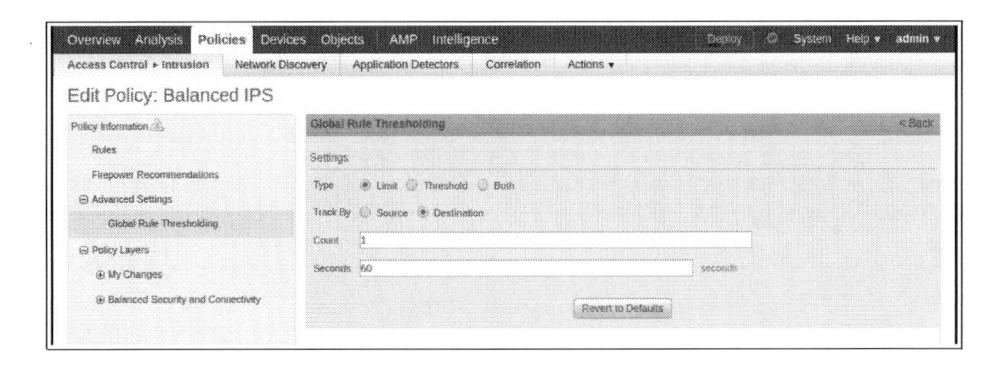

If you edit this setting you'll see that the devices are only sending one intrusion event per destination IP address every 60 seconds (per rule). This means a single rule will only alert for a destination IP address once per minute on a device. If multiple rules alert on a destination IP you'll see multiple events so this only applies to repeated rule matches for a single IP.

The idea is you shouldn't need 100 events to let you know that something evil is occurring. However, where this makes a difference is in rules that trigger for attacks like a brute force password attack. Say you have a rule triggering on this activity. It may look like a low and slow attack because the attacker is only trying one password every minute. In fact, it's probably hundreds or thousands but the system is limiting the alerts from that rule.

I call this "good to know" information. Cisco support recommends against it but I have no problem recommending that folks disable this threshold ONCE YOUR EVENTS ARE TUNED. Keep in mind that when you disable this your event count may jump up 10 fold so be ready for that. Tune out the majority of your false positives first and then you can feel confident disabling this threshold. Personally, I like to see an alert every time a rule triggers.

> BP48 - Don't be afraid to disable the Global Rule Threshold.

To disable the threshold, click on the **Advanced Settings** link (not the little + to the left) and select the **Disabled** radio button under **Intrusion Rule Thresholds**.

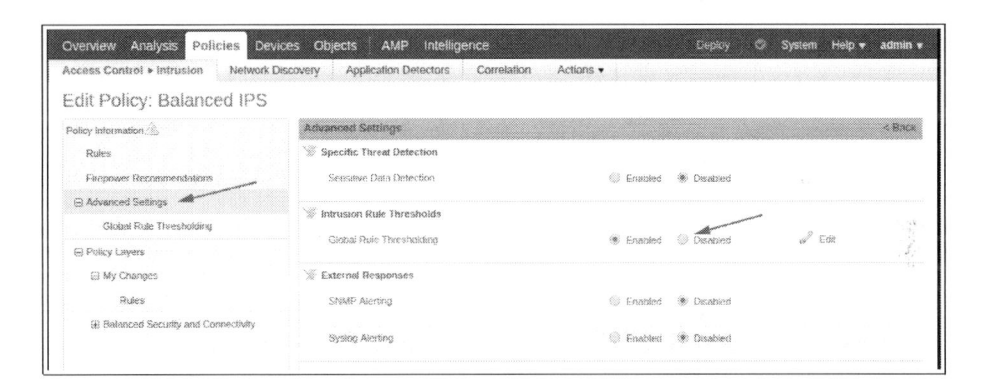

Chapter 9 - Network Analysis Policy

History

I mentioned earlier that the Network Analysis policy is new as of Firepower 5.4. Prior to this, the settings in this policy were part of the Intrusion policy. Now, I don't have any inside information on the reason for this split but it is plain to see that Cisco has made finding and editing this policy a bit of a treasure hunt. There is no menu entry for this policy anywhere on the FMC. It's clear the settings in this policy were separated and tucked away. Why? To keep people from changing them.

In fact, this is what the online help says about this policy:

> In most cases, preprocessors require specific expertise to configure and typically require little or no modification. Tailoring preprocessing, especially using multiple custom network analysis policies, is an **advanced** task. Because preprocessing and intrusion inspection are so closely related, the network analysis and intrusion policies examining a single packet **must** complement each other.

The Network Analysis policy contains what can be called "advanced" Snort settings. In reality, open source Snort has a single logical configuration. This contains all the variables, preprocessor configurations, logging, thresholds and all of the rules. It's distributed as a single snort.conf file with "include" statements which pull in the other configuration files and Snort rules. So, even though it is distributed with several files, it's all really one big configuration.

This is how the Sourcefire 3D System existed prior to 5.4. The

Intrusion policy provided a GUI configuration for the entries in snort.conf. The Intrusion and Network Analysis policies still work the same way today with their settings being written out to numerous text configuration files when you deploy policies to a device. As with Snort, these are all linked by a single central file which now pretty much just contains "include" statements.

I could make this a very short chapter by just saying, "Leave the Network Analysis policy (NAP) alone." Honestly, I don't think your detection would suffer much and you would not fall into the same traps so many others have. However, I think there is some value in understanding how the NAP works and where you really could make changes that can enhance your packet inspection. In addition, if you've already made some questionable changes to this policy this might be your chance to make it right!

Finding It

As I mentioned already, the NAP has purposely been made difficult to find. It is not available from the menu and there are only two pages on the FMC GUI where you can navigate to it. You can get there by clicking on the quick access link near the top right of the screen from the Access Control policy or Intrusion policy pages. You'll find these at **Policies → Access Control → Access Control** and **Policies → Access Control → Intrusion** respectively.

The figure below shows where to find this link.

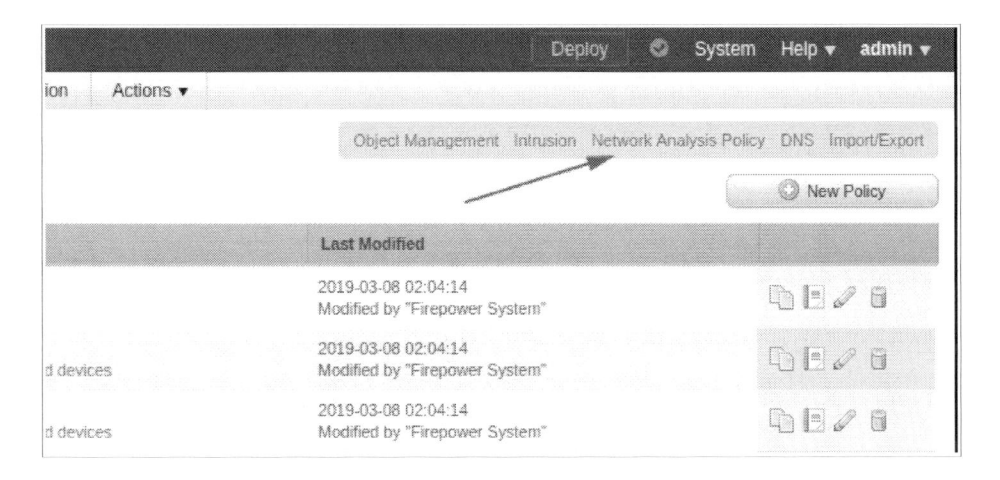

Essential Firepower

Clicking the **Network Analysis Policy** link will bring you to the policy list. This looks very similar to the Intrusion policy page. There you can create a new policy or edit an existing one.

Once you edit or create a policy you will again experience deja vu as the user interface is very close to what you've seen in the Intrusion policy, you will have **Settings** and **Policy Layers** on the left as well as other intrusion-reminiscent fields and options on the right. You can see this in the figure below.

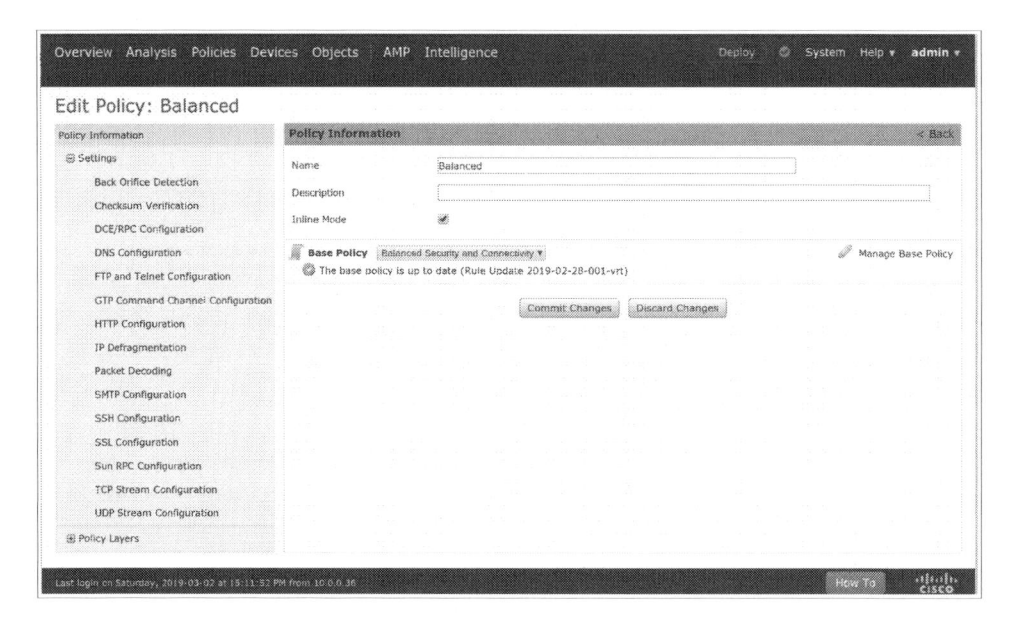

The Network Analysis policy has Talos base layers which come in the same sizes as the Intrusion policy. Each one also has the same name as it's Intrusion policy sibling. As you can guess, the recommended configuration is to use the same-named Intrusion and Network Analysis policy base layers together. You would do this via the Access Control policy which will be discussed in Chapter 14.

There's an important UI quirk that I want to point out. When you first look at the NAP you'll notice that there are a number of items under **Settings**. At first, you may think that these are all of the settings that are available. Not so! This list only shows the *enabled* preprocessors/settings. If a particular preprocessor is disabled it will not show in this list.

To view all the available settings you have to click on the word **Settings** itself. Note that this works the same as it does in Intrusion policy but the Network Analysis list is much longer so it's easier to miss something. Once you click **Settings** you will see all the available preprocessors regardless of their current state as shown below.

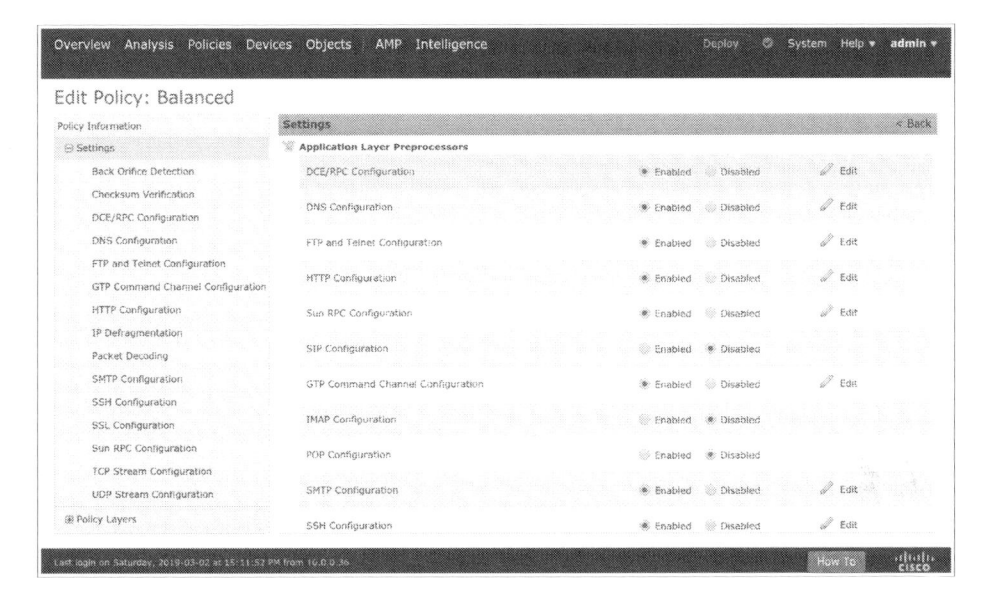

In the screenshot above you'll notice that the SIP, IMAP and POP preprocessors are missing from the list on the left because they are currently disabled.

Comparing this to the Intrusion policy, you will also notice there are a lot more settings listed on the left and no rules anywhere to be found. This can be a little inconvenient because if you want to enable the rules (alerts) for a given preprocessor you will have to know or lookup its Generator ID (GID) and look for those rules in the Intrusion policy. To make it easier, don't forget Appendix A which contains a list of all the preprocessors and their GIDs.

But wait, I'm getting ahead of myself! Let's talk about what a preprocessor is.

Pre What?

I've already used a made-up word so I should probably explain it. Snort uses what are called preprocessors. These are (mostly) application specific modules designed to deal with specific types of traffic. Their main purpose is to "normalize" traffic to allow Snort rules to - well - work. Some preprocessors actually don't normalize but for now we won't quibble about those. Let's say that most preprocessors provide an important service - removing or compensating for evasion techniques, defragmenting packets, reassembling streams and decoding complex protocols. Books have been written (by myself and others) on how and why these preprocessors are important. Since we're focusing on essentials here let's suffice to say that *if the preprocessor doesn't function correctly then Snort rules won't either.*

That last statement alone should be reason enough to keep a very light hand when making any changes to the NAP. Here is my number one rule when editing this policy, "If you don't know what it does, leave it alone!" In fact let's make that a best practice.

> BP49 - When editing the Network Analysis policy, if you don't know what a setting is for - leave it alone!

To expand a bit on this advice. If you think there's a setting you need to change in the NAP and aren't 100% sure of what it does or if you should change it then investigate first. The first thing you can check is the built-in help. As I mentioned earlier, it is quite good at explaining some of the nuances of the system. That might be enough to help you decide what to do. Beyond that you can visit www.snort.org and read the Snort User Guide. Another good source is the Snort source code. I'm not saying you need to learn to read the source code itself, but there are quite a few README files included which describe the preprocessors and their settings.

Preprocessor Run-Down

Preprocessors fall into several categories, these are:

- **Application Layer Preprocessors** - these work at layer 7 of the Open Systems Interconnection (OSI) model. You'll see all the usual suspects, HTTP, Telnet, FTP, etc.
- **SCADA Preprocessors** - SCADA stands for Supervisory Control and Data Acquisition. This means control systems like power, water, chemical, etc. These preprocessors apply to the industrial control protocols and will not be

needed for most deployments.
- **Transport/Network Layer Preprocessors** - just like it says, these work at the transport and network layers of the OSI model. They are very important for packet and stream reassembly among other things.
- **Specific Threat Detection** - these are the black sheep of the family. They aren't technically preprocessors although they fall into that bucket. These are used for activity which cannot be detected using Snort rules alone.

I am fighting the urge to write a paragraph or two about every preprocessor. I don't want to dive into the weeds and start spewing data that may be impressive but isn't relevant. If I skip a preprocessor below it doesn't lessen its importance. It is because it is not commonly changed and probably shouldn't be. I will mention some that are commonly modified along with my recommendation on whether that's a good idea. Spoiler alert - it usually isn't. So if I skip a preprocessor below that's your cue that it is better left at its defaults. With that, let's discuss some selected NAP settings.

Inline Mode

The **Inline Mode** check box is found on the main policy page. If your devices are deployed inline, that is they are using routed, switched, or transparent interfaces, or inline interface pairs, then some preprocessors can modify and block traffic. Chief among these are:

- **The inline normalization preprocessor** - it normalizes packets to prepare them for analysis by other preprocessors and the rules engine. It's one of the few that can also modify packets on the wire if **Inline Mode** is checked.
- **Checksum Verification** - this allows the system to drop packets with invalid checksums (note that FTD routed and transparent interfaces always drop packets that fail IP checksum verification regardless of whether Inline Mode is enabled).
- **Rate-Based Attack Prevention** - can drop packets matching rate-based attack prevention settings

Checking the **Inline Mode** box is what enables the above preprocessors to drop or change packets. You may or may not receive alerts for this activity depending on the reason for the drop and whether the associated rule(s) are enabled. Some types of drops such as invalid checksums will never generate intrusion events. On the other hand, **Rate-Based Attack Prevention** allows you to create rules in the NAP to detect or block certain types of attacks - these will generate intrusion events.

> Note: **Rate-Based Attack Prevention** does not mean Firepower is effective as a Denial of Service (DoS) mitigation - it's not. These may be helpful for detecting or slowing down certain types of activity but Cisco does not make any claims about Firepower's DoS protection capabilities.

Cisco's recommendation is to enable **Inline Mode** for inline deployments. I'm not going to argue with this. They also recommend enabling the **Inline Normalization** preprocessor which will be discussed later in this chapter.

|BP50 - Enable NAP Inline Mode for inline type deployments

HTTP Configuration

The HTTP preprocessor (HTTP Inspect) is one of the most important preprocessors in Snort. This is due to the ubiquity of HTTP and therefore the tendency to use it for malicious purposes. The settings in this preprocessor vary somewhat between the Talos base policies. The important numbers here are the inspection depth. That is, how deep into the HTTP request/response Snort will normalize/inspect traffic. In the Connectivity and Balanced policies these numbers are conservative. However, in the Security and Max Detection policies this preprocessor goes much deeper, especially into the HTTP response. This belies the fact that performance is much less of a consideration with the Security and Max Detection policies. Or you might say, "Damn the performance - inspect everything!"

In the policy, the numbers I'm talking about are the client and server flow depths:

- **Client Flow Depth** - how deep to normalize/inspect client

requests
- **Server Flow Depth** - how deep to normalize/inspect server responses

The figure below shows these values from the Balanced Security and Connectity policy.

HTTP Configuration

Global Settings

Detect Anomalous HTTP Servers	☐	
Detect HTTP Proxy Servers	☐	
Maximum Compressed Data Depth	1460	bytes
Maximum Decompressed Data Depth	2920	bytes

Targets — Configuration

Servers — default

Networks	default	
Ports	80, 443, 1220, 1741, 2301, 2980, 3:	
Oversize Dir Length	500	(1 or greater)
Client Flow Depth	300	bytes
Server Flow Depth	500	bytes

There are some nuances here you can read for yourself in the help but when it comes to flow depth:

Bigger Numbers = Deeper Inspection = Reduced Performance

There is a significant jump in the flow depth defaults from the Balanced to the Security policy. Personally, I have not seen evidence that this increased depth makes a significant impact on the detection rate of the Talos rule set. I am still of the opinion that you should use the NAP that is the namesake of your Intrusion policy.

Whatever you do, don't decrease these numbers but also don't arbitrarily increase them assuming your device will suddenly be able to detect more evil than before.

> BP51 - HTTP preprocessor settings can have a significant performance impact don't change them without clear justification

What might justify changing these depths? If you have specific knowledge of a particular Snort rule or rules that may be missing attacks because this depth is too small then you should change it. When I say specific I mean packet captures showing the attack and the applicable Snort rule not triggering.

Another possibility is if you have written your own Snort rules that require deeper inspection for HTTP traffic. If this is the case, then feel free to update these depth numbers as needed. However, never forget that there's no such thing as a free lunch with Snort. If you inspect traffic more deeply you are always going to pay a performance penalty.

SCADA Preprocessors

The SCADA preprocessors are only useful in conjunction with industrial control systems. If you don't work for a power utility, water treatment plant or use Firepower on an industrial control network then skip this section. This category includes the following preprocessors:

- **Modbus** - GID:144
- **DNP3** - GID:145
- **CIP** - GID:148

If you use these industrial protocols then you should enable the appropriate preprocessor. However, you're not finished. You must also enable the appropriate Intrusion rules using the GIDs shown in the list above. You can set these rules to alert or drop depending on your preferences. Most folks are pretty squeamish about dropping packets on a control network. - for good reasons.

It's important to remember that most of the alerts generated by preprocessors are for anomalous traffic. Anomalous does not mean evil, it just means unusual. Be very careful before you start blocking *unusual* traffic.

For the CIP preprocessor you also have some changes to make to the

TCP Stream preprocessor. The Firepower online help is again your friend as it lists a number of considerations when enabling this feature. I'm not going to restate them here so please refer to the help or configuration guide if you enable this preprocessor.

> BP52 - If you know what SCADA means then consider the SCADA preprocessors, if you don't, leave them disabled

Information on enabling these SCADA rules in the Intrusion policy is contained in the Intrusion Policy chapter. However, let's run through the steps below.

1. Edit the Intrusion policy (**Policies** → **Access Control** → **Intrusion**)
2. Click the **Rules** link on the left to edit your active rules.
3. Click in the **Filter** bar and type in "GID:<your_GID>" where your_GID is the GID of the preprocessor you want to enable rules for. You can also locate the preprocessor in the **Preprocessors** predefined search list.
4. The rules list will now contain all the rules from this preprocessor generator ID.
5. Select the check boxes by the rules you want to enable.
6. Click the **Rule State** button and change the state for the selected rules.
7. Return to the **Policy Information** page (click **Policy Information** in the upper left) and **Commit Changes**.
8. **Deploy** your policy changes.

Inline Normalization

Cisco recommends enabling the **Inline Normalization** preprocessor if your device is deployed inline - that is, if it has the capability to block traffic. Enabling this setting allows Firepower to take a more active role in blocking malicious behavior. If you deploy an inline device without this preprocessor enabled, Snort will still drop packets that match drop rules. However, the drop behavior will be slightly different.

The Firepower help makes this recommendation for inline traffic:

> In an inline deployment, Cisco recommends that you enable inline mode and configure the inline normalization preprocessor with the **Normalize**

TCP Payload option enabled.

That's pretty specific and to the point. If your device is deployed inline then you should probably follow this advice. Note that the Security Over Connectivity policy already enables these settings so if you're using it then no changes are needed.

> BP53 - If your devices are inline then use inline policy settings

You can enable alerting for the **Inline Normalization** preprocessor by setting the GID:116 rules to alert in your Intrusion policy. Be aware that some of these will be noisy and may not be actionable.

Inline Normalization has quite a number of settings, If you are considering changing the defaults my advice is to look at the online help. There you'll find a great description of all of the options.

As for what this preprocessor actually does, it falls into three categories.

1. Blocking or correcting miscellaneous traffic anomalies
2. Performing TCP reassembly and dropping improperly fragmented traffic (check **Normalize TCP Payload**)
3. Changing Snort's blocking behavior from post-ack to pre-ack (check **Normalize TCP Payload**)

The first two categories are handy for dealing with evasions or other attempts to confuse Snort or manipulate traffic in an evil way. The last one is not well-known but does have ramifications in some networks. Let's discuss it for a bit.

Drop Events

When a Snort drop rule triggers, you see an intrusion event in Firepower and the event shows that Snort blocked the packet. Sounds pretty simple right? Ha! Nothing is simple in Firepower haven't you learned that yet?

First let me say that yes, when you see a Snort drop event the packet was dropped and the attack was thwarted. But, it may not be the packet you think it was. When a Snort rule triggers, the event you see in the FMC contains the datagram that triggered the event. It could be a single packet or several reassembled packets. Either way, you can examine the contents of this datagram, compare the Snort rule keywords and find exactly where Snort matched the rule to the data. An example of a drop event packet view is shown below.

I know the figure is hard to read but believe me, the Snort rule is there and below you can expand the Packet Text or the Packet Bytes and see exactly what Snort detected.

But, you might assume that when Snort says it dropped the packet it's talking about THIS packet - that's not always the case.

Pre-ack and Post-ack

Snort actually behaves differently when the inline settings are configured following Cisco's recommendations versus the default Balanced or Connectivity policies. One of the important differences is its pre-ack/post-ack behavior. First, let's look at post-ack which is the behavior *without* **Inline Normalization** enabled and **Normalize TCP Payload** checked.

In a typical web-based attack we have an evil packet - in this case an HTTP GET coming from a client to a server. Snort detects the attack and blocks the packet. It looks like this:

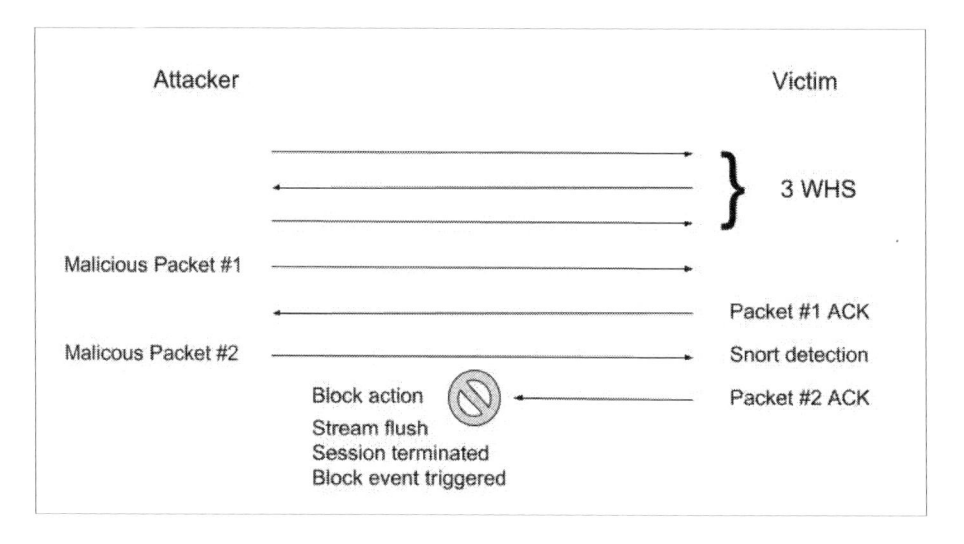

```
           Attacker                                    Victim

                          ───────────────────────→  ⎫
                          ←───────────────────────  ⎬  3 WHS
                          ───────────────────────→  ⎭

Malicious Packet #1  ───────────────────────────→

                          ←───────────────────────   Packet #1 ACK

Malicous Packet #2   ───────────────────────────→   Snort detection

                     Block action    🚫  ←────────   Packet #2 ACK
                     Stream flush
                     Session terminated
                     Block event triggered
```

1. First, the three way handshake (3WHS) establishes the TCP session.
2. The attack occurs in Malicious Packet #2
3. Snort detects the attack
4. The ACK packet from the server (Victim) is dropped and the session is terminated. The intrusion event shows drop and the packet in the event is Malicious Packet #2 (and possibly 1 also if this attack was spread across two packets as shown).

The result is that the attack was detected and the session terminated. However, what isn't obvious from the event is that the server actually received the attack packet and responded. If you were running a packet sniffer on the server you might think Snort was not operating correctly. However, this is expected behavior in the post-ack configuration.

Once you configure the **Inline Normalization** preprocessor and enable **Normalize TCP Payload** it looks like this:

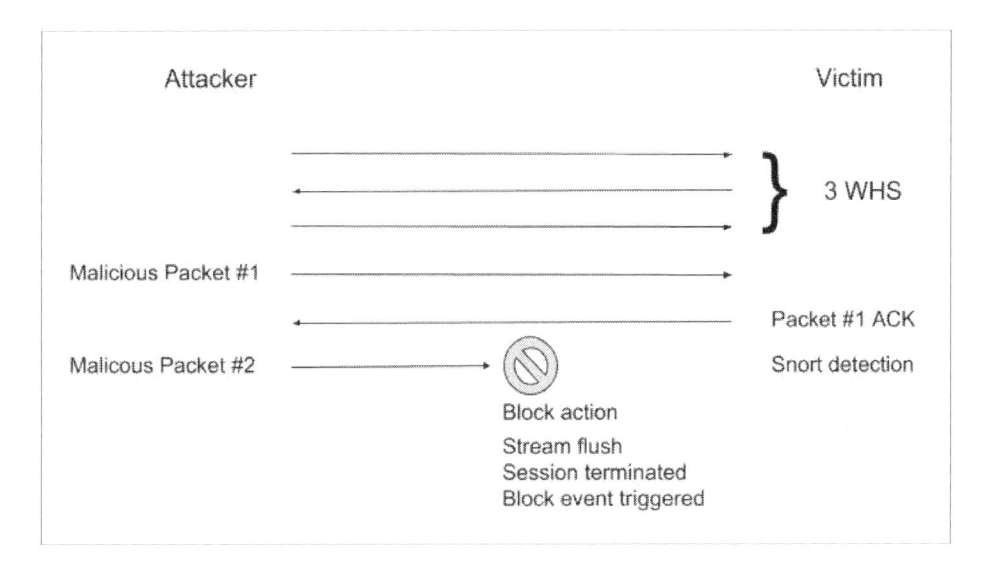

```
Attacker                                              Victim

                    ─────────────────────────▶  ⎫
                    ◀─────────────────────────  ⎬  3 WHS
                    ─────────────────────────▶  ⎭

Malicious Packet #1 ─────────────────────────▶

                    ◀─────────────────────────     Packet #1 ACK
Malicous Packet #2  ─────────────────▶  ⊘          Snort detection
                                         Block action
                                         Stream flush
                                         Session terminated
                                         Block event triggered
```

As you can see, this is the preferred behavior since the victim server is never subjected to the complete attack. This is one advantage of using **Inline Normalization** with the **Normalize TCP Payload** setting enabled. If that second packet contained a denial of service attack that may have crashed the server, the pre-ack mode is the only one that would have stopped the attack before it impacted the server.

The ability to drop attacks in the pre-ack mode is an important benefit of proper configuration of the **Inline Normalization** preprocessor.

IP Defragmentation and TCP Stream

I lumped the IP Defragmentation and TCP Stream preprocessors together because they perform somewhat similar actions on different parts of the packet. Also, they are very important to ensuring Snort can detect and avoid fragmentation-based evasions. In addition, they illustrate something which most people don't realize - the GUI doesn't always tell the truth.

If you read the help for the NAP you'll find this sentence:

> If you disable a preprocessor but the system needs to evaluate preprocessed packets against an enabled intrusion or preprocessor rule, the system automatically enables and uses the preprocessor although it remains disabled in the network analysis policy web interface.

Umm, what? The web interface shows something is disabled yet the system automatically enables it? Reading further you'll also find:

> When tailoring a network analysis policy, especially when disabling preprocessors, keep in mind that some preprocessors and intrusion rules require that traffic first be decoded or preprocessed in a certain way. If you disable a required preprocessor, the system automatically uses it with its current settings, although the preprocessor remains disabled in the network analysis policy web interface.

This says the same thing with a little more detail. Most notably - the preprocessor remains disabled in the web interface but the system still uses it. The help doesn't list what a "required preprocessor" is but I can take a guess. It's probably any preprocessor that is required for the Talos rule set to function. Among the major ones I would suspect are:

- DCE/RPC
- HTTP Inspection
- IP Defragmentation
- TCP Stream Reassembly
- UDP Stream Reassembly

There may be others but the key takeaway here is the system will do its best to keep you from shooting yourself in the foot. Even if that means allowing you to disable a critical preprocessor in the UI and then enabling it behind your back.

Portscan Detection

Probably the most enabled and least understood preprocessor is Portscan. It's disabled by default in all policies but I see customers turning this on all the time. It sounds like a good idea on the surface – sure I want to detect port scans – right?

The problem is that the Portscan preprocessor was conceived back when Snort was young and multi-CPU systems were rare. In those days a single Snort process handled all the traffic on a sensor. However, the traffic volume quickly outpaced this single CPU. As a result, parallel Snort processes were used to increase the sensor throughput. That is still how we gain performance today. It works slightly differently on a classic Firepower (7000/8000) device versus an FTD device but the outcome is the same. Flows are divided across CPUs as they are processed in parallel to gain improved throughput.

The normal criteria used to split flows across CPUs is a 5-tuple consisting of:

1. Source IP
2. Source Port
3. Destination IP
4. Destination Port
5. Protocol

Firepower actually adds another tuple - VLAN ID which is on by default and can be enabled/disabled in the **Advanced Settings** of the Access Control policy.

All of this information is hashed together, then packets that have the same hash value are dispatched to the same CPU. In this way, each CPU can maintain flow and state information for packets as they are processed.

If you are looking for something deep within a single packet or a single flow this architecture is great. However, a port scan or port sweep is a behavior across multiple connections, it's not something you can detect in a single packet. A single attacker scanning a victim might look like this.

```
     Attacker                                              Victim

   SYN TCP/21    ──────────────────────────────────▶
                 ◀──────────────────────────────────    RST
   SYN TCP/22    ──────────────────────────────────▶
                 ◀──────────────────────────────────    RST
   SYN TCP/23    ──────────────────────────────────▶
                 ◀──────────────────────────────────    RST
   SYN TCP/25    ──────────────────────────────────▶
                 ◀──────────────────────────────────    RST
```

The attacker may randomize or pick different ports but the result is still the majority of the scanned ports are closed on the victim. This means the victim sends numerous reset (RST) packets to the attacker. There will be some SYN/ACK packets but they will only be sent from listening ports.

My example above only covers Transmission Control Protocol (TCP) but the same applies to User Datagram Protocol (UDP) scans and the ICMP responses sent for closed UDP ports.

The Portscan preprocessor is designed to detect this type of activity and alert. Depending on the settings it will detect a large number of RST packets targeting a host (the attacker). It can also detect a large number of SYN packets originating from a given host (also the attacker).

The problem is when you have a multi-CPU system these SYN packets do not hash to the same CPU because the 5/6-tuple is different. There is no central Portscan process that somehow has visibility to all the traffic coming in an interface. As a result, the Portscan preprocessor (running on each individual CPU) does not get a complete picture of the scan traffic.

To make matters worse, the Portscan preprocessor will behave differently on different models of appliances. If your appliance only has 4 Snort CPUs it will behave much differently than if your device has 40 CPUs. Because scans will be spread across so many processors, the 40 CPU device has little chance of ever detecting a port scan unless it's simply massive.

This is why the Portscan preprocessor is disabled by default and why you should probably leave it that way. It might trigger now and then but it will not be consistent or as sensitive as it should be.

> |BP54 - Leave the Portscan preprocessor disabled

If you do insist on enabling this preprocessor remember to enable the associated GID:122 rules. Otherwise, you're just spending CPU cycles with no chance of ever alerting.

One last thing, you can never stop a port scan using Snort. Even if you had a single CPU system the best you could hope for is detection but not blocking of this activity.

Chapter 10 - Malware & File Policy

In this chapter we'll discuss some of the considerations when editing the Malware & File policy. This policy is fairly simple, there are just a few nuances that are worth mentioning.

First of all, this policy - like many others - is invoked by rule(s) in the Access Control policy. When you specify file inspection in an Allow rule, you have an option to select the file policy to be used. In most deployments there is only one Malware & File policy in use. However, in complex deployments you may have more than one. Keep in mind that you will need the Malware license to use the malware detection capabilities of this policy, although you can use the file detection or file type blocking capability with just the threat license.

Overview

Access the Malware & File policy from the FMC at **Policies → Access Control → Malware & File**. There you can edit your existing policy or click the **New File Policy** button to create a new one. If you create a new one you'll be presented with the opportunity to give your policy a name and optional description. After this you'll be taken to the main policy edit screen as shown below. In this example, I'm editing an existing policy which already has an inspection rule.

Essential Firepower

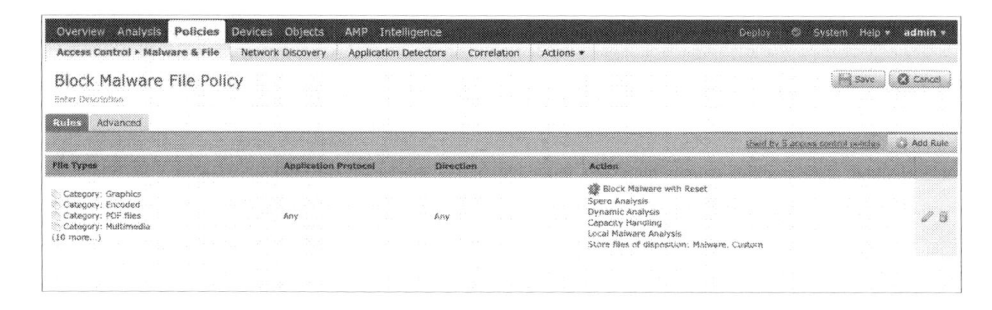

Before we dive into the policy, let's go over the basics of what it does. As you can guess from the name, this policy is all about files. It "carves" files out of network flows and checks them to see if they are malicious. This action is performed only on supported file transfer protocols. Currently these are:

- **HTTP** (Hyper Text Transfer Protocol)
- **SMTP** (Simple Mail Transport Protocol)
- **IMAP** (Internet Message Access Protocol)
- **POP3** (Post Office Protocol version 3)
- **FTP** (File Transfer Protocol)
- **NetBIOS-ssn SMB** (Server Message Block)

Some of these protocols are supported for upload and download of files while some only support only one or the other.

Once the file is carved out of the flow the system can check it to see if it is malicious. This is done using one or more of the following techniques:

- **SHA-256** - the file's SHA-256 hash is calculated and sent to the FMC where it is relayed to the AMP (Advanced Malware Protection) cloud. The cloud returns the hash disposition (clean, unknown, malware).
- **Spero** - static file structure analysis. This only applies to Microsoft executable (MSEXE) files. A hash of the file's static characteristics is sent to the FMC which forwards it to the AMP cloud for analysis.
- **Local Malware Analysis** - this uses the ClamAV engine to inspect the file's properties and embedded objects for evidence of malware. This is not the full signature-based ClamAV.
- **Dynamic Analysis** - if the Spero or Local Malware Analysis evaluation deems the file is possible malware it is uploaded to the AMP cloud for Threat Grid analysis. The file is executed or

opened (in the case of documents) in a sandbox environment and its behavior is evaluated.

Once a file is evaluated by one or more of these techniques it is given a disposition:

- **Clean** - the file has been deemed to be clean by the AMP cloud or the user added the file to a clean list. Note that this requires human intervention and as a result only a tiny fraction of files receive this disposition.
- **Unknown** - the file's malware disposition is unknown. This means it has not been deemed as clean or malicious. It's possible it has been analyzed and not shown signs of malicious activity or that it has not been seen previously. The vast majority of files will have an unknown disposition for their entire existence. A less confusing word for this disposition might be "unclassified".
- **Malware** - the file has been classified as malware.
- **Custom Detection** - a user added the file to a custom detection list.
- **Unavailable** - the system was unable to query the AMP cloud. This is probably due to an intermittent connectivity issue. Cisco says a small number of these is expected behavior.

Finally, you can create rules that detect files but don't perform malware analysis. File types matching these rules are not actually carved out of the traffic. Well, at least not the entire file. Actually only the first 1460 bytes of the file are inspected (configurable in the Access Control policy **Advanced** tab). To do this, AMP looks for the "file magic" to determine what type of file is being transferred. To register the file event, AMP doesn't need the entire file, just the first 1460 bytes where it looks for specific signatures to identify what type of file is being transferred.

Now that you know the basics of how Malware & File policy works, let's dive into the settings.

Advanced Settings

I always start at Advanced Settings when creating a new policy. That

Essential Firepower

way you get this part out of the way and can concentrate on the rules. Clicking the **Advanced** tab displays the screen below:

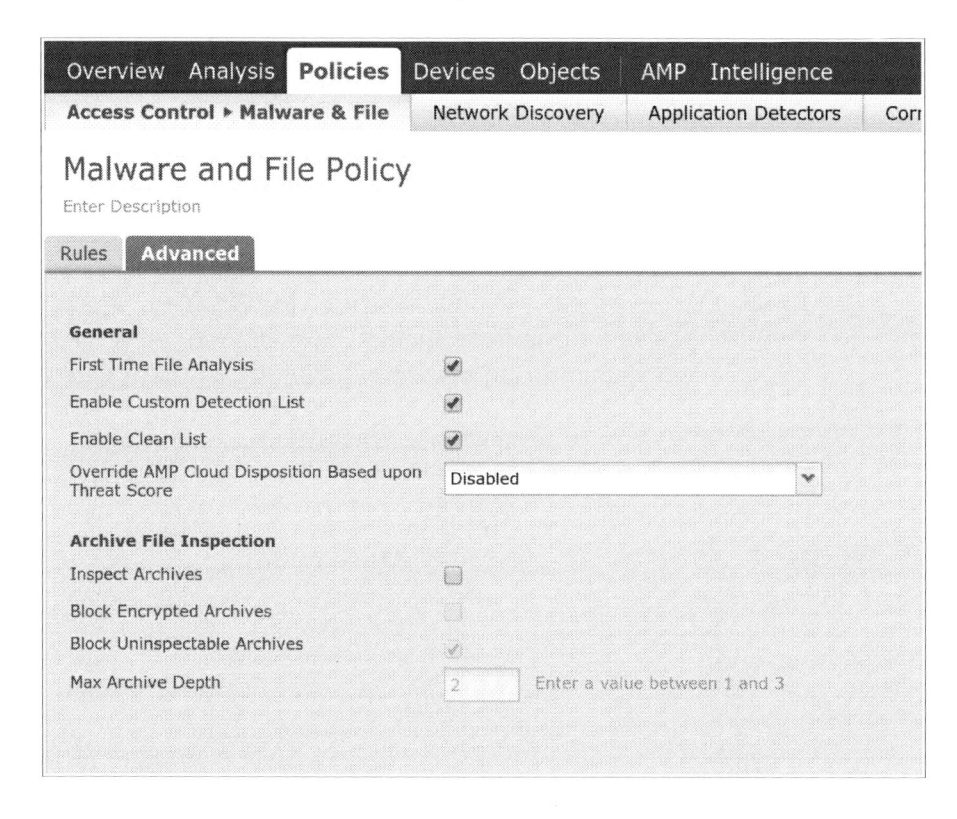

There are just a couple of noteworthy settings on this page. First, there is an option to **Override AMP Cloud Disposition Based upon Threat Score**. This setting can be disabled or set to several levels as shown below:

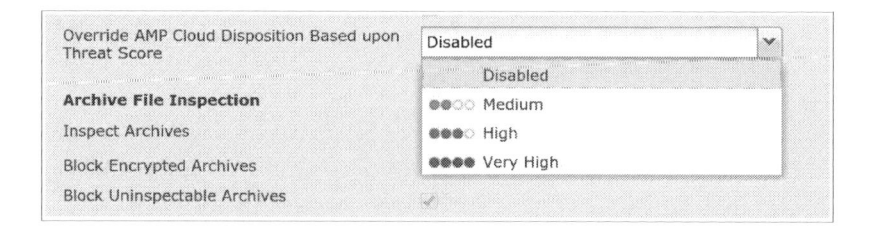

The key takeaway here is **this setting doesn't do anything**. It was designed for the old Joe Sandbox file analysis on version 5.x of Firepower (actually called FireSIGHT at the time). It currently has no impact on whether Threat Grid deems a file as malicious or not.

> BP55 - You can't override the Threat Grid malicious threat score in Malware & File policy

The **Archive File Inspection** section contains settings for inspecting file archives (zip, lha, rar, mscab, etc.). Note that by default, inspection of archives is disabled. You can enable this inspection and optionally configure the **Max Archive Depth** (archive within an archive) and what to do for uninspectable archives or encrypted (password protected) archives. Uninspectable means the archive depth exceeds the maximum setting, it doesn't mean an unsupported file archive format. The default settings are shown below.

Archive File Inspection	
Inspect Archives	☐
Block Encrypted Archives	☐
Block Uninspectable Archives	☑
Max Archive Depth	2 Enter a value between 1 and 3

The options are pretty clear. It's another security versus connectivity situation where you decide how intrusive you want your inspection to be. It may be worth considering that there's probably not much business need for someone to send a file with more than 3 nested archives. Stuffing malware into a file deeper than AMP can inspect or putting a password on the archive can be used to evade AMP analysis depending on the settings you choose here. However, before you start blocking archives here you should test thoroughly. You may find there are applications that do interesting archive tricks as part of their normal operation.

> BP56 - Consider your archive file inspection settings in the Malware & FIle policy.

Malware & File Rule Options

The **Rules** tab is where you determine what to do with traffic that is processed by this policy. When you click the **Add Rule** button in the upper right you will see a dialog like the one below.

Essential Firepower

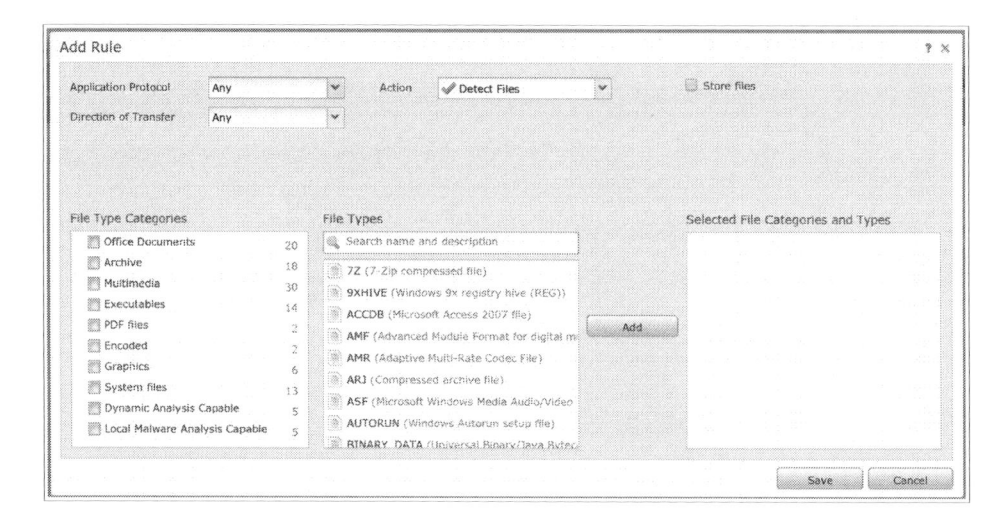

By default, this rule will apply to all supported application protocols and any direction of transfer (subject to whether that direction is supported for the particular protocol). You can improve the performance of your device by only selecting specific protocols (one per rule) but most of the time the **Application Protocol** and **Direction of Transfer** are set to Any.

Rule Action

The **Action** is where you decide what to do with the files that are detected with this rule. Clicking the **Action** drop-down shows the options below.

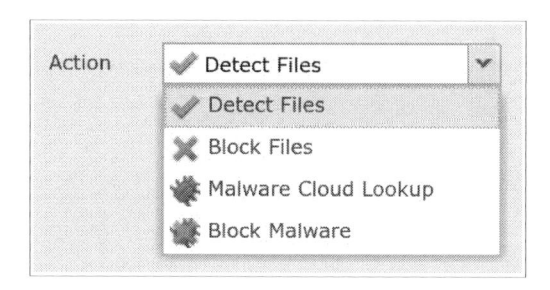

- **Detect Files** - look at the file magic and record a file event showing the file was transferred.
- **Block Files** - look at the file magic and block the file type.
- **Malware Cloud Lookup** - carve the entire file out of the stream and check to see if it's malicious, if it is, then generate a malware event.

138

- **Block Malware** - carve the entire file out of the stream and check to see if it's malicious, if it is, then drop the file and generate a malware event.

Underneath the Action drop-down there are some more options. Let's take a look.

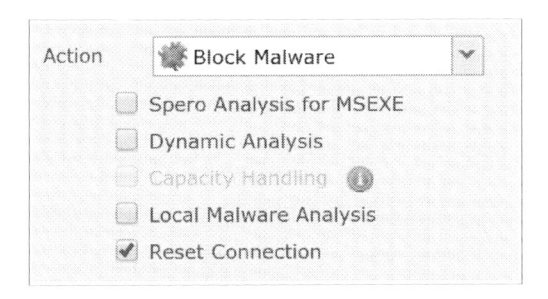

- **Spero Analysis for MSEXE** - perform Spero analysis on the file if it's a Microsoft executable
- **Dynamic Analysis** - upload the file to the Threat Grid sandbox for dynamic analysis if it's deemed to be possible malware by Spero or Local Malware Analysis
- **Capacity Handling** - Threat Grid submissions have a daily limit per device. If your device exceeds this limit additional files cannot be uploaded until the next day. If this box is checked and you exceed the limit, the device will store the file(s) until the malware submission limit is reset and try re-submitting it.
- **Local Malware Analysis** - ClamAV local malware checks
- **Reset Connection** - sent a TCP reset to the source and destination if the file is blocked.

Blocking Files

It's important to understand how Firepower works when it decides to block a malicious file. In order to carve a file out of a flow, Firepower must allow that file to pass through it. However, what if the file is malicious? Well, Firepower allows *almost* the entire file to pass through. If the file type and protocol matches a **Block Malware** rule, Firepower holds the final packet (the one it needed to fully reassemble the file) and waits for the AMP cloud disposition (up to two seconds by default). If that disposition comes back as malicious then that last packet is dropped.

This means the receiving host never gets the entire file. It may send requests to the other host to try and get that last packet but Firepower will catch this and continue to drop these packets. Firepower can also reset the connection if you check the **Reset Connection** check box. This makes it easier on everyone involved - that way the file transfer fails quickly.

Uploading Files to Threat Grid

Something worth noting here is the device network communication requirements for **Dynamic Analysis**. When a device performs a SHA-256 lookup or sends a file Spero hash to the AMP cloud, this communication is proxied by the FMC. The device does not require an Internet connection. This is shown in the diagram below.

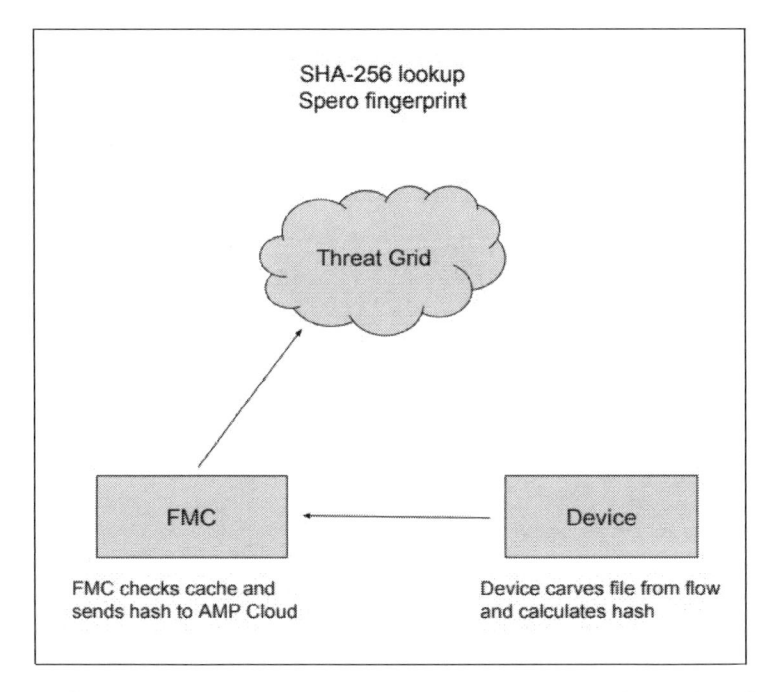

However, if you select **Dynamic Analysis** in your policy, the *device* sends files directly to Threat Grid. They do not pass through the FMC as shown below.

10 – Malware & File Policy

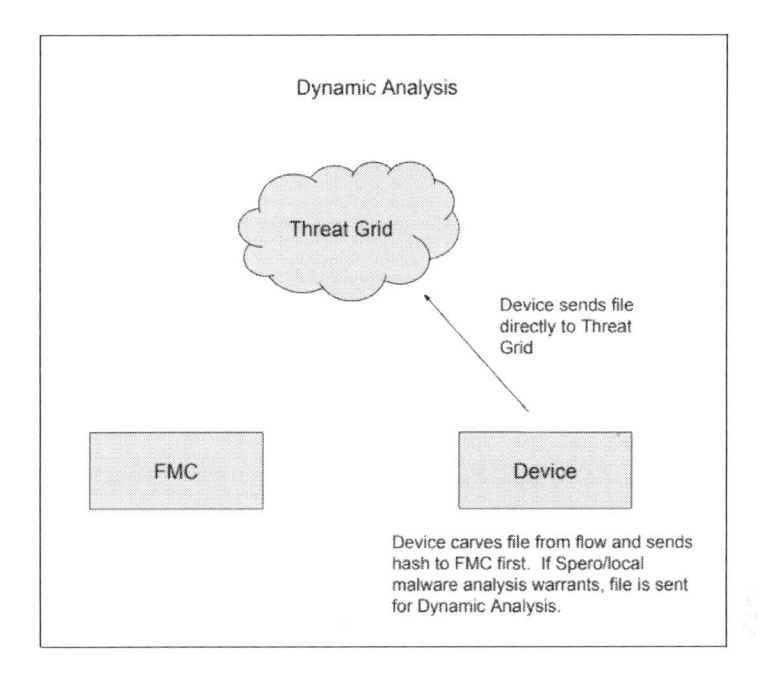

```
                    Dynamic Analysis

                    ╭─────────╮
                   (  Threat Grid  )
                    ╰─────────╯
                              ↖
                               Device sends file
                               directly to Threat
                               Grid

         ┌─────────┐          ┌─────────┐
         │   FMC   │          │  Device │
         └─────────┘          └─────────┘

                    Device carves file from flow and sends
                    hash to FMC first. If Spero/local
                    malware analysis warrants, file is sent
                    for Dynamic Analysis.
```

This is important because it's one of the few times a device ever needs to communicate directly back to Cisco. Keep this in mind if you decide to enable **Dynamic Analysis** in your environment.

> BP57 - Ensure your device can communicate to Threat Grid if using file Dynamic Analysis.

Store Files

The Store Files section determines what to do with the carved out files. You can check the box next to a file disposition to have that file stored.

```
Store Files
  ⬢ Malware   ☐
  ○ Unknown   ☐
  ○ Clean     ☐
  ○ Custom    ☐
```

The files will be stored on the device where they were detected.

Duplicate files will not be stored on a device but they could be duplicated across devices.

There may be a use-case to store malware files if the security team wants to have some fun with them. However, I don't recommend storing clean files or especially unknown files. This will simply use up your file storage which decreases the amount of file history available on a device. Some additional CPU cycles will be used as well in this storage.

> BP58 - Consider the "why" when storing files in the Malware & File policy, avoid storing Unknown file types unless you have a good reason

File Types and Categories

The rest of the rule is simply selecting the types of files this rule will apply to. Again, for many deployments, a single rule in which all file categories are selected is fairly common. There is only one thing that I always mention when selecting file types - think about **Dynamic Analysis**.

What I mean is, think about what happens to files if you are using the public Threat Grid cloud. (A private Threat Grid appliance is also available for on-site sandbox analysis) If you select **Dynamic Analysis** then, any supported file type might be uploaded to Threat Grid for analysis. These file samples are marked private by default meaning other customers cannot see them or see the detailed file analysis results. However, the fact remains that you are uploading *your* files to the cloud. We know the cloud just means - somebody else's computers. These files will persist for an indeterminate amount of time on Cisco's Threat Grid cloud infrastructure.

For some of these file types that's not really an issue. For instance, most companies don't keep any private or proprietary information in Microsoft executable files. However, there are other file types which may contain sensitive data. Let's look at what file types are supported for **Dynamic Analysis**.

If you check the **Dynamic Analysis Capable** check box in your file rule you'll see the file type list below:

10 – Malware & File Policy

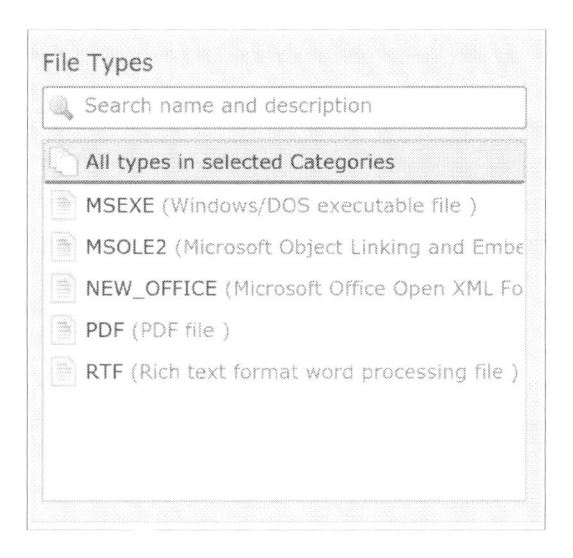

```
File Types
🔍 Search name and description

    All types in selected Categories
    MSEXE (Windows/DOS executable file )
    MSOLE2 (Microsoft Object Linking and Embe
    NEW_OFFICE (Microsoft Office Open XML Fo
    PDF (PDF file )
    RTF (Rich text format word processing file )
```

Of particular interest here are files types such as NEW_OFFICE and PDF. These includes files with extensions like:

- DOCX
- PPTX
- XLSX
- PDF

Keep in mind that the extension doesn't matter, Firepower looks at the file magic - right? I just used them to illustrate that these types of files are all candidates for **Dynamic Analysis** and therefore might be uploaded to Threat Grid and stored there.

Many customers are ok with this - or honestly haven't given it much thought. However, it's something you should be aware of especially if you have compliance requirements that prevent cloud storage of such files. This isn't a huge, dark secret that Cisco is trying to hide. There is documentation available that outlines the measures that have been taken to protect this data. However, it is something to consider as you create your file rules.

> BP59 - Understand the possible privacy ramifications of Dynamic Analysis for document type files.

If this is something that concerns you, there are a couple of options.

1. Don't perform Dynamic Analysis of these document files.

143

This carries with it some risk as these files could contain malware and go undetected.
2. Use a local Threat Grid appliance for your file Dynamic Analysis needs. See your Cisco sales rep and tell them I sent you.

If you select #1 above you can do this with two rules in your policy. One rule would include the **Dynamic Analysis** option and the other would not. You would simply exclude the document file types from the rule where you enable **Dynamic Analysis**.

To create the first rule, In the **Selected File Categories and Types** select everything except the document files you don't want to send to the cloud. A second rule would then not include **Dynamic Analysis** and you would only select the document file types. An example policy is shown below.

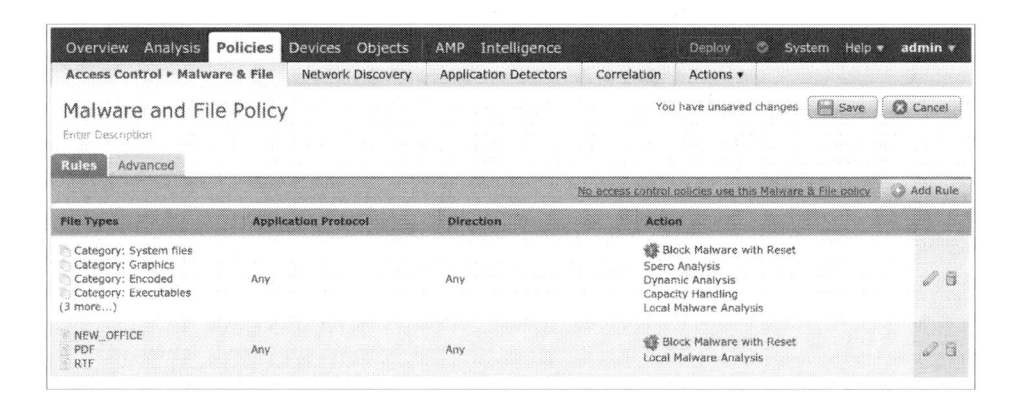

Notice that the second rule does not include Dynamic Analysis and only applies to the document file types. Note that Malware & File rules are unordered so it doesn't matter which rule comes first or second. If you did create a policy where two rules conflicted (say, a rule that blocked PDF with another rule to analyze PDF) you would get a notification in the policy that the rules are incompatible.

Be aware that a file type can occur in more than one **File Type Categories** list. For example the various Microsoft document files (DOCX, PPTX and XLSX) appear in the **Office Documents**, **Dynamic Analysis Capable** and **Local Malware Analysis Capable** categories. This is shown in the three screenshots below.

10 – Malware & File Policy

File Type Categories		File Types
✓ Office Documents	20	🔍 Search name and description
☐ Archive	18	
☐ Multimedia	30	MSCHM (Microsoft Compiled HTML Help File)
☐ Executables	14	MSHTML (Proprietary layout engine for Micro
☐ PDF files	2	MSWORD_MAC5 (Microsoft Word for Mac 5)
☐ Encoded	2	MWL (Metastock technical analysis program
☐ Graphics	6	NEW_OFFICE (Microsoft Office Open XML Fo
☐ System files	13	ONE (Microsoft OneNote note)
☐ Dynamic Analysis Capable	5	PST (Microsoft Outlook Personal Folder File)
☐ Local Malware Analysis Capable	5	RTF (Rich text format word processing file)

Above you can see that the Office Documents file type category contains the NEW_OFFICE file types. In the figure below you can see that the **Dynamic Analysis Capable** category also contains NEW_OFFICE as well as PDF file types.

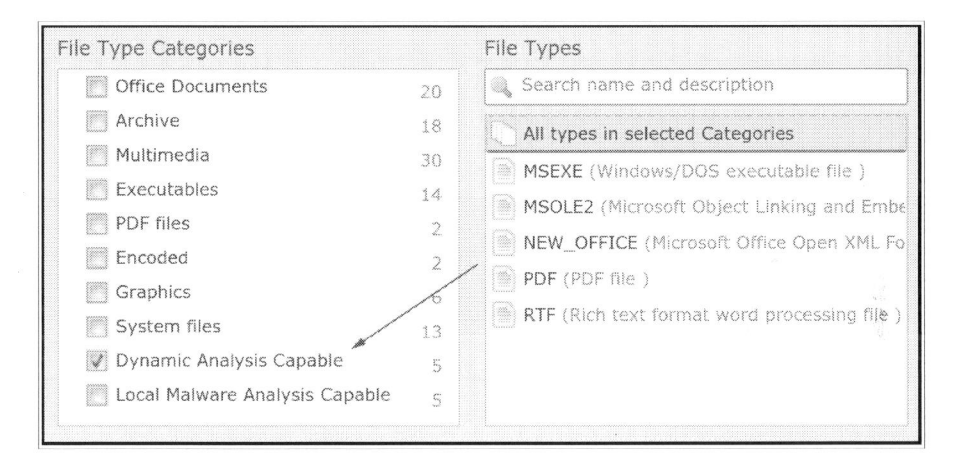

File Type Categories		File Types
☐ Office Documents	20	🔍 Search name and description
☐ Archive	18	All types in selected Categories
☐ Multimedia	30	
☐ Executables	14	MSEXE (Windows/DOS executable file)
☐ PDF files	2	MSOLE2 (Microsoft Object Linking and Embe
☐ Encoded	2	NEW_OFFICE (Microsoft Office Open XML Fo
☐ Graphics	6	PDF (PDF file)
☐ System files	13	RTF (Rich text format word processing file)
✓ Dynamic Analysis Capable	5	
☐ Local Malware Analysis Capable	5	

Finally in the third figure below the Local Malware Analysis Capable category also contains NEW_OFFICE and PDF file types.

Essential Firepower

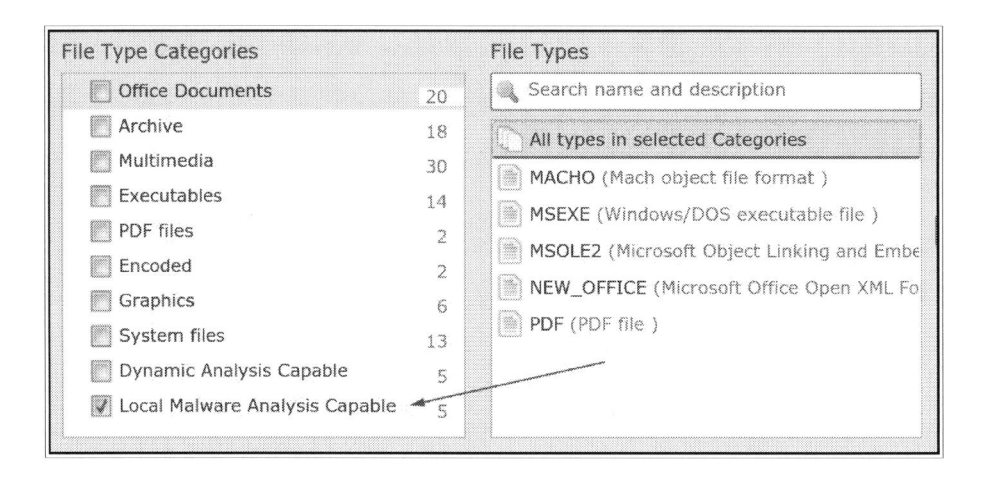

File Type Categories		File Types
☐ Office Documents	20	🔍 Search name and description
☐ Archive	18	All types in selected Categories
☐ Multimedia	30	MACHO (Mach object file format)
☐ Executables	14	MSEXE (Windows/DOS executable file)
☐ PDF files	2	MSOLE2 (Microsoft Object Linking and Embe
☐ Encoded	2	NEW_OFFICE (Microsoft Office Open XML Fo
☐ Graphics	6	PDF (PDF file)
☐ System files	13	
☐ Dynamic Analysis Capable	5	
☑ Local Malware Analysis Capable	5	

As with most things the devil is in the details so be certain your Malware & File policy is performing the type of inspection you want it to.

Chapter 11 - Prefilter Policy

In this chapter, we will focus on the Prefilter policy. This policy processes traffic before it is sent to the Access Control policy or even before it is evaluated by Security Intelligence. It is only used on Firepower Threat Defense (FTD) systems not on classic Firepower appliances. The reason for this is this policy targets the Adaptive Security Appliance (ASA) portion of an FTD device. This is a component that a classic Firepower appliance does not have.

The Prefilter policy is generally used to either fast path or block traffic before it is sent to the Access Control policy. If you don't have a requirement to do either of these you can just leave the **Default Prefilter Policy** in effect and skip this feature altogether.

In fact, a very large number of FTD deployments do just that. If you don't have a need to use the Prefilter policy features or you are running classic Firepower devices then you can skip this chapter. Because this is an "essentials" book I am not going to spend much time on this policy. We will hit some of the important highlights, especially when NOT to use this policy.

If you are ready to use Prefilter or just learn more about it - read on!

The Default Prefilter Policy

You will find the Prefilter policy on the FMC under **Policies → Access Control → Prefilter**. If you haven't been here before you'll see that there is a single **Default Prefilter Policy** already in existence. In the figure below you'll see this **Default Prefilter Policy** in addition to a custom policy I have created called FTD Prefilter.

Essential Firepower

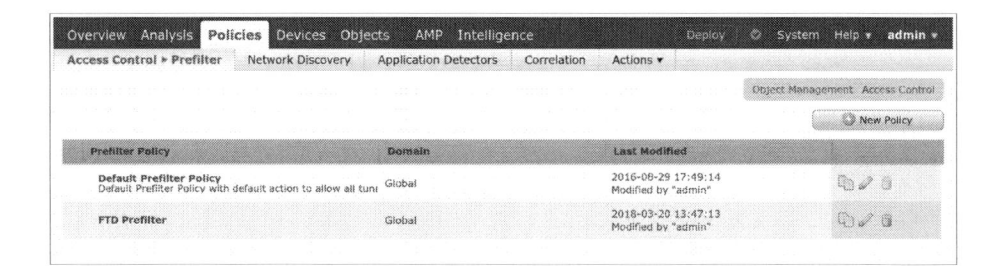

The **Default Prefilter Policy** cannot be modified other than to change the **Default Action** from **Analyze all tunnel traffic** to **Block all tunnel traffic**. It's really only here as a placeholder for folks who don't want to use Prefilter at all. If you are going to take advantage of any of the features you'll want to create a new policy.

Customizing the Prefilter Policy

As with the other policies, to customize the Prefilter policy you will click the **New Policy** button in the upper right, then enter a name and optional description. This will bring you to the rule editing page below.

Note that this policy doesn't have any fancy advanced settings - you just add rules. These rules can be Tunnel Rules or Prefilter Rules.

Tunnel Rules are used to identify tunneled traffic and "tag" it for rules in the Access Control policy. If you need to create specific Access Control rules for tunneled traffic then you'll need rules(s) here to tag

148

the traffic. This is a very unusual use-case, in fact I've never seen anyone use this in real-life. When we say tunnels we mean:

- **Generic Routing Encapsulation (GRE)** - IP protocol 47
- **IP-in-IP** - IP protocol 4
- **IPv6-in-IP** - IP protocol 41
- **Teredo** (UDP (17)/3455)

The other type of rule is simply called a Prefilter Rule. This is the rule type (if any) you are more likely to use.

When you think of a Prefilter Rule think of a firewall working at OSI layer 3 and 4. These firewalls basically allow or block traffic purely based on the source and destination port, IP address and (transport) protocol. Honestly, if all you wanted to do with your Firepower system was to use it like a traditional firewall you could do it all in the Prefilter policy - but that doesn't mean it's a good idea. (It doesn't mean it's a bad idea either, just an option)

When you click the **Add Prefilter Rule** button you will see the dialog shown below.

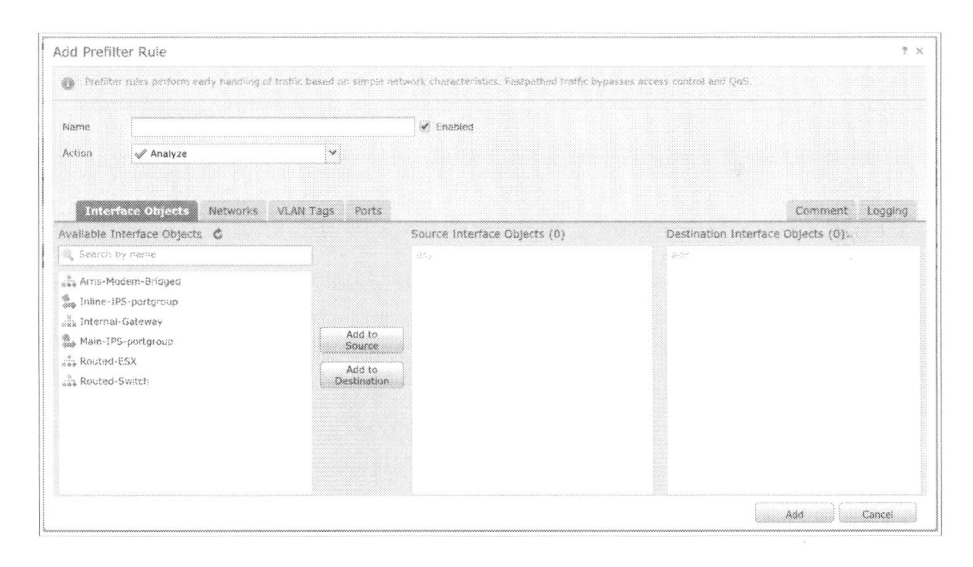

Your options for selecting what traffic your rules will process include:

- Interface
- Networks
- VLAN Tags
- Ports

The rule actions available are:

- **Analyze** - the traffic will be sent on to the Access Control policy
- **Block** - block the traffic
- **Fastpath** - exempt traffic from all further inspection and control, this includes Security Intelligence, Access Control, Identity etc.

Why would you want to Block or Fastpath traffic in the Prefilter policy? Well, to start with, a block is a block regardless of whether you do it here or later in the Access Control policy. I can't come up with a good reason to block traffic here instead of doing it later in Access Control. I've asked the experts, and it doesn't appear to be measurably faster or more efficient in Prefilter versus Access Control policy.

The Analyze function just means "process this traffic by the Access Control policy" so it has a very limited use-case as well. Basically if you wanted to Fastpath or Block an IP range but within that range you wanted to analyze some traffic you could use a combination of Fastpath, Block and Analyze rules to do that.

This brings us to the feature I see most used in Prefilter - Fastpath. This can be used to speed traffic through the device which you do not want to inspect. Why would you want to pass traffic through without inspection? Reasons may include:

- A protocol or application that is latency sensitive such as Session Initiation Protocol (SIP) which is used for Voice Over IP (VOIP).
- Large encrypted flows such as backups or replication traffic between hosts/data centers
- Vulnerability scanners
- Any long running flow you don't want to impact by pinning it to a single Snort CPU

These are examples of types of flows you may want to Fastpath through your device without inspection. However, it doesn't mean that Prefilter is the right place to do this.

When you Fastpath a flow in Prefilter - depending on the device hardware - the system may take advantage of the "Smart NIC" (Network Interface Card). This is special network hardware which can actually be programmed to block or pass traffic without routing it through the device at all.

In layman's terms, here's what happens when traffic matches a Fastpath rule. (By the way, I'm a layman when it comes to what happens at this level in Firepower so I'm not talking down to anyone) Firepower identifies the traffic as a flow that needs to be bypassed. It does this very early in the flow - like the first packet. When this happens, it sends a message to the Smart NIC telling it that this flow should be Fastpathed. The Smart NIC then implements that action and the flow is now forwarded without actually being processed by the ASA or Snort code at all. Limited connection data is still logged for this connection and can be viewed in Connection Events on the FMC.

This is all good - right? The answer is, it depends.

If you have a very small flow such as a UDP DNS request that "connection" may only consist of a single packet. There is no handshake at the beginning or tear down of the connection at the end. If this traffic was to match a Prefilter Fastpath rule then by the time Firepower instructed the Smart NIC to Fastpath the traffic the flow would be finished. This also applies to very short TCP flows which may only consist of a handful of packets. The system actually spends more CPU cycles instructing the Smart NIC to bypass the flow then it would have taken to process the flow through Access Control normally. This defeats one of the primary purposes of bypassing flows in the first place - to reduce overhead on Firepower.

If the flow is a large and long lived one then it makes perfect sense to use a rule with the Fastpath action in Prefilter and offload that flow via the Smart NIC. This leads to the primary best practice when using Prefilter rules:

> BP60 - Don't use Prefilter Fastpath rules for tiny flows.

So where would you create rules to bypass tiny flows like DNS? At the risk of stealing my own thunder from the Access Control Policy chapter; you would do this in the Access Control policy via a Trust rule. More on that later.

To round out this chapter, Prefilter rules contain additional options for

Essential Firepower

logging and comments which are self-explanatory or explained in the online help. There isn't anything else that falls into the essential category for this policy.

That about wraps it up for Prefilter - see I told you it would be short!

Chapter 12 - SSL and Identity Policy

I am combining SSL and Identity into the same chapter because these are seldom-used policies and there aren't many essentials to mention about them. As you might guess, the SSL policy controls how SSL decryption is performed. The Identity policy is used if you have the requirement to create Access Control rules that only match traffic generated by certain users or groups. Both of these are heavily dependent on additional configuration outside of the policies themselves. In the case of SSL there will be certificate management and for Identity you'll have to configure an identity source.

SSL Policy

This policy is named for the Secure Sockets Layer (SSL) which is an older cryptographic protocol. It was replaced almost 20 years ago by Transport Layer Security (TLS). Even though SSL is no longer used on modern networks, everybody knows it means encrypted traffic so the term is still widely seen when we talk about encrypted connections.

Before you create an SSL policy you will need to decide what traffic you plan to decrypt. At a high level your choices are:

- **Inbound** - traffic initiated from external clients to your SSL servers
- **Outbound** - traffic initiated from within your network to external SSL servers

Each of these carries its own requirements and challenges. I would say that decrypting inbound traffic is a more common and less complex task in most cases. I'm going to assume you know something about SSL communications and what decryption involves. It's basically a man-in-the-middle (MITM) attack on SSL connections which fools the client and server into thinking they are talking directly to each other privately when in fact they are not. Calling this an attack is really a misnomer in this case since it's an authorized attack and we're really not trying to do anything evil here. But whether it's authorized or not the mechanics are the same.

Here are some considerations when decrypting traffic with Firepower.

- **Decryption carries processing overhead**. We're not just talking about a little overhead, be prepared to take an 85% or higher performance hit on your device throughput compared to plain text inspection. Your mileage may vary but make no mistake, even with hardware decryption enabled your device throughput capability will take a massive dive.

- **Certificates**. You will have to manage certificates for this to work. It will either involve importing the private keys for your web servers or getting your FMC Certificate Authority (CA) certificate signed in the case of re-signing outbound connections.

- **Not everything can be decrypted.** Applications that use certificate pinning cannot be decrypted using MITM. This isn't a Firepower shortcoming, it's just a fact of life. Defeating MITM is what certificate pinning is for.

- **It's probably harder than you think.** You really should have a firm mandate to start down this path. If you don't, it's likely you'll realize what a royal pain it is and decide it wasn't such a great idea after all.

- **You will have to forego decryption of some traffic.** Whether it's due to certificate or key pinning, privacy issues or application incompatibility you will likely have to exempt some traffic from decryption or risk interfering with the traffic/application.

- **Consider privacy when decrypting outbound sessions.** If you're planning to decrypt your users' outbound SSL traffic there are likely going to be some connections you should not be peeking into. Anything relating to privacy such as banking, shopping (credit card transactions), health related sites, etc. should probably not be decrypted. Doing so can lead to legal liability, consult your legal department before you go down this path.

You may have noticed a theme in the considerations above - decrypting SSL traffic is fraught with peril!

> BP61 - SSL decryption is fraught with peril, proceed only if you have a clear business need.

If you remain undaunted, you will find SSL policy on the FMC under **Policies → Access Control → SSL.** There is no default SSL policy. As with other policies you can create a new one by clicking the **New Policy** button in the upper right. When you do you get the chance to give your policy a **Name**, **Description** and select the **Default Action** as shown below.

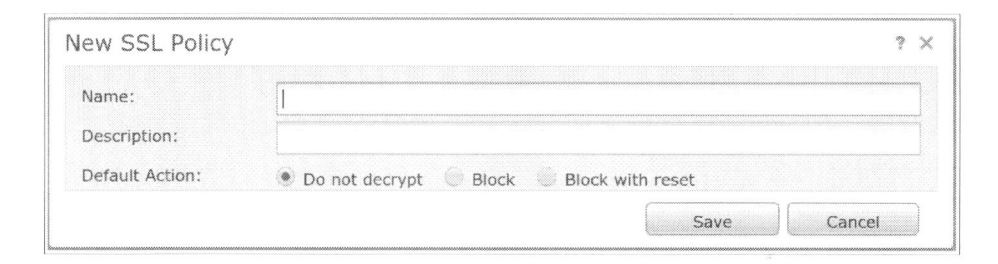

New SSL Policy	? ×
Name:	
Description:	
Default Action:	● Do not decrypt ○ Block ○ Block with reset
	Save Cancel

After saving the new policy you will see the main Rules screen as shown below. Rather than restate the help here I'm just going to show you what a very simple policy might look like.

Essential Firepower

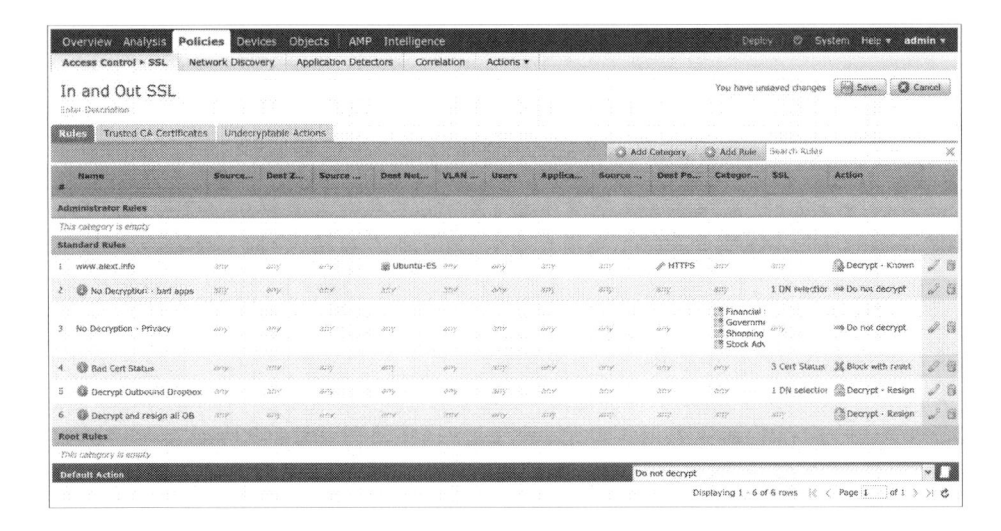

The policy above enables inbound (known key) and outbound (resign) rules. It avoids decryption of certain URL categories (this require a URL license), blocks invalid certificates and attempts to decrypt all outbound sessions. If sessions cannot be decrypted for various reasons (except decryption errors) then the **Default Action** of Do not decrypt would be taken.

Clicking the **Undecryptable Actions** tab shows the actions for undecryptable sessions.

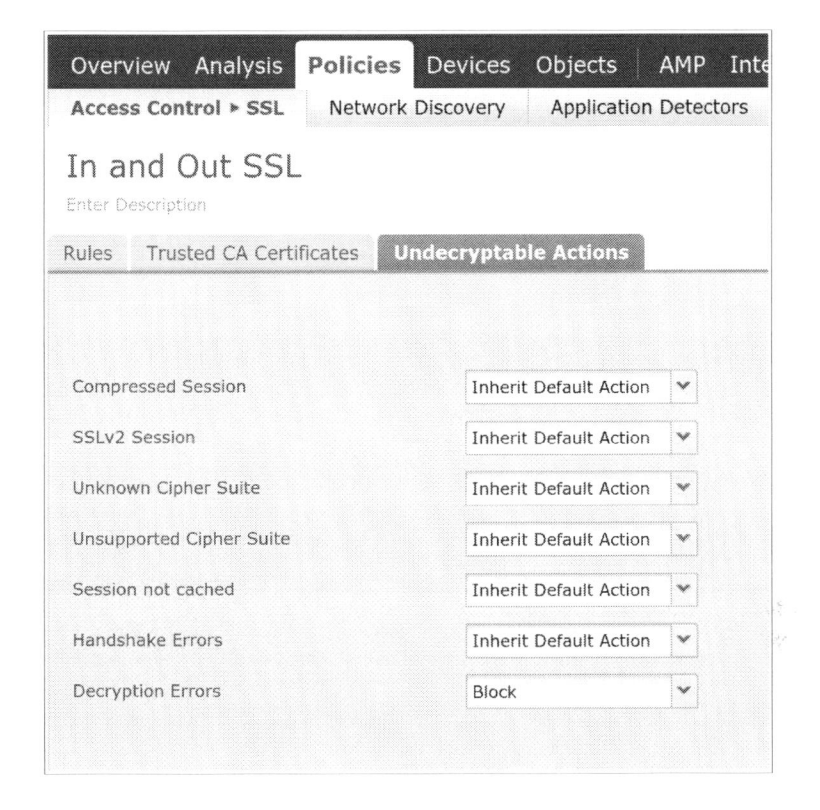

12 – SSL and Identity Policy

```
Overview  Analysis  Policies  Devices  Objects  AMP  Inte
Access Control ▶ SSL     Network Discovery   Application Detectors
```

In and Out SSL
Enter Description

| Rules | Trusted CA Certificates | **Undecryptable Actions** |

Compressed Session	Inherit Default Action
SSLv2 Session	Inherit Default Action
Unknown Cipher Suite	Inherit Default Action
Unsupported Cipher Suite	Inherit Default Action
Session not cached	Inherit Default Action
Handshake Errors	Inherit Default Action
Decryption Errors	Block

SSL rules are evaluated in sequence from top to bottom. You have numerous options for selecting what traffic will match a given SSL rule.

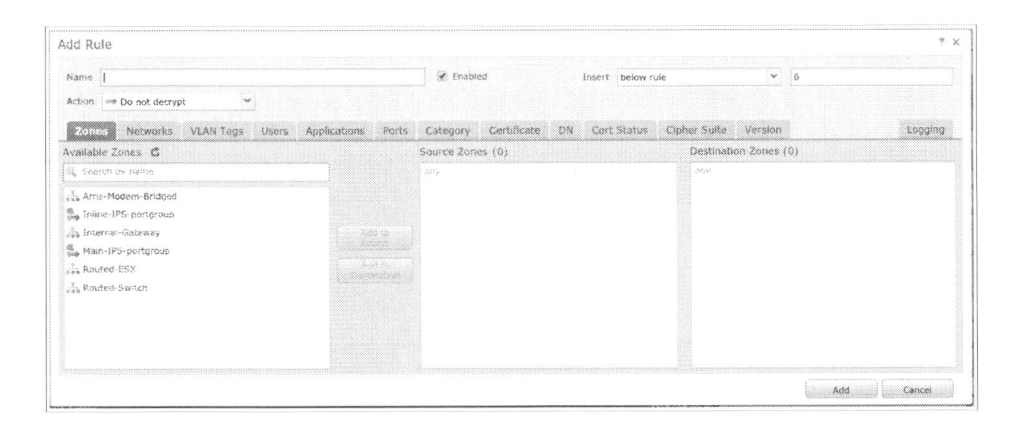

If you are planning to enable SSL decryption in your deployment, I recommend reading the Configuration Guide thoroughly and maybe buying a book on SSL to get a solid understanding of decryption protocols.

157

Identity Policy

Identity is one of the least-used Firepower policies. If you want to create Access Control rules that match traffic for specific users or groups you'll need this policy. However, like SSL policy, doing this may be harder than it looks.

The first thing to keep in mind is that it's impossible to identify the user for network connections simply from the traffic alone. Network traffic consists of packets, with source and destination addresses and possibly some data attached. I say "possibly" because some packets such as SYN, SYN/ACK, FIN, etc. which build up or tear down connections don't have data in them at all (at least they shouldn't). This means we must have some other way to associate this traffic with a user. Even if we could peer into the data packets and discern the user it may be too late at that point to decide whether the traffic should be allowed or blocked. This generally means we need to associate a user with an IP address on the network before we see traffic from that IP.

Cisco introduced Security Group Tags (SGT) some time ago to identify traffic from specific users. If you have all the right network equipment you can assign a numeric tag to traffic which can then be allowed/blocked on your network. Firepower can use SGT as well, if you only want to allow/block traffic for specific SGTs you can do that without an Identity policy. All you have to do is create a Security Group Tag object, give it a name and assign the SGT number. However, if you want to identify users, there still must be a lookup to tie the SGT number to a user.

Authoritative Users

It's important that you don't cofuse the identity we're talking about here with the users discovered through passive analysis. Remember that the Discovery policy has a Users tab where you can select the clear text logins that will be inspected. If a user name is detected in these logins that user will be associated with the host in the host database. These are not sufficient for user-based Access Control rules. These are not what Firepower calls "authoritative users".

12 – SSL and Identity Policy

To put it into perspective here are the steps required to start identifying authoritative users and creating identity based rules in your Access Control policy:

1. **Create a realm** - this is a trusted user and group store, typically a Microsoft Active Directory repository.
2. **Create a directory in the realm** - an Active Directory domain controller that organizes information about a computer network's users and network shares.
3. **Download users/groups from the realm** - this is pretty easy once you have the realm setup. You typically schedule this to update periodically so your FMC keeps an updated list of users and groups.
4. **Create a method to retrieve user and group data** (the identity source) - this is where it starts getting a little sticky. The steps above provide the FMC with information about the users in your directory. Now you need to find a way to associate them with traffic.
5. **Create an Identity policy** with rules to use the identity sources above.
6. **Associate your Identity policy** with an Access Control policy.

Now you can create Access Control rules using user/group criteria.

Step 4 above is arguably the most difficult. This is because it requires an external mechanism to identify users. This can be:

- **Cisco Identity Services Engine (ISE)** - your FMC connects to an ISE or ISE-PIC server to receive user-awareness information. You must already have this ISE infrastructure deployed and working.
- **User Agent** - this is an agent running on one or more Windows hosts that forwards login events to the FMC from an Active Directory server. These login events contain the IP address of the user.
- **Captive portal** - A web page hosted on one or more Firepower devices which requires the user to authenticate.
- **Remote Access VPN** - remote user VPN authentications.

The Firepower help provides details on how to setup an Identity policy depending on the identity source you select. The purpose of including it here is simply to give you an idea of the external requirements you will have to satisfy.

As with SSL policy, my advice is not to journey down this path unless you have a clear requirement to do so. It will require some external integration and can be quite complex.

> BP62 - Identity policy requires coordination/setup of external authentication mechanisms, make sure you understand them if this is a requirement.

Chapter 13 - DNS Policy

Overview

DNS policy is the way DNS blacklists are implemented in Firepower. As you will see, IP and URL blacklisting is done on a tab in the Access Control policy. However, since you can respond a number of ways to DNS requests this has been given its own policy. With DNS policy you can decide how you want to respond to DNS requests. Your options are:

- **Whitelist** - allow the DNS request and skip any DNS blacklists
- **Monitor** - generate a Security Intelligence event only
- Domain Not Found - drop the request and impersonate a NXDOMAIN response from the DNS server
- **Block** - drop the request and send no network response to the requestor
- **Sinkhole** - drop the request, impersonate a response from the DNS server but return the IP address specified in a sinkhole object

You will find DNS policy under **Policies → Access Control → DNS**. There is a Default DNS Policy which you can use and add rules to. Or if you prefer, you can create a new one. A sample DNS policy is shown below.

Essential Firepower

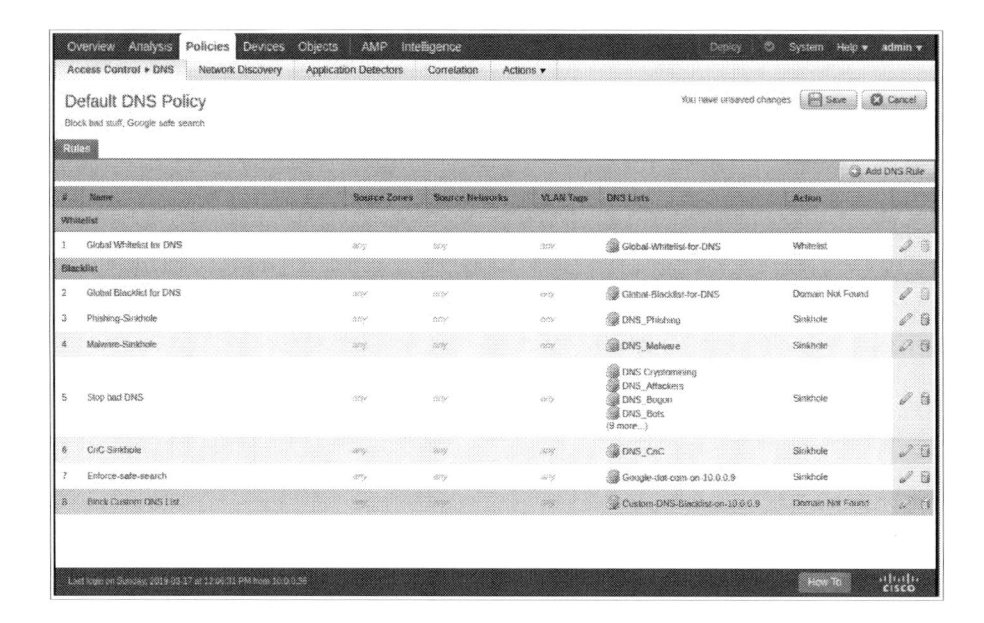

In the sample above I have added a number of custom rules. Your Default DNS policy will only contain the default whitelist and blacklist rules for the Global Whitelist and Global Blacklist.

Clicking **Add DNS Rule** in the upper right will bring up the rule dialog as shown below.

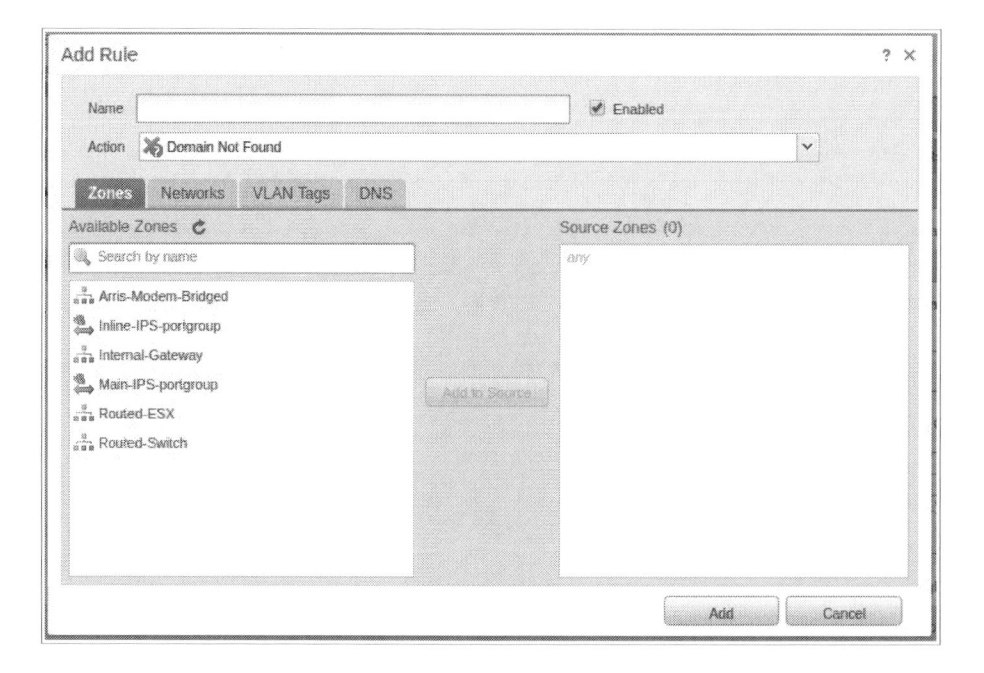

Clicking the Action drop-down will allow you to pick the actions for the rule.

```
Action      ✗ Domain Not Found
            ✓ Whitelist
Zones       ↓ Monitor
vailable    ✗ Domain Not Found
  Search    ✗ Drop
  Arris-N   ⊙ Sinkhole
  Inline-IPS-portgroup
```

Consult the help if you want more details on what the actions do. Here are my recommendations.

Depending on your network design and the placement of your Firepower device(s) you may want to simply add a Drop or Domain Not Found rule and add all the Talos Security Intelligence categories. This is ok if your device can see the actual DNS request from your hosts. However, if your Firepower device is positioned outside or North of your DNS servers then you may want to consider a sinkhole instead.

Before we go to sinkholes there's one important thing I want to note about DNS Security Intelligence rule actions. If you select one of the drop actions:

- Domain Not Found
- Drop
- Sinkhole

The system will drop the traffic and cease any further inspection. This is fine if your device really is inline. However it if is deployed in passive mode the packet will not actually be dropped. Because of this, It might be beneficial to run it through the rest of your intrusion policy rules. This isn't as critical as it might be with IP Security Intelligence but it's still something to consider.

> BP63 - use the DNS Security Intelligence drop actions only on devices which can actually drop

To Sinkhole or Not to Sinkhole

There's no way to explain sinkholes without a couple of diagrams. The first example shows a situation *without* DNS security intelligence or a sinkhole.

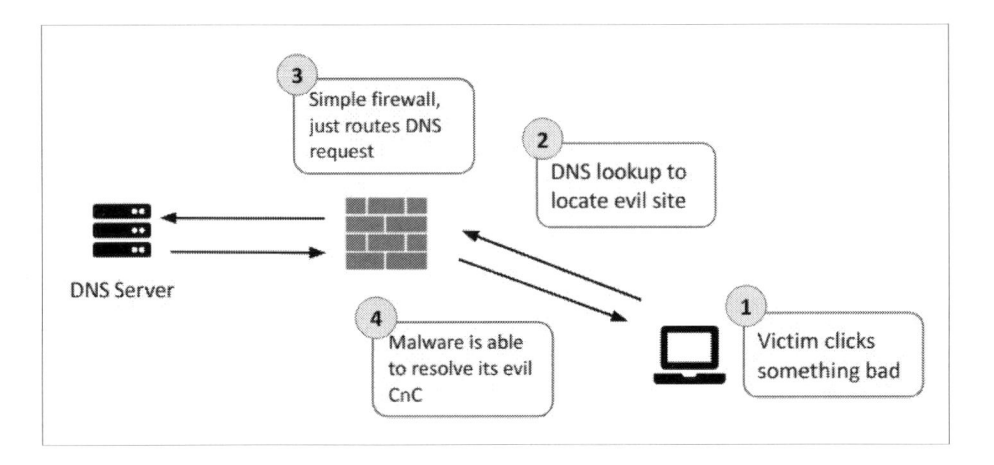

In the diagram above the victim clicks something bad or has some malware running on their computer. The malware performs a DNS lookup using an external DNS server. That query is sent through the (dumb) firewall. Since there is no DNS Security Intelligence the query succeeds and evil is allowed to spread.

Next, let's look at a simple situation where there is no internal DNS server between the victim host and the Firepower NGFW. In this case there is still no sinkhole is needed. If something evil happens, the Firewall can block the bad DNS request before it even gets to a DNS server.

13 – DNS Policy

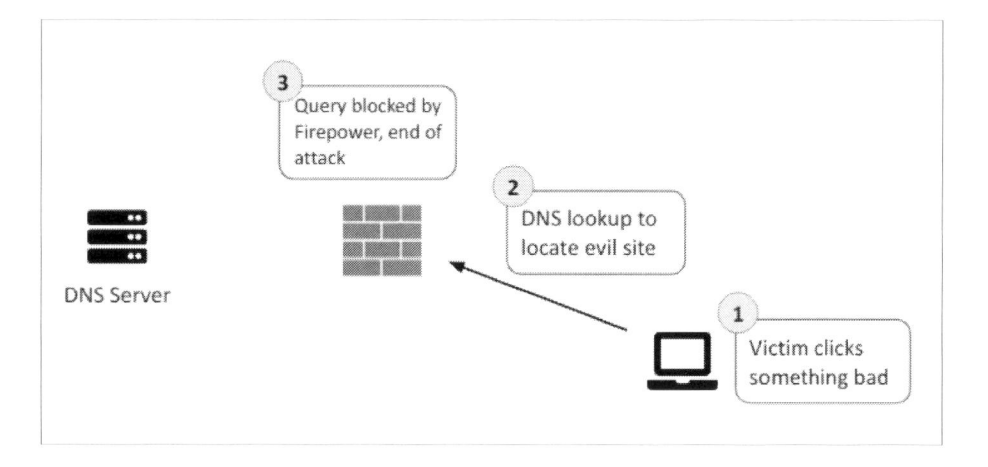

DNS Server

3. Query blocked by Firepower, end of attack
2. DNS lookup to locate evil site
1. Victim clicks something bad

It's important to remember that this is only half the battle. If the victim simply clicked on a malicious link then the threat has been averted and all you may have is some user training left to do. However, if the DNS request was the result of something evil already running on the victim's computer then **blocking the DNS request did not solve the problem**. You may have slowed the malware down but if the victim's computer moves off the network where Firepower isn't blocking the DNS request the malware could try again and this time it might work. Then it can call all of it's malware buddies and completely infest the victim.

When the DNS request is blocked in the example above you will receive a Security Intelligence event on your FMC. Depending on the severity of the event you may want to pay the user a visit and remediate the malware infection. You may not care for Possibly Unwanted Applications (PUA) but if this is a request to a Command and Control (CnC) server then it might be something worth looking into.

Tracking down the user should be fairly easy because your Security Intelligence event shows their IP address in the Initiator IP field for the event. The screenshot below shows some of the fields you might find in a Security Intelligence event.

Essential Firepower

Reason ✕	Initiator IP ✕	Responder IP ✕	Responder Country ✕
DNS Block	10.0.0.205	8.8.8.8 (google-public-dns-a.google.com)	USA
DNS Block	10.0.0.205	8.8.8.8 (google-public-dns-a.google.com)	USA
DNS Block	10.0.0.49	208.67.222.222 (resolver1.opendns.com)	USA

Ahh, but no network is as simple as the ones above right? At a minimum your Firepower device is likely to be positioned outside of your internal DNS server. Revisiting an example **without** a Firepower device, the diagram below shows what might happen.

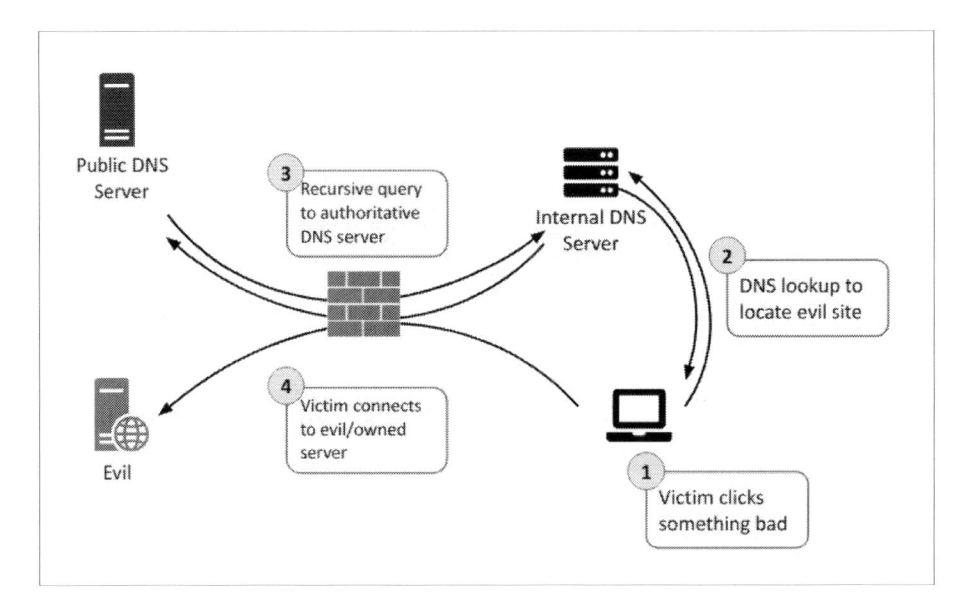

It's pretty similar to the non-Firepower example before. The only difference is that there's an internal DNS server doing a recursive lookup for the victim. The malware is still successful and it's not somewhere you want to be.

Let's look at what happens when we have a Firepower device that is configured to respond with a Domain Not Found rule action.

166

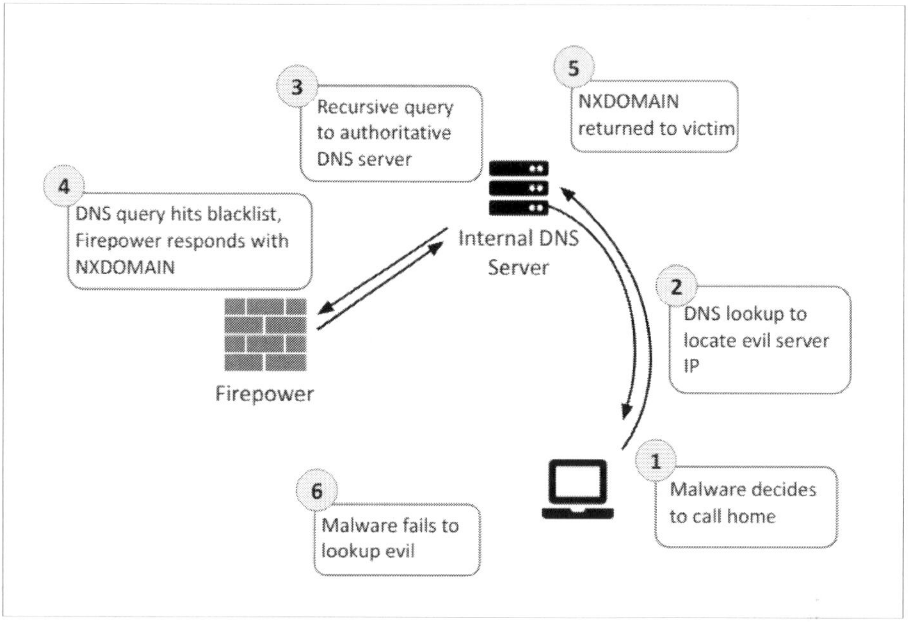
3
Recursive query to authoritative DNS server
5
NXDOMAIN returned to victim
4
DNS query hits blacklist, Firepower responds with NXDOMAIN
Internal DNS Server
2
DNS lookup to locate evil server IP
Firepower
1
Malware decides to call home
6
Malware fails to lookup evil

In the example above the Firepower device detects the blacklisted DNS lookup and replies with a NXDOMAIN message. This is relayed to the victim and the malware fails to lookup it's evil CnC or whatever it was looking for. The malware probably has a plan B but at least we've stopped this immediate action.

You will receive a Security Intelligence event just like we saw previously. However, this time the source IP address will be the DNS server instead of the victim. In fact, you will never see a victim IP address in your DNS events. You will still get the events but now there's a challenge locating the infected host.

You may be able to cross-reference your DNS logs for a lookup at the same time as your event. However, this is usually difficult at best and not foolproof.

Enter the DNS Sinkhole!

By using a DNS Sinkhole rule and associated object you can return a custom IP address to your victim. The malware will think its query was successful and then attempt to contact the evil server at the IP you gave it. It's this second attempt that you can see and then track back to the victim. It looks like this:

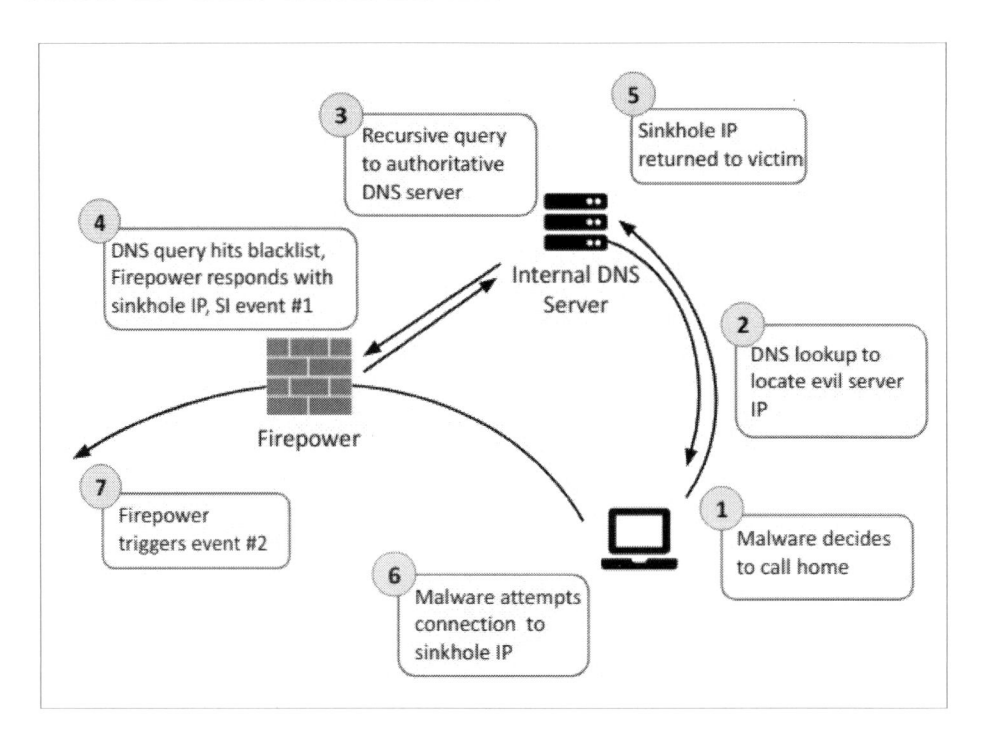

```
3 - Recursive query to authoritative DNS server
5 - Sinkhole IP returned to victim
4 - DNS query hits blacklist, Firepower responds with sinkhole IP, SI event #1
  Internal DNS Server
  Firepower
2 - DNS lookup to locate evil server IP
7 - Firepower triggers event #2
1 - Malware decides to call home
6 - Malware attempts connection to sinkhole IP
```

You will receive a similar Security Intelligence event as before with the internal DNS server's IP address as the source. However, this time it will be a sinkhole event.

Action	Reason	Initiator IP	Responder IP	Responder Country
Sinkhole	DNS Block	10.0.0.205	8.8.8.8 (google-public-dns-a.google.com)	USA
Sinkhole	DNS Block	10.0.0.205	8.8.8.8 (google-public-dns-a.google.com)	USA
Sinkhole	DNS Block	10.0.0.49	208.67.222.222 (resolver1.opendns.com)	USA
Sinkhole	DNS Block	10.0.0.49	208.67.222.222 (resolver1.opendns.com)	USA

There will then be a follow-up connection event to the custom IP address you assigned to your sinkhole object.

Honestly, sometimes I struggle finding the follow-up event. You have to have the sinkhole object configured correctly and it has to be either Command and Control, Malware or Phishing.

If you are serious about locating the victims in your environment, you might consider another way. Setup your own "honeypot" server. This would not be a host you would advertise. The IP address assigned should not be well-known or published. The idea is that the only way anyone would get that IP is if you gave it to them via a sinkhole event. Any connection you see coming to that host is a result of a malicious DNS lookup. You would have to listen on several ports because you don't know what protocol the malware will use. However, it's a good bet that 80 and 443 will be on the short list.

Here's what it might look like:

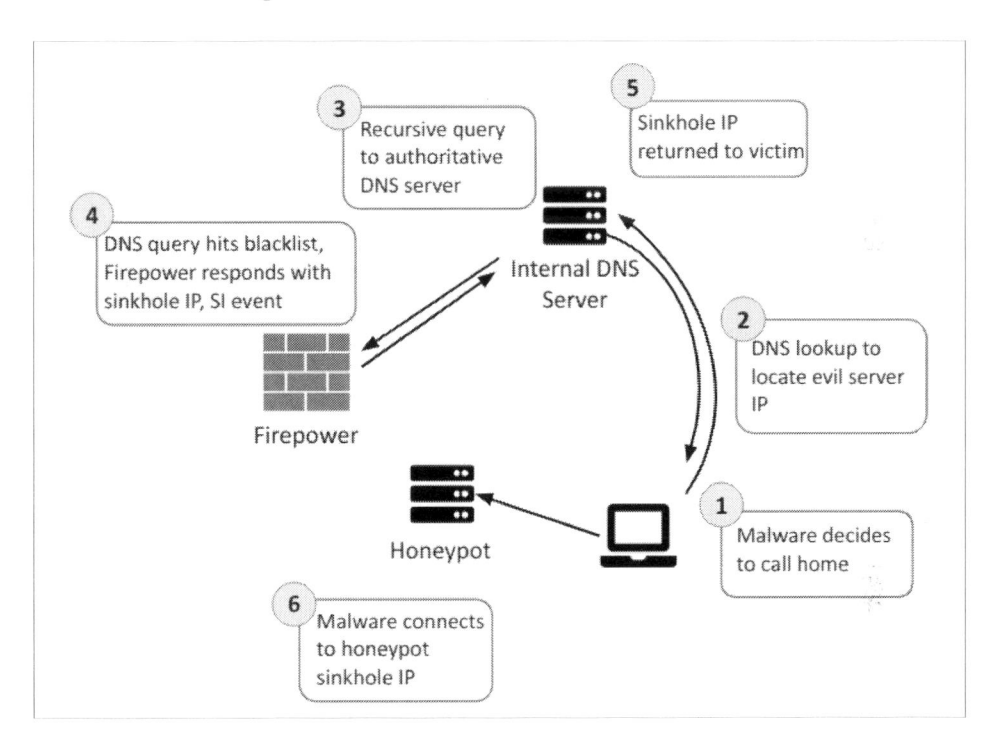

Now you can look at the connection logs on your honeypot and identify the source IP of the victim. You can also gather additional intelligence on the malware activity depending on the sophistication of your honeypot server.

This finally leads me to my last recommendation for DNS policy.

>BP64 - Try out the sinkhole, you may like it

Chapter 14 - Access Control Policy

Welcome to the chapter on the "mother of all policies" - Access Control. This is the primary policy responsible for determining how traffic passing through devices will be processed. When configuring the system, it is tempting to start here since it is the central traffic management point. However, as we have learned, Access Control depends on multiple other policies and settings to perform threat detection and deep packet inspection. As such, these other items must be configured before we can use Access Control to direct traffic to the various inspection types available.

Within the policy itself, my technique is generally to start with the Advanced and Security Intelligence settings and then configure rules last. That way, once the other settings are configured we can concentrate on rule creation.

You may have noticed that in Firepower we use the word "rules" a lot. This is often confusing because there are quite a few types of rules in the system. You will find the following major rule types:

- Intrusion (Snort)
- Access Control
- Discovery
- Correlation
- DNS
- SSL
- Malware & File

There are other less common rules within some of the policies but the point is you can't just say "rules" without somehow qualifying what you mean. The Access Control, rule set is the one that most closely approximates an Access Control List (ACL) on a typical router or firewall. Of course, there are more options for traffic processing on Firepower but this rule set is processed from top to bottom in the same way as those other ACLs you may be more familiar with.

Overview

You will find Access Control policy on the FMC under **Policies → Access Control → Access Control**. When you create a new policy or edit an existing one you will find yourself at the **Rules** tab as shown below.

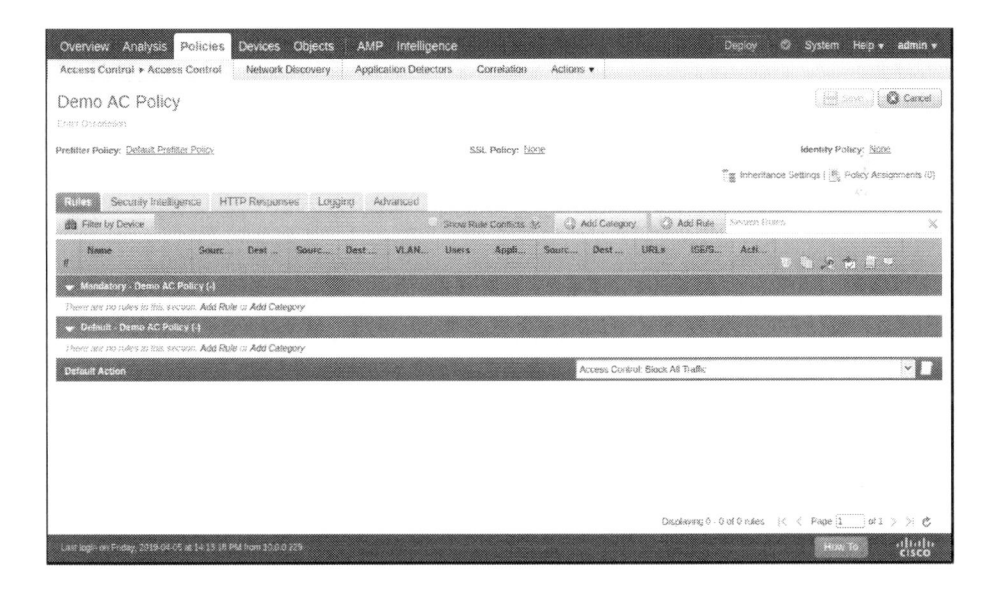

Before we configure any rules, let's look at the other policy settings. Notice on this page near the top you have links where you can configure the Prefilter, SSL and Identity policies. By clicking the links there, you associate these other policies with your Access Control policy. You also have **Inheritance Settings** and **Policy Assignments**.

The **Policy Assignments** setting is pretty simple, you have to target one or more devices where you want to deploy it. Each device must have an Access Control policy assigned to it. You assign an Access Control policy to the device when you first register it to the FMC. From that point on, the device will always have one Access Control policy associated with it. You can assign a single policy to multiple devices but each device can have only one.

Essential Firepower

When you click the **Policy Assignments** link you will see a dialog like the one below. This shows all of your devices on the left and any Selected or Impacted devices on the right.

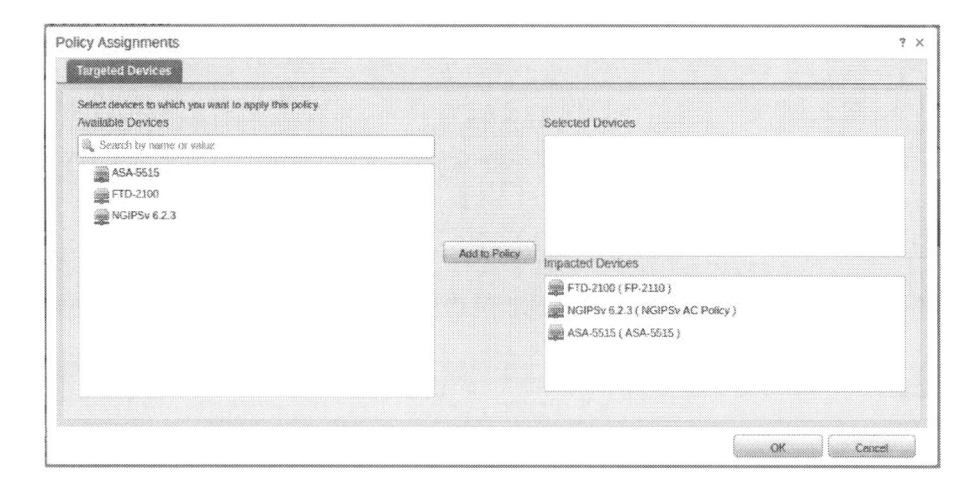

What is the difference between Selected and Impacted?
In the dialog above, when you select a device on the left and click the **Add to Policy** button, the device appears in the **Selected Devices** list. If you just want to assign the policy to a device this is how you do it. The only way policies appear in the **Impacted Devices** list is if you are using Master/Child policies.

The tabs available here are **Rules**, **Security Intelligence**, **HTTP Responses**, **Logging** (6.3 and later), and **Advanced**. We will deal with each of these in this chapter.

Parent/Child Policies

I am a fan of hierarchical policy design. I showed an example of this in the Intrusion Policy chapter. By using a base policy you can make changes across a number of other policies without duplicating your efforts. Access Control has a similar capability, however it is a bit more refined than what is available with Intrusion policy.

The terminology for Access Control hierarchy in Firepower is a bit convoluted. What I mean is that Cisco calls the parent policy the "Base" and the descendant policy the "Child". This makes no sense to me. Base seems like it should be below with layers built on top - as with Intrusion policy. The help also refers to the base as the "parent" so I'll use that term because I think it's more clear. Just be aware that you'll see Base in the UI and the Child is a descendent of the Base.

To configure parent/child policies click the **Inheritance Settings** link when editing an Access Control policy. This will bring up a dialog like the one below.

What you select here depends on whether you are editing a Parent (Base) or a Child policy. If this is a Child policy, then you will only use the **Select Base Policy** drop down at the top. By doing so, you are selecting the Parent which this policy will fall under. The Parent can be any other policy so when you click this drop down it will contain every other Access Control policy on your FMC.

In the example below you can see that every other policy on my FMC is available as a Parent policy.

Essential Firepower

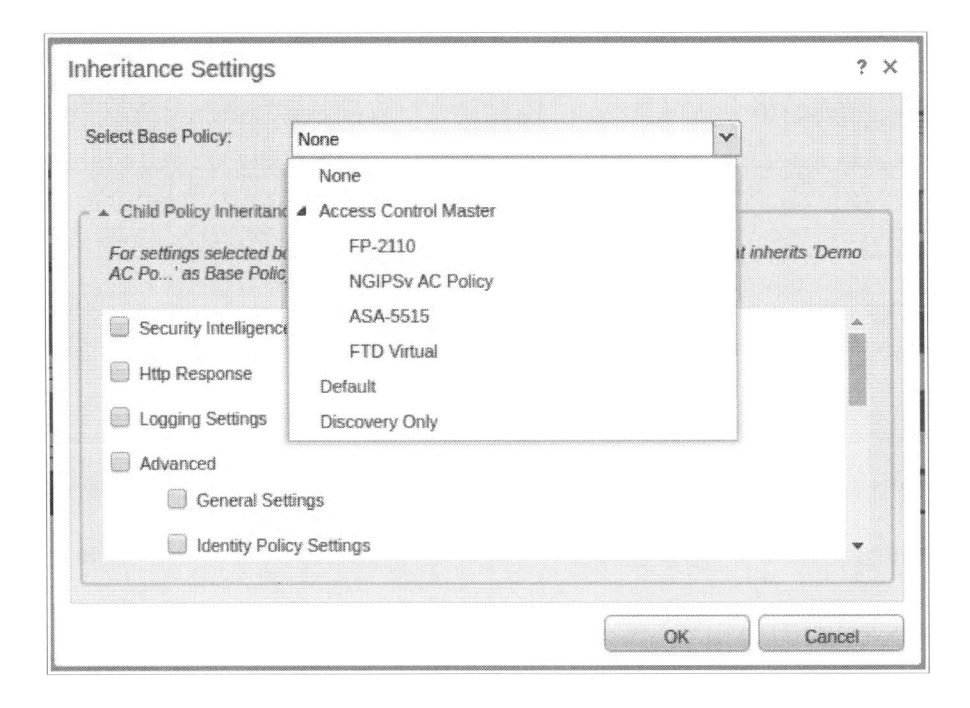

[Inheritance Settings dialog showing Select Base Policy dropdown with options: None, Access Control Master, FP-2110, NGIPSv AC Policy, ASA-5515, FTD Virtual, Default, Discovery Only. Child Policy Inheritance section shows checkboxes for Security Intelligence, Http Response, Logging Settings, Advanced, General Settings, Identity Policy Settings.]

Once you make a policy a Child of another policy it will inherit any settings that are enforced from the Parent.

If the policy you are editing is to be a Parent (Base) policy then the items that apply are all under the **Child Policy Inheritance Settings** list. By selecting the checkbox by items in this list you are enforcing the Parent policy settings on the Child and not allowing them to be set at the Child policy level.

You can enforce the settings on each one of the tabs such as **Security Intelligence**, **Http Response**, **Logging** and **Advanced**. You can also enforce just some of the **Advanced** setting categories if you prefer.

Let's talk about recommendations for using Access Control hierarchy. First, I think using this feature can be beneficial even for small deployments. By small I mean even if you only have two or three Access Control policies. The main areas I see where this is helpful are the **Security Intelligence** and **Advanced** settings. By enforcing inheritance for these settings, you can ensure consistency between your policies.

Security Intelligence and **Advanced** settings are often consistent across all of your policies. By inheriting these settings you save a time and effort keeping your policies in sync. You also avoid the problem of someone changing a setting in one of the policies without changing the others. If you create a new policy, you don't have to go and duplicate all the Security Intelligence feed settings, you just add it as a Child and the settings will be pushed down automatically.

> *Note: While you can deploy a Parent policy to a device you probably won't. As with Intrusion policy, the Parent (Base) exists only to enforce settings on the descendant policies.*

My recommendation would be:

- Create a Parent (Base) policy where you define your **Security Intelligence** and **Advanced** settings.
- Configure your device-specific policies as Child policies of your Parent and inherit these settings.

BP65 - Consider using a Parent/Master Access Control policy, especially for Security Intelligence and Advanced settings.

This leads me to my second recommendation - don't get carried away with inheritance. You will find that you can inherit rules as well as the settings on the various policy tabs. This means you could have layers upon layers of Parent/Child policies with rules at each layer. This would be a nightmare to manage! The idea of policy hierarchy is to make management easier not more complex. Start small with a single parent and then the rest of your policies as children. Once you get used to this, if you feel like you would benefit from more layers then go ahead.

The list below shows how Parent/Child policies appear in the policy list. As you can see, unlike Intrusion policy, it's easy to see who the Parent and Child policies are.

Essential Firepower

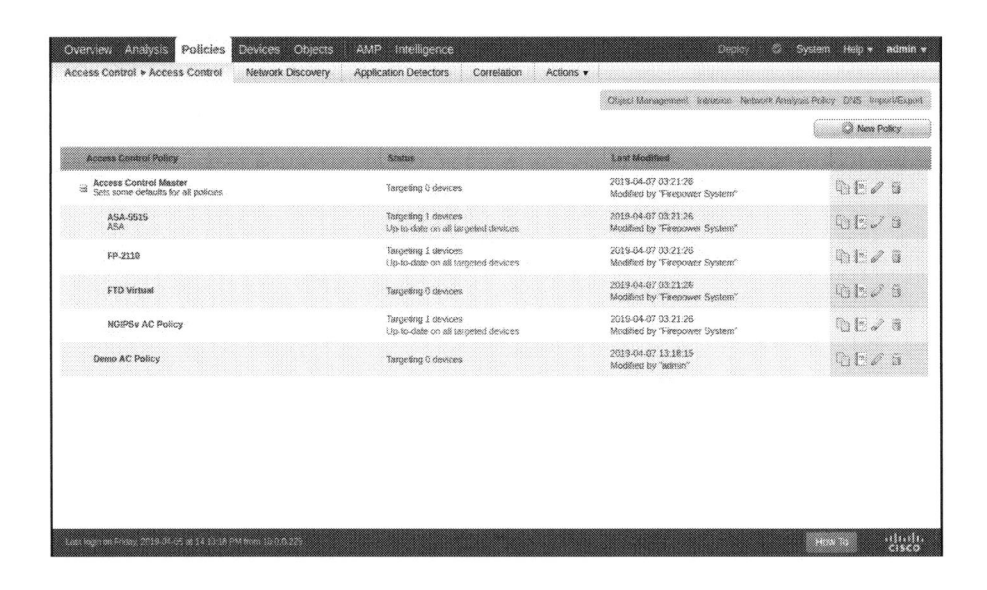

Security Intelligence Settings

The **Security Intelligence** tab controls the IP, URL and DNS blacklisting capabilities of Firepower. This feature uses the Talos lists which are constantly updated on your FMC as well as any customer lists, feeds or objects you have created. I recommend that customers start out using the entire Talos category list, even if you only want to alert and not block traffic. However, to gain the most benefit in an inline configuration you should configure at least some of the categories to block. When you first visit the Security Intelligence tab it will look something like the figure below.

14 – Access Control Policy

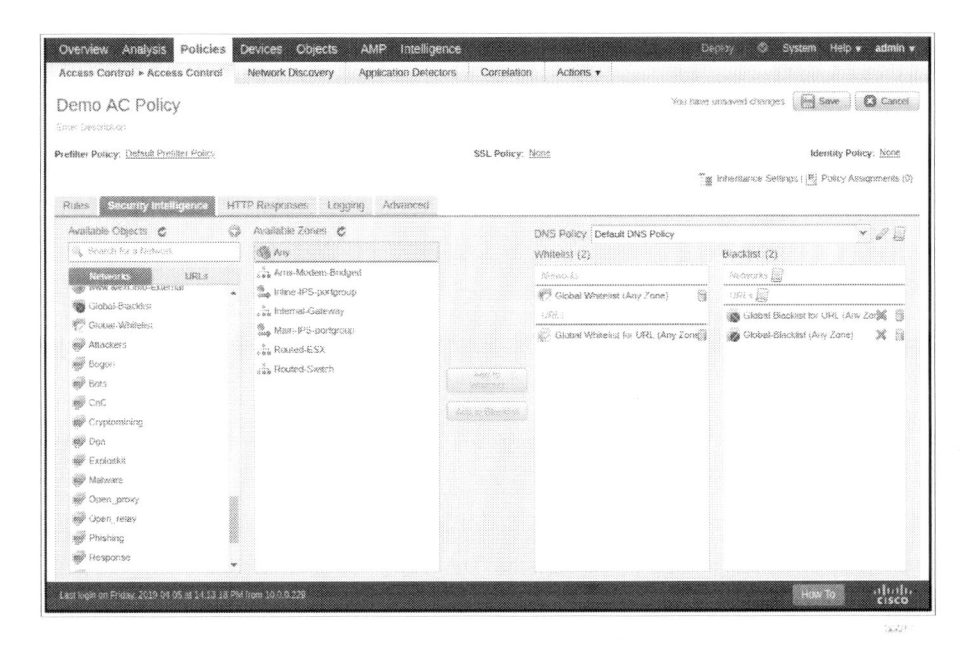

In the figure above I have scrolled down on the left to the Talos category list. This will be at the bottom of your **Networks** and **URLs** tabs.

I recommend adding all of the Talos categories to your IP and URL blacklists. You can click on **Attackers** and then scroll down to the last item (currently this is **Tor_exit_node**) and shift-click. This will select all the Talos categories. Then click the **Add to Blacklist** button.

After you do this for the **Networks** tab, click the **URLs** tab and do the same thing for the Talos URL categories. You will then see all the selected items under the Blacklist column on the right. See the figure below.

Essential Firepower

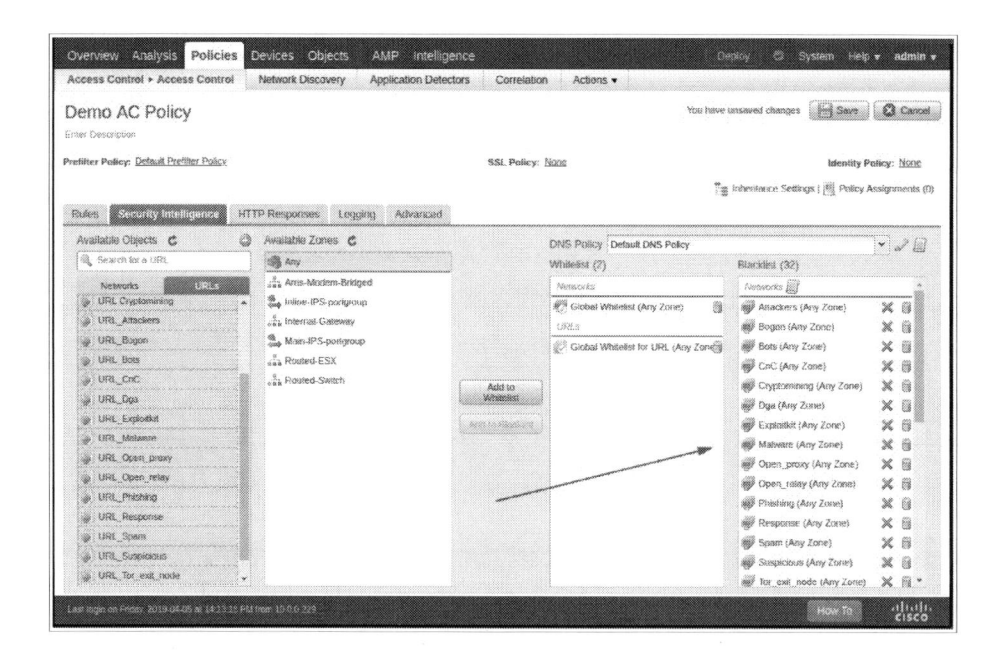

By scrolling down the list on the right you'll see the URL categories are shown below the network categories.

The default state is to **Block** and generate a Security Intelligence event for these categories. You can change one or more of the categories by right-clicking on the category and selecting an option from the pop-up menu as shown below.

In the example above after right-clicking on Dga (Domain Generation Algorithm) you can change the action from **Block** to **Monitor-only (do not block)** if desired. You may want to do this for some categories if you're not sure you want to block the traffic.
Some of the Security Intelligence categories are self-explanatory while

178

14 – Access Control Policy

others are less so. Appendix C contains the Talos descriptions for the various categories.

When it comes to deciding whether to select Block or Monitor-only here are some considerations:

- Blocking is obviously the most effective option. Especially for the more malicious lists like Exploitkit, CnC, Bots, etc. this is the recommended setting. Give careful consideration to other categories such as Tor_exit_node as these may impact legitimate traffic.
- Security Intelligence blocking falls between Prefilter and Access Control rules. So if you fastpath a connection via Prefilter, it will skip Security Intelligence. Likewise, if you block a connection with Security Intelligence, it will never get a chance to match any Access Control rules.
- If your device is deployed in passive mode **do not** select Block as the action. See the previous bullet. If the device is passive, a Block action at Security Intelligence means the traffic is not blocked and does not hit rules in Access Control. This means the traffic is not subject to Intrusion or File policy inspection. For passive devices, use Monitor-only for the action.
- A common tactic is to start out in Monitor-only mode and then move some or all categories to Block once events are reviewed for false positives.

> BP66 - Use the Block action for enabled Security Intelligence categories when inline
>
> BP67 - Use the Monitor-only action for Security Intelligence when in passive mode

Logging

The Logging tab is only available in Firepower 6.3 and higher. It is a first step to consolidate the scattered logging capabilities of Firepower. It allows selecting the syslog destination for all Access Control rules where external logging is enabled on the rule **Logging** tab. There are two configurations here, one for FTD version 6.3 and later devices, and one for all other devices.

Essential Firepower

It's not really that simple however. The two logging settings are shown below.

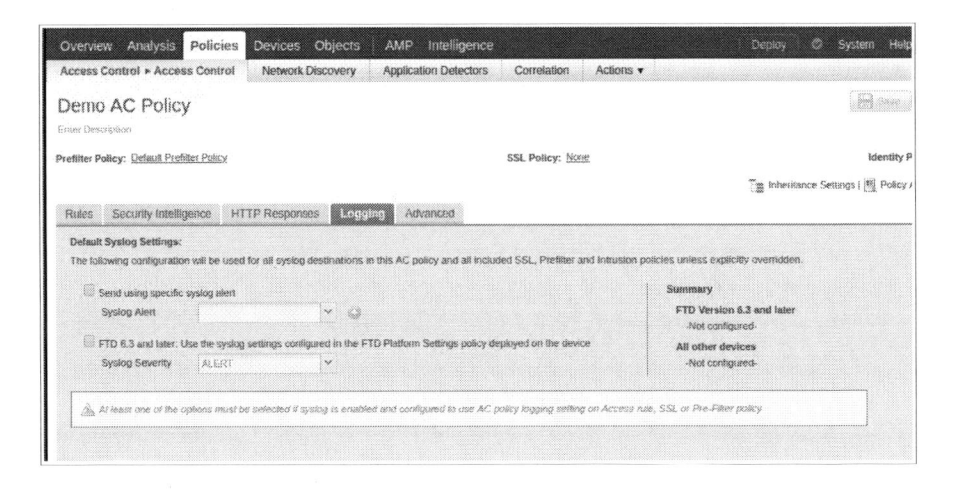

There are two checkboxes to configure your logging destinations. Depending on what you select, the Summary on the right will tell you where your logs will go.

If you select **Send using specific syslog alert** then you would check the box and select a log destination from the drop down. Note that you have to have these log destinations already setup via **Policies → Actions → Alerts**. Once you do this the screen would look similar to the one below. Note the Summary tells you that your log destination is the same for all devices whether they are 6.3 and later, or previous versions.

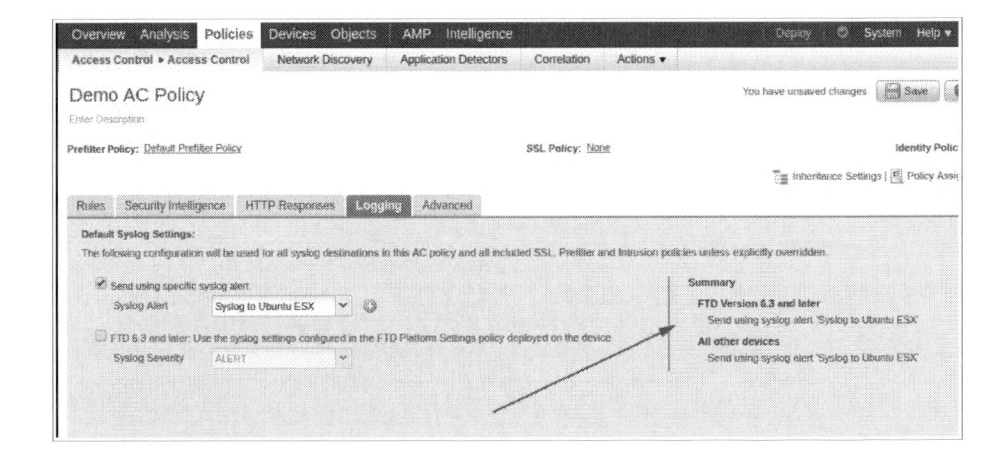

You can also check the second option for FTD 6.3 and later devices.

This causes the system to use the syslog settings which are configured in the Platform Settings for that device. The idea is that this limits the syslog configuration for each 6.3 device to just what is in Platform Settings rather than using the FMC and device settings for different types of syslog events. I know it doesn't sound that tremendous at this point but the idea is that syslog will become easier and more unified in future FTD versions. Checking the second box changes the Summary as shown below.

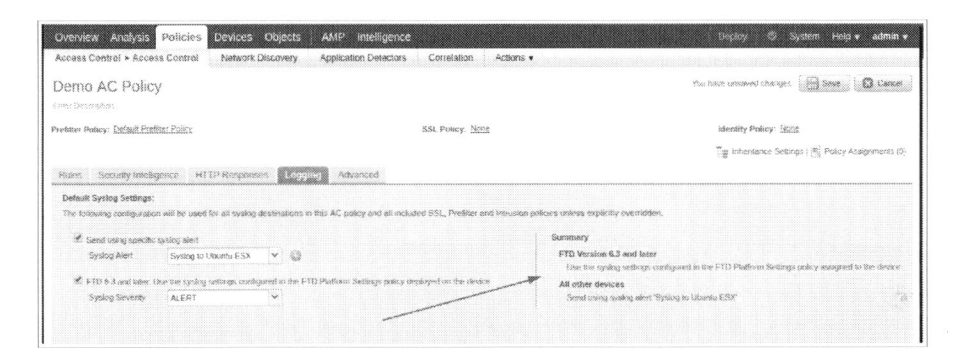

This is telling you what your log destinations will be if you apply this policy to FTD 6.3 and later or older device versions. I don't have a best practice here, I just wanted to go over this since it's a new (and slightly confusing) feature.

Advanced Settings

There are quite a number of advanced settings available in the Access Control policy. The vast majority should not be changed. Let's hit just a few that you may want to tweak yourself.

Network Analysis and Intrusion Policies

There are four settings in the Network Analysis and Intrusion Policies section to consider.

Intrusion Policy used before Access Control rule is determined - this is a rather long winded setting which controls how packets will be treated during application identification. The reason for this setting is that application identification generally requires that the firewall leak some packets. The reason is that applications are usually identified by the 4th or later packet(s) in the connection. (The 4th packet would be the first data packet after the initial three-way-handshake) Identifying some applications may require even more packets to pass through the firewall.

This setting determines if these packets will pass through the device uninspected or if they will be processed through an Intrusion policy. The default is to pass uninspected. If you want to inspect this traffic then select an Intrusion policy from the drop-down.

- **Intrusion Policy Variable Set** - if you select a policy in the setting above, this is the variable set that will be used with that policy.
- **Network Analysis Rules** - you can create custom rules to determine which Network Analysis policy will be used for traffic. If you don't select anything here, then all traffic will use the **Default Network Analysis Policy** configured below. You can create rules for traffic to use different Network Analysis policies based on zones, networks and/or VLAN tags. This setting is only for the most sophisticated users and you should probably leave it alone. I never configure this setting.
- **Default Network Analysis Policy** - of all the settings in this section, this is the only one I would recommend changing. My recommendation here is to use whichever Network Analysis policy matches your Intrusion policy. The default is Balanced Security and Connectivity so if you followed my recommendation for the Balanced Intrusion policy then you can just leave this at the default. If you are using one of the other policies or you customized your Network Analysis policy then you should select the appropriate policy here.

BP68 - Ensure your Default Network Analysis Policy setting matches your Intrusion policy.

Intelligent Application Bypass Settings

Intelligent Application Bypass (IAB) has been around for some time but is now receiving more attention from Firepower engineering. What I mean is that in newer Firepower versions there are default values even though the feature is still disabled by default. IAB provides the ability to intelligently bypass large traffic flows so the flow speed and/or the device performance is not impacted. You may recall that flows are load balanced across CPUs on a Firepower device. Multi-CPU architecture is what provides increased throughput, however a flow (connection) cannot span multiple CPUs. Fortunately, most flows are ok with this design and the single CPU does not impact the traffic. However, some large "elephant" flows can be negatively impacted if they are restricted to a single CPU. This will restrict the flow throughput for an inline device and will also possibly spike the CPU usage at or near 100% for the life of the flow.

As it turns out, these large flows generally don't warrant deep packet inspection so bypassing them can alleviate the negative impact to both the flow and the device without sacrificing security. Before IAB, the method to bypass these flows was (and still is) to identify the flow based on source/destination IP/port and then create either a Prefilter fastpath rule or a trust rule. This method still works fine but has the disadvantage of being labor intensive. It requires identifying each flow and manually adding rules to bypass inspection. IAB can address this elephant flow problem automatically.

To configure this setting click the pencil by Intelligent Application Bypass Settings. This brings up the dialog shown below.

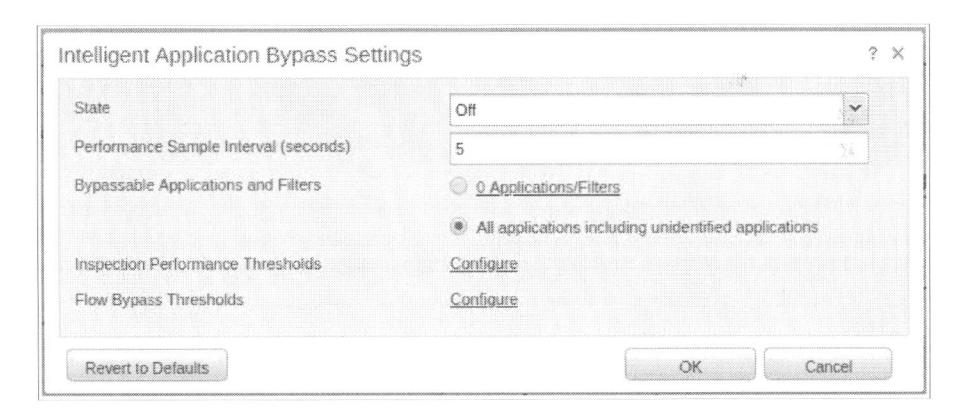

Let's go over some of the settings here:

- **State** (Off/Test/On) - the state of the IAB process. This is off by default. You can set it to **Test** which will generate bypass connection events without actually bypassing any traffic or **On** which will bypass traffic matching the criteria. Note that the connection events look the same for either setting.

- **Performance Sample Interval (seconds)** - how often IAB samples traffic. The default is 5 seconds which seems pretty good to me. This means the device will check once every 5 seconds to see if the bypass criteria has been met for flows currently being processed.
- **Bypassable Applications and Filters** - This can be set to all applications or to a list of selected applications. The default is all applications but you could limit IAB to just the ones you select here if desired. In that case a flow would have to match one of the selected applications as well as the other bypass criteria you set.

There are two **Configure** links for the other settings. Clicking these expands the dialog to include these other settings. Let's click both of these to expand everything fully. The figure below shows the default values.

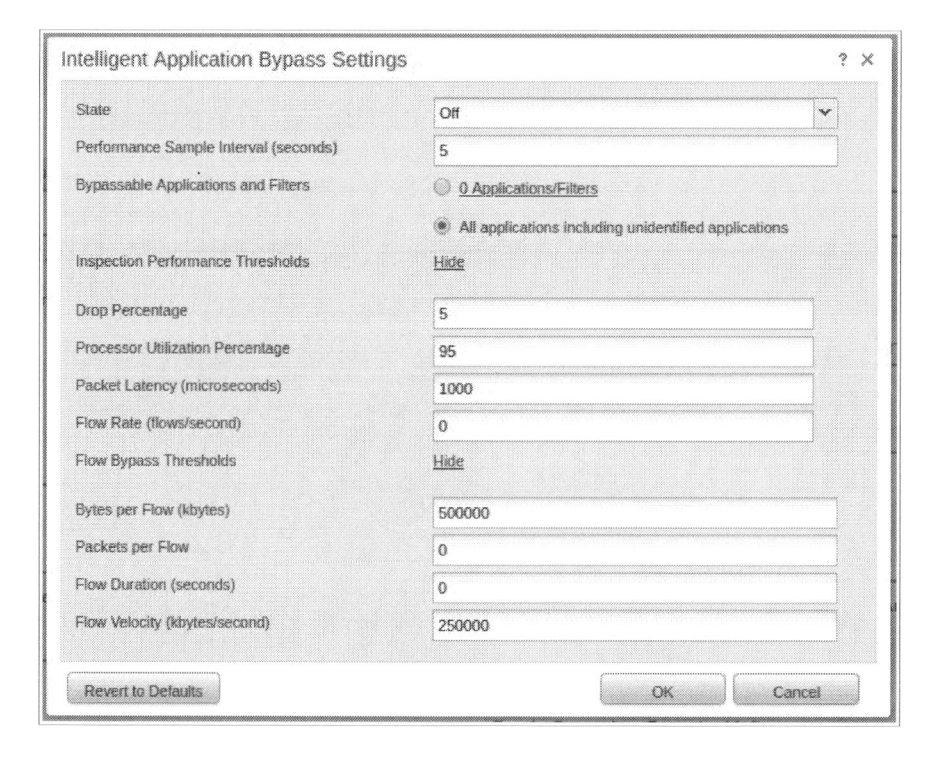

Intelligent Application Bypass Settings	
State	Off
Performance Sample Interval (seconds)	5
Bypassable Applications and Filters	○ 0 Applications/Filters
	● All applications including unidentified applications
Inspection Performance Thresholds	Hide
Drop Percentage	5
Processor Utilization Percentage	95
Packet Latency (microseconds)	1000
Flow Rate (flows/second)	0
Flow Bypass Thresholds	Hide
Bytes per Flow (kbytes)	500000
Packets per Flow	0
Flow Duration (seconds)	0
Flow Velocity (kbytes/second)	250000

The top four settings (**Inspection Performance Thresholds**) relate to device performance and the bottom four (**Flow Bypass Thresholds**) are flow characteristics. If you have questions, the online help gives good descriptions of each one. The idea is that this is the criteria that a flow must match to be bypassed. It's important to note that all eight of these fields are ANDed together. This means every one of them has to be true for a flow to be bypassed. Flows are checked at the sample interval (5 seconds by default) and if any are found to meet the criteria listed here then they will be bypassed (assuming the **State** is **On**).

My advice here is to experiment with these settings and see if IAB can benefit you. Chances are you have some flows which should be bypassed such as backups, replication traffic, etc. To reduce the number of conditions needed to bypass, you can remove a criteria by just entering a zero value. Maybe start in Test mode by bypassing any flow where the **Flow Rate** is 1 and the **Flow Duration** exceeds 20 seconds.

> Note: For IAB to work you must configure at least one item from **Inspection Performance Thresholds** and one from **Flow Bypass Thresholds**. The rest can be set to zero.

Once you start seeing bypass events you can tweak your settings until just the large flows are identified. After that you can move from **Test** to **On** mode and offload elephant flows from your devices.

Once you're in **Test** mode you can find the bypass events under **Analysis → Connections → Events**. Just look for events with **Intelligent App Bypass** in the **Reason** column as shown below.

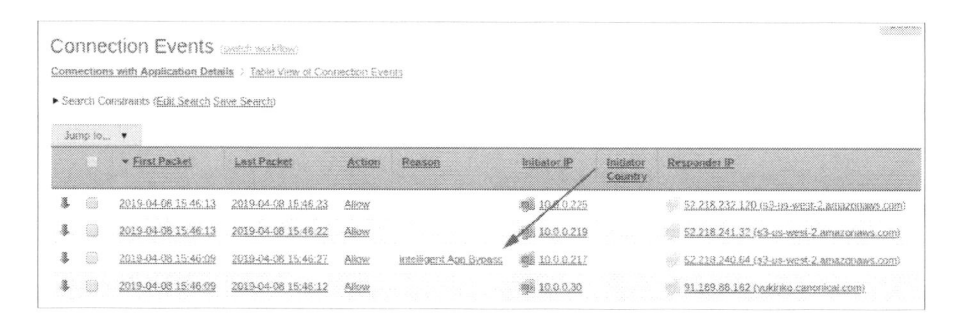

After you're satisfied that your IAB settings are correct you can change the mode to **On**.

> BP69 - Consider Intelligent Application Bypass to automatically bypass large flows

Rules

We are finally here - Access Control rules. If you've been following the book from start to finish you have finally arrived at the core of Firepower's traffic inspection. Access Control rules is the central crossroads for most of the traffic passing to or through your devices. The only traffic that doesn't make it this far was blocked by either Prefilter or Security Intelligence or maybe fastpathed by a Prefilter rule. In most deployments the majority of traffic makes it to the Access Control rule set where it is blocked, allowed, trusted, etc. In this section we will discuss some general practices when configuring your Access Control rule set.

To get started, let's look at the default empty rule set (shown below) when creating a new policy.

You will see there are two rule categories by default. They are named **Mandatory** and **Default**. These default categories cannot be deleted or renamed. You can, however, add new categories if desired. This is actually a good idea if you are going to have more than just a few rules. By creating categories like Trust Rules, Block rules, etc. it may be easier for admins to understand where a given rule type should go. It can also make it easier to track down a rule if you know what category it should be in.

Access Control rules are evaluated from top to bottom like a typical router or firewall access control list (ACL). Because of this, sometimes the categories break down and you can't always put a given rule type within a category. Categories can still help to keep the chaos to a minimum.

If you do add your own custom categories remember that once they are created they cannot be moved. Rules can be moved up or down or from one category to another. However, the category itself cannot be moved above or below another category.

Rules and Hierarchy

If you do use Access Control hierarchy - a Parent policy with one or more Child policies - you will notice a "sandwich" effect with the default categories. What I mean is that Child policy categories are inserted between the **Mandatory** and **Default** categories of the Parent policies.

The screenshot below illustrates how this works. It shows three policies:

1. AC Master
2. Child
3. Grandchild

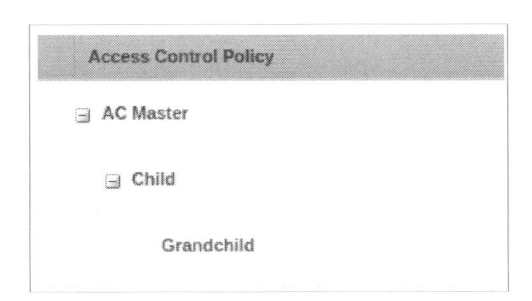

Access Control Policy

- AC Master
  - Child
    - Grandchild

These are setup in a three level hierarchy so the AC Master is the parent of the Child and the Child is the parent of the Grandchild. The

Essential Firepower

screenshot below shows the **Rules** tab on the Grandchild policy.

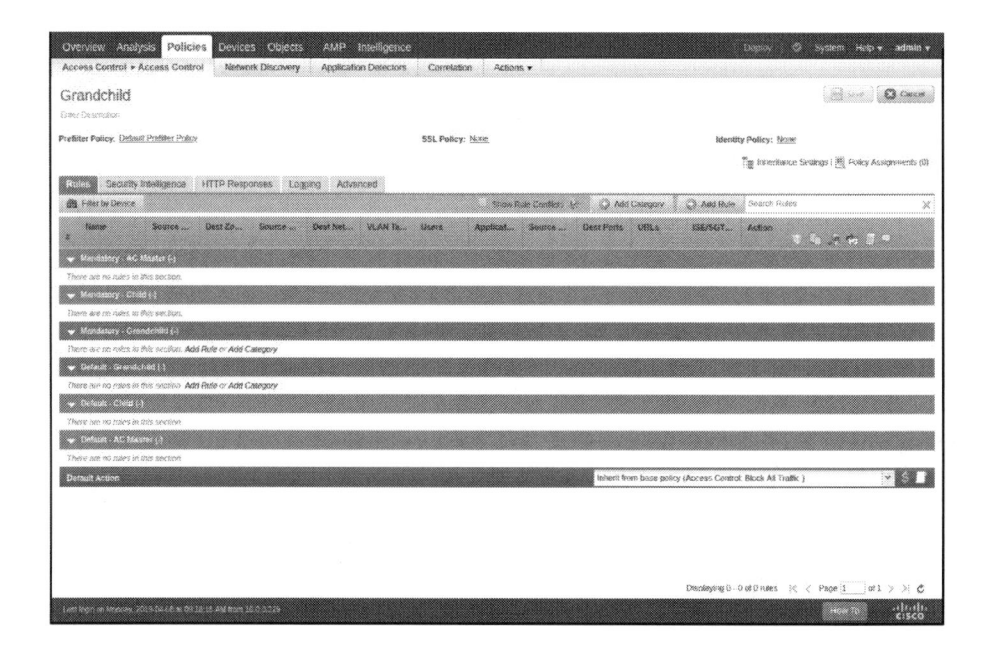

You can see that there are now three Mandatory categories and three Default categories. The Grandchild policy is sandwiched inside the Child policy which is inside the AC Master. Before, you might have wondered why the categories were named Mandatory and Default. Now, it becomes a little more clear. Once you start layering them you can see that the highest level policy - AC Master in our case - always gets first priority for rules in the Child policies. Since the parent policy Mandatory layers come first, the child policies cannot override any of the parent rules.

By the same token, the AC Master gets the last shot at traffic as well. If these are deployed to firewalls, the Grandchild policy may have a "block all" rule as the last rule in its policy. In this case the other Default categories will never see any traffic. But you still might want to place a rule in your master policy Default category just in case there's a misconfiguration in one of the Child policies and traffic slips through. Depending on your deployment the master's default rule might be a block rule or maybe just a rule to ensure any traffic dropping through is inspected.

This also illustrates why I recommend keeping your policy hierarchy as flat as possible. As you stack on child policies you sandwich more and more layers and the resultant rule set gets more and more "interesting" to try and interpret.

Rules and Actions

Use the Add Rule button to insert rules into your Access Control policy. The Add Rule dialog is shown below.

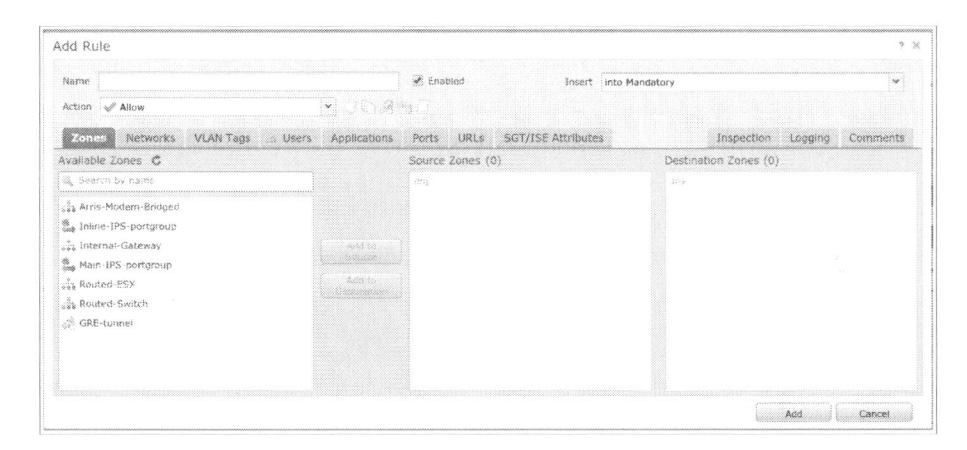

You rule will need a name and an Action. Firepower rules have several actions:

- **Allow** - allow traffic to pass through the device subject to Intrusion and/or Malware & File policy inspection. Technically, you can create Allow rules with no inspection but these really should be Trust rules. When migrating rule sets from other firewalls they generally are imported as Allow rules.
- **Trust** - allow traffic to pass through the device with no inspection or network discovery.
- **Monitor** - log a connection event for the traffic but keep processing through the rule set. The Monitor rule is the only rule type that can match traffic yet allow other rules to match after it. With other rules, once traffic is matched the traffic is not processed through subsequent rules.
- **Block** - block traffic without sending any external signal such as a reset packet. Note that Block rules do not automatically have Logging enabled so you should always enable this. Of course there may be rare exceptions but blocking traffic without generating events can be a recipe

for disaster.
- **Block with reset** - block traffic and send a reset to the source and destination. Generally this is preferred for outbound traffic. For inbound traffic we usually don't send the reset so we can keep the attacker in the dark regarding the status of the connection.
- **Interactive Block** - block traffic and if this is web traffic send an interactive web page to the client. The user can then elect to bypass the block and proceed to the site. This bypass will remain in effect for 10 minutes after which the interactive block page will be displayed again.
- **Interactive Block with reset** - this will block all non-web traffic and send a reset. Web traffic will be treated the same as the Interactive block rule.

Here are some rule recommendations:

> BP70 - Don't forget to enable logging on any Block rules

When it comes to Access Control rules there are a few common types of rules found in policies. The list below describes some of the rule usage and rule types you might consider.

- **Normal firewall rules:** These would be the type you typically see in a conventional firewall. In a firewall you would typically have a Block All action at the end of the policy and the rules would serve as exceptions to allow the traffic you want to pass. In a NGFW like Firepower, most of these would have the Allow action and you would assign an Intrusion and Malware & File policy to inspect the traffic.
- **Block rules:** As already stated above. These rules should have the **Log at beginning of connection** checkbox checked on the **Logging** tab. You can't perform Intrusion inspection on a Block rule although you can on an Interactive Block rule.
- **Trust rules:** These would be used for traffic which you want to pass but not inspect. It could be that you need the traffic to pass with low latency or it could be that you just don't want to inspect the flows. One example of the latter is traffic from your vulnerability scanners. Typically, we want to allow these scans to reach the endpoint hosts unmolested and without lighting up Intrusion events. If you have hierarchical policies you could place these trust rules in the master policy.
- **Application identification rules:** I have already mentioned

the caveat when using rules with application identification enabled. Remember that a policy with these rules will "leak" traffic. This is necessary to identify the application. When deploying Firepower at the network edge, keep your application identification rules specific to outbound traffic by using **Zones** or **Networks**.
- **HTTP Responses:** Keep in mind that if you enable the Custom or System-provided Block Response Page you will send a web page response anytime HTTP traffic is blocked. If you are not careful you may be sending that page in response to inbound external traffic. I don't have a good solution to this as the HTTP Responses configuration is policy-wide and can't be limited by zone or network.
- **Rule categories:** Using categories can be helpful in rule organization. Common categories include Inbound, Outbound, Trusted Connections, etc. Remember, once created, you can't reorder or move a category.
- **Non-firewall devices:** Rule sets are typically much smaller on devices deployed in the NGIPS role. Often you will see a few Trust and Block rules with a single Allow rule at the end that performs Intrusion and Malware & File inspection.
- **High connection rate traffic:** Sometimes, your connection events seem to consist mainly of traffic like DNS requests. These are typically unremarkable and take up a large percentage of the connection event storage in your database. However, it's important to inspect DNS traffic so trusting it is not generally a good idea. If you want to inspect but not log connections for some traffic simply create an Allow rule with the usual **Inspection** options. Then don't enable logging on the **Logging** tab. This means the traffic will be sent to the Intrusion policy for inspection but connection events will not be logged.

Chapter 15 - Miscellaneous Tips and Tricks

This chapter will cover a few additional tips and tricks. These are the result of using Firepower for over a decade and represent some of the common questions or scenarios I've seen over the years.

Chapter Contents

Moving from IDS to IPS Mode..193
Tap Mode...198
High Volume Event Logging...199
Trust/Fastpath/Bypass..205
Admin Preferences..207
Hit Counts..209
Reduce Annoying Pop-up Notifications..215
Minimizing Network Impact..217

Moving from IDS to IPS Mode

One of the common methods to deploy a new Firepower security device is to first deploy the device on the network in passive mode. Then, after the settings have been confirmed and tuned, the device mode is changed to active. This comes up most often with a NGIPS deployed inline, however it can also apply to a NGFW deployment. Changing the system from detection to blocking mode is not just throwing a master switch. Several policies have their own settings which control detection or blocking. The following policies can be configured to drop malicious or unwanted traffic:

- Prefilter
- SSL
- DNS
- Malware & File
- Intrusion
- Network Analysis
- Access Control

In a typical NGIPS mode deployment, the Prefilter and SSL policies are not configured to drop traffic - this is something normally left to the firewalls. The NGIPS is there to perform deep packet inspection and threat detection/blocking. In this case, the Access Control policy is configured just to facilitate intrusion/file inspection and may only contain a few trust and allow rules. Basically, we're going to allow most, if not all, of the traffic to pass subject to Firepower threat detection.

If you are replacing a traditional firewall with a Firepower NGFW then you will likely migrate your Access Control Lists (ACLs) or firewall rules to Firepower Access Control rules. In this case, you will probably want to perform deep packet inspection on the traffic you allow to pass through the firewall. Once again, since the "next generation" features of the firewall are new and untested in your environment, you may want to hold back initially on allowing the device to drop traffic other than the ACLs inherited from the previous firewall.

Now that we know some of the use-cases for initially deploying without blocking enabled, let's discuss how you would go about making the transition. Simply run down the list of policies below, making the necessary adjustments to move them from inspection/alerting only to blocking mode.

Prefilter
If you want to block any traffic with your prefilter policy, simply add in some block rules. Chances are you've already got this policy adjusted the way you want it but I'm mentioning it here in the interest of completeness.

SSL
SSL policy actually doesn't work well at all unless you are already inline and modifying traffic. Passive SSL inspection won't work at all for resigning mode (outbound traffic) and is very limited for known private key decryption. Again, mentioned here for completeness, you probably won't change this as part of your move from detection to blocking. It will likely come later or at least separately because SSL implementation is a specific effort and is different from many of the threat detection features.

DNS
The DNS policy provides the ability to alert, block or respond to evil DNS requests. When you move from alert to block you may want to adjust your DNS rules to take an active role (block or respond) rather than just alerting.

Malware & File
The biggest change here is to adjust your Malware & File rule(s) from detect malware to block malware. You may want to look at the archive inspection features in the **Advanced** tab as well, but the biggest change will be moving your rules from detect to block.

In the figure below (editing a Malware & File rule) you would change the **Action** to **Block Malware** instead of **Malware Cloud Lookup.**

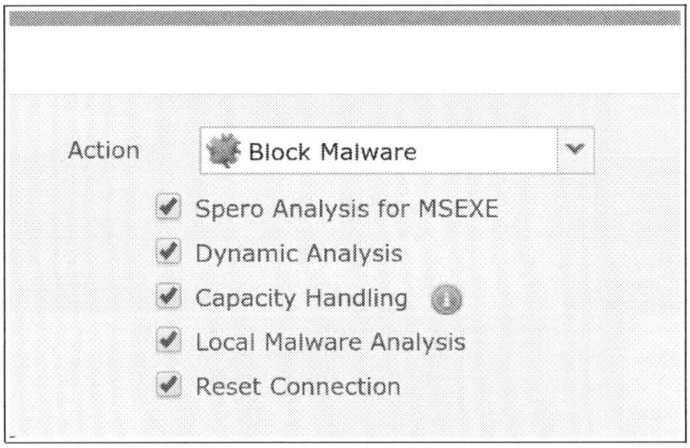
Action
Block Malware
Spero Analysis for MSEXE
Dynamic Analysis
Capacity Handling
Local Malware Analysis
Reset Connection

Intrusion
For Intrusion policy, just check the **Drop when Inline** checkbox on the main page of your Intrusion policy. Drop rules won't drop traffic until you check this box.

You'll find the **Drop when Inline** box on the main policy page as shown below.

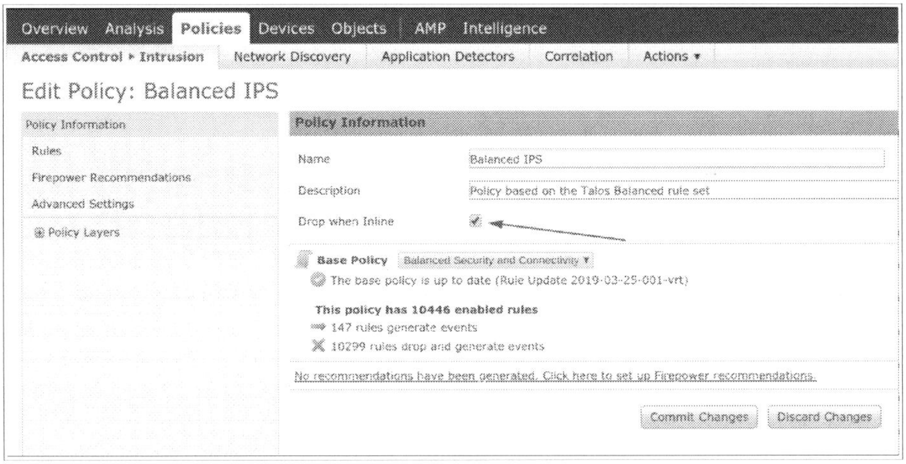
Overview Analysis Policies Devices Objects AMP Intelligence
Access Control ▸ Intrusion Network Discovery Application Detectors Correlation Actions ▾
Edit Policy: Balanced IPS
Policy Information
Rules
Firepower Recommendations
Advanced Settings
Policy Layers
Policy Information
Name
Balanced IPS
Description
Policy based on the Talos Balanced rule set
Drop when Inline
Base Policy
Balanced Security and Connectivity
The base policy is up to date (Rule Update 2019-03-25-001-vrt)
This policy has 10446 enabled rules
147 rules generate events
10299 rules drop and generate events
No recommendations have been generated. Click here to set up Firepower recommendations.
Commit Changes
Discard Changes

Network Analysis
There are three Network Analysis policy settings that are recommended if you are inline.

1. Enable **Inline mode** on the main page as shown below.

Essential Firepower

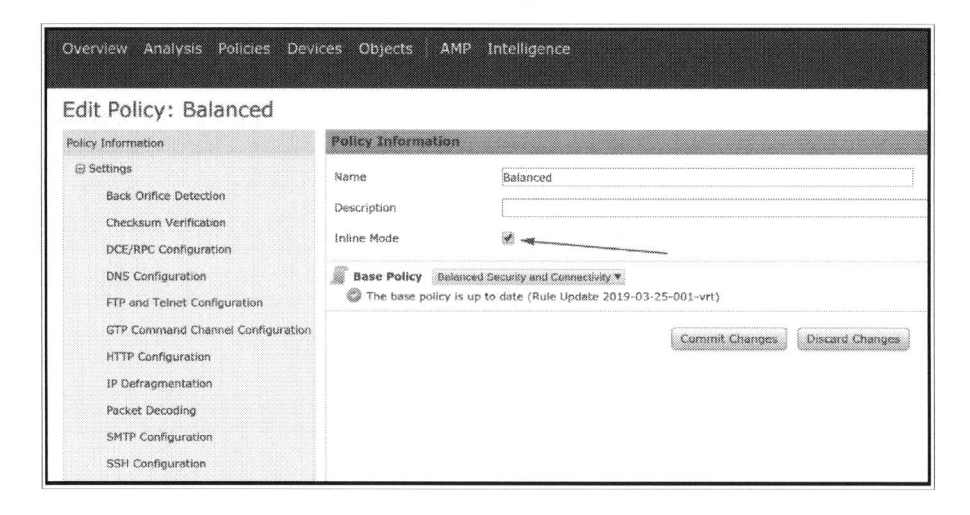

2. Enable the **Inline Normalization** preprocessor. You'll find it under **Transport/Network Layer Preprocessors**.

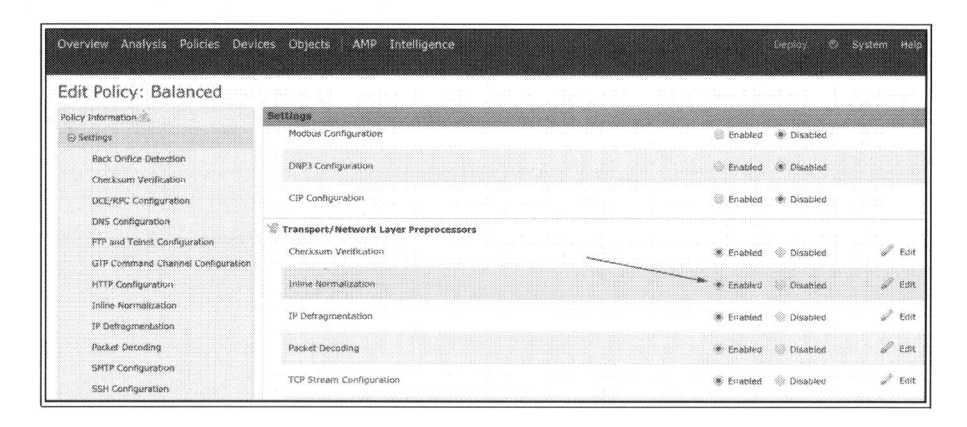

3. After enabling **Inline Normalization**, click the pencil and check the **Normalize TCP Payload** checkbox in the settings.

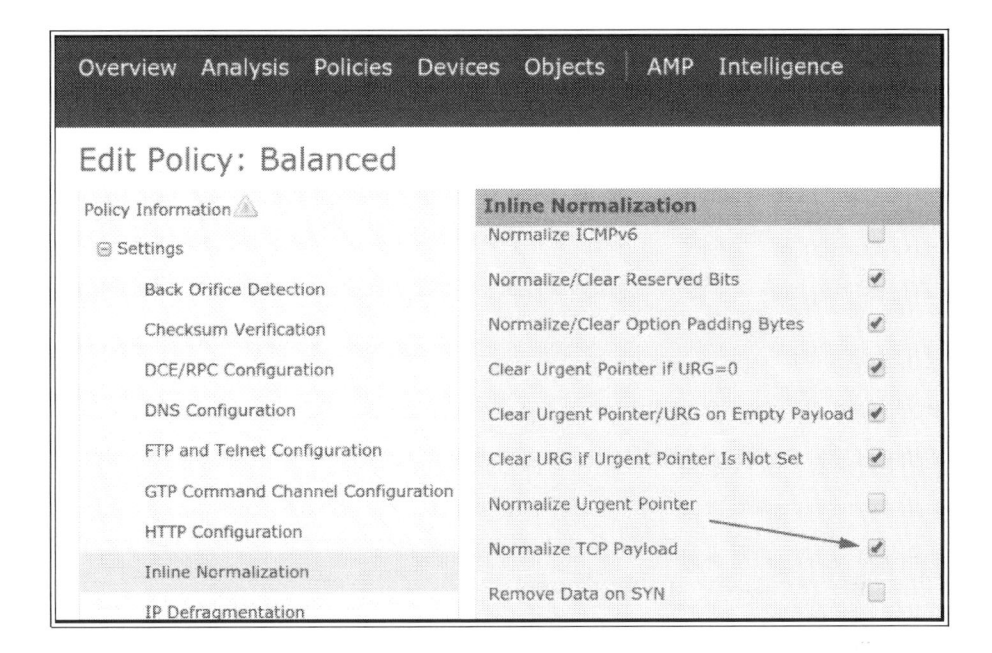

Access Control

As with Prefilter, you may want to adjust your rules and start blocking some traffic. However, the most common change here would be to change your Security Intelligence settings from alert to block. This applies to your IP and URL Security Intelligence lists (DNS SI lists are handled by the DNS policy). To make this change, navigate to the **Security Intelligence** tab in your Access Control policy. If you've followed the previous best practice you already have all - or nearly all - the SI categories added to the blacklist column. However, these are probably set to **Monitor-only** and not to **Block** connections.

For this change, you would right-click on the category in the Blacklist column, then select **Block** from the context menu. This is shown in the figure below.

Essential Firepower

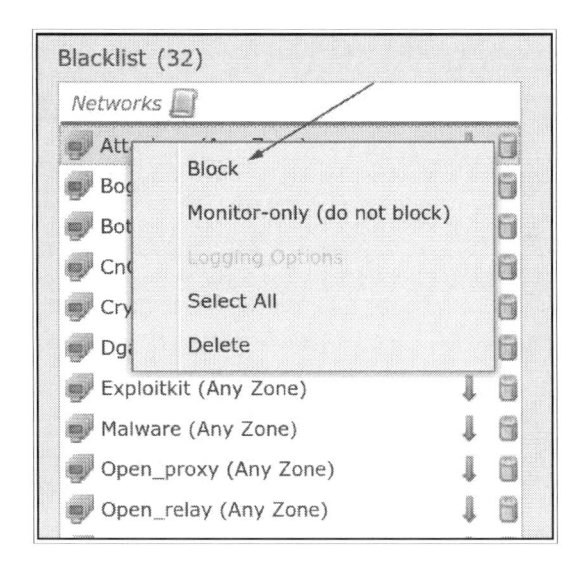

```
Blacklist (32)
Networks
  Att┌─────────────────────────┐
  Bo│ Block                   │
  Bot│ Monitor-only (do not block)│
  Cn│ Logging Options         │
  Cry│ Select All              │
  Dg│ Delete                  │
  └─────────────────────────┘
  Exploitkit (Any Zone)           ↓
  Malware (Any Zone)              ↓
  Open_proxy (Any Zone)           ↓
  Open_relay (Any Zone)           ↓
```

Note, you can also select multiple categories by using the Shift or Ctrl keys and then right-click so you don't have to change each one individually.

There you have it! By running down the list above you will hit all the high points to consider when transitioning from alerting to block mode on your Firepower device.

Tap Mode

Another feature that can be used to place an inline device on to the network without risk of impacting traffic is **Tap Mode**. This is an interface mode available if you use an inline set. It basically turns the inline device into an inline tap. Packets are sent through the inline interfaces and a copy is then inspected with the various policies. By using this mode you can test any settings without fear of impacting legitimate (or evil) traffic in any way. If you do deploy block or drop rules your device will think it is blocking traffic and the events you see on the FMC will also indicate this. However, the inline tap interface prevents this from actually happening.

You will find the **Tap Mode** configuration on the **Interface Set** tab. This is on your FMC under **Devices → Device Management**. Click the pencil icon by the device you want to edit, then click the **Inline Sets** tab. (You will need an inline set configured already) Click the pencil icon next to your inline set then click the **Advanced** tab.

Finally, this will bring you to the page where you can check the **Tap Mode** box at the top. This dialog is shown below.

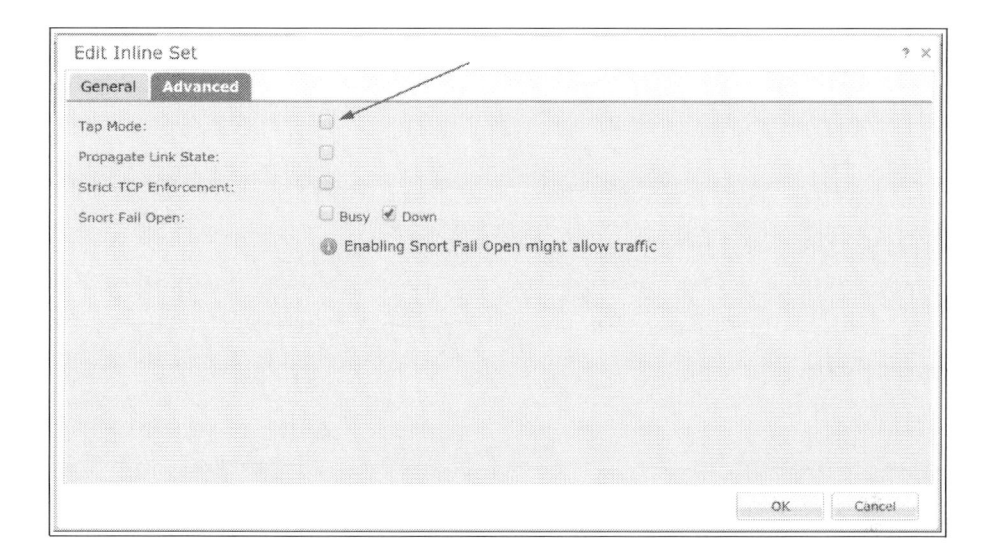

High Volume Event Logging

Something that comes up quite often in Firepower deployments is the desire to log all connections passing through devices. If the Access Control policy is configured appropriately, the system can create a connection event for each successful or blocked connection. When you are dealing with a NGIPS, logging these events may only be a "nice to have". However, if you are setting up a firewall this becomes more of a necessity.

The issue that often arises is that the rate of connection events can quickly exceed the FMC's ability to collect and store them. It doesn't take much for a moderately busy network to saturate even the largest FMC models. The FS4000/4500 or similar models are rated at 20,000 events per second – which sounds like a lot. However, if you are collecting events at or near that rate, connection database growth can become an issue. At just 10,000 events per second you are looking at 36 million events per hour. Remember the default storage setting for the connection database? It's only 1 million events. You can modify the database settings allowing a FS4000/4500 to store up to 1 billion connection events. However, we generally don't recommend that you set the limit that high. Even if you increase this storage to 50% of the maximum, or 500 million events, you're only looking at just over 13 hours of connection event history.

This seems like a serious flaw in the system. How can one setup a firewall and only retain a short connection history? The reason for this is due to the NGIPS lineage of Firepower. If you insert an IPS into your network, the main purpose is deep packet/threat inspection. You already have firewalls logging the passed/blocked connections. Logging connections from an NGIPS is nice to have but not something you really need. However, since Firepower is now often setup as a firewall, we need a solution to this issue.
For now, there isn't a good way to log these connections within the system itself. There are enhanced logging capabilities coming to Firepower in the future, but we need a solution now. Fortunately for you, you bought this book!

The answer isn't terribly complex. It involves logging connection events via syslog directly from the devices. These events would be sent to your security information and event management (SIEM) system. There are two important benefits to configuring logging directly from your devices to the SIEM. 1) You remove the event load from your FMC and avoid the event per second limitation associated with your FMC model, 2) Your SIEM has more storage and can provide more event history than the FMC.

You could choose to log your intrusion and malware events to the SIEM as well but it wouldn't be because of the event rate. Logging security events to the SIEM is usually for the purpose of correlating these with other events or simply detecting malicious activity. Even without much tuning, the intrusion event rate should be far below that of connection events. Logging intrusion and other security events to the SIEM is usually done because the cyber security team uses the SIEM as their primary logging and analysis tool rather than using the FMC's event analysis features. I'm not going to address this configuration for now, this discussion will focus only on high volume connection events.

What we're going to do is configure our devices to send only connection events to the SIEM via syslog. The rest of the event types (intrusion, security intelligence, etc.) will still be sent to the FMC. At that point you may want to forward these to your SIEM as well. It will look like the figure below.

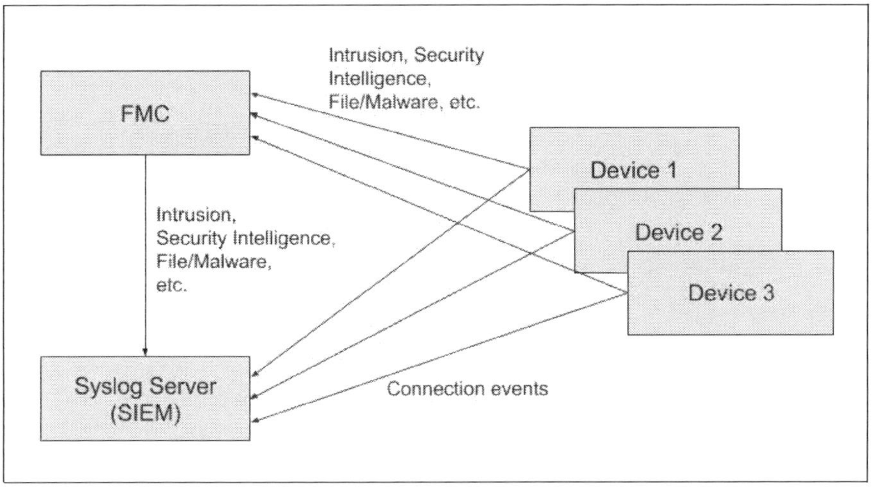
FMC
Intrusion, Security
Intelligence,
File/Malware, etc.
Device 1
Device 2
Device 3
Intrusion,
Security Intelligence,
File/Malware,
etc.
Syslog Server
(SIEM)
Connection events

The effect of logging configured this way is your high volume connection events skip the FMC entirely. This means there is more storage and processing capacity for the security related events. Also, you are now not limited to the event processing rate of your FMC. In the diagram above we have also configured the FMC to forward the various security events to the SIEM as well so it has a more holistic event view.

Connection logging is controlled by the Access Control policy. However, we can't start there. Before we can configure syslog for connection events we need to define the syslog destination. The first step then is to navigate to **Policies → Actions → Alerts**. This page looks similar to the figure below.

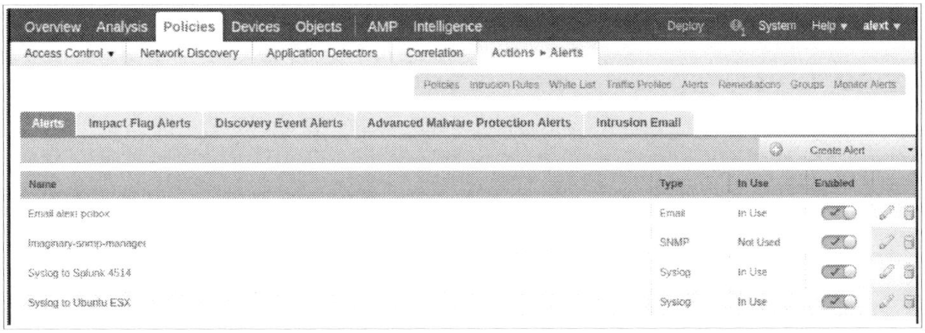
Overview Analysis Policies Devices Objects AMP Intelligence
Deploy System Help alext
Access Control Network Discovery Application Detectors Correlation Actions ▸ Alerts
Alerts Impact Flag Alerts Discovery Event Alerts Advanced Malware Protection Alerts Intrusion Email
Create Alert
Name Type In Use Enabled
Syslog to Splunk 4514 Syslog In Use
Syslog to Ubuntu ESX Syslog In Use

As you can see, I've already setup a few alerts. Alerts can be email, SNMP or syslog destinations.

Once here, we need to make sure there's an entry defining the syslog parameters for our connection events. To add a new destination click the **Create Alert** button then select **Create Syslog Alert**. This brings up the dialog shown below.

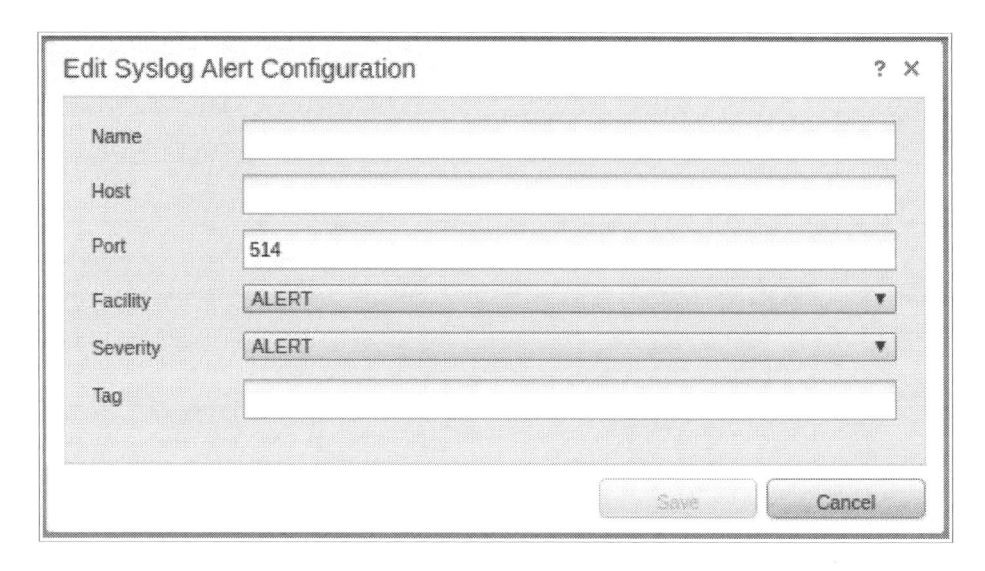

```
Edit Syslog Alert Configuration                        ? X

   Name    [                                          ]
   Host    [                                          ]
   Port    [ 514                                      ]
   Facility [ ALERT                                 ▼ ]
   Severity [ ALERT                                 ▼ ]
   Tag     [                                          ]

                                        [ Save ] [ Cancel ]
```

Give your alert a **Name** (something describing the alert destination) and enter the IP or host name in the **Host** field. Change the **Port** if desired. The syslog messages will be sent with the **Facility** and **Severity** you select here.

After your alert is setup, go to the Access Control policy (**Policies → Access Control → Access Control**). Edit your policy and then configure the **Logging** tab on the rule(s) where you want to log connection events. If you already have a lot of rules then you may want to just add a Monitor rule near the top of your policy and configure the syslog destination there.

Once the alert is set up we can go to the Access Control policy and configure our rules for logging. You will find two different techniques for this, on for versions prior to 6.3 and one for version 6.3 and later.

Versions Prior to 6.3

For versions of Firepower older than 6.3 it's a simple selection on the Logging tab for the rules you need to configure. In the figure below you simply:

15 – Misc. Tips and Tricks

1. Check your logging preference (Beginning/End/both).
2. Uncheck **Event Viewer** as a logging destination. This means we won't send the connection event to the FMC.
3. Check **Syslog Server** and select your syslog alert from the drop-down.

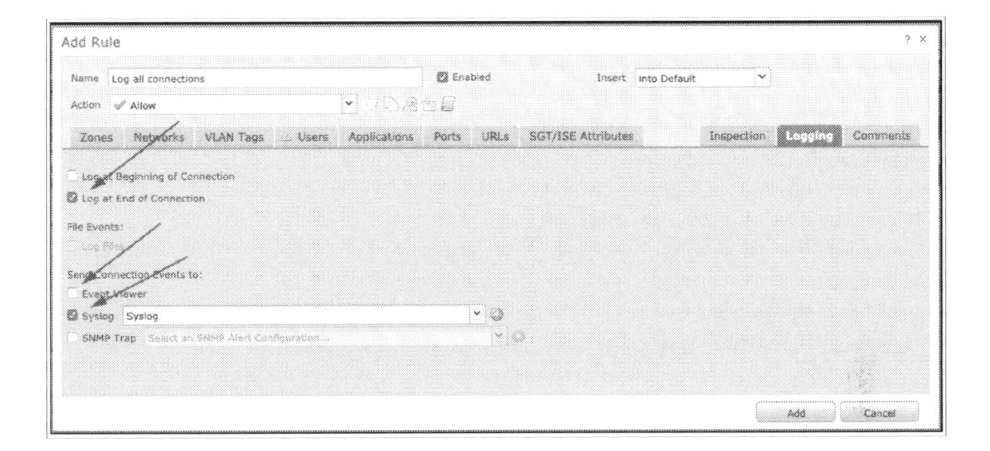

> Note: The log settings above only apply to connection events. Intrusion, malware and security intelligence events are always sent to the FMC.

Do this for every rule for which you want to send events only to the SIEM. Note that you can still send some connection events to the FMC and the SIEM if you want. Maybe there are some critical servers you want to always log to the FMC. To do this, just leave the **Event Viewer** box checked and check the **Syslog** box in addition to it.

Version 6.3 and Later

For version 6.3 and later of Firepower there are some additional options. Syslog settings have been centralized on the **Logging** tab. You should go there first and decide how you want to setup your logging. Your options are:

- Set a syslog destination that will be used by all your devices whether they are 6.3 and later or not.

203

Essential Firepower

- Set the syslog destination for your 6.3 devices via the Platform Settings policy, and set a syslog destination for all your other devices which will be used by the AC policy.

> Note, there have been some syslog changes in version 6.3 and more are coming. The direction FTD is heading is to centralize logging within the Platform Settings policy for Firepower Threat Defense devices. The settings described in this section will work on all Firepower versions. This includes the "classic" 7000/8000 devices as well as FTD.

For now we will assume you are going to pick #1 above and set the syslog destination in the Access Control policy for all devices.
To do this you would check the **Send using specific syslog alert** box and then select the **Syslog Alert** from the drop down as shown below.

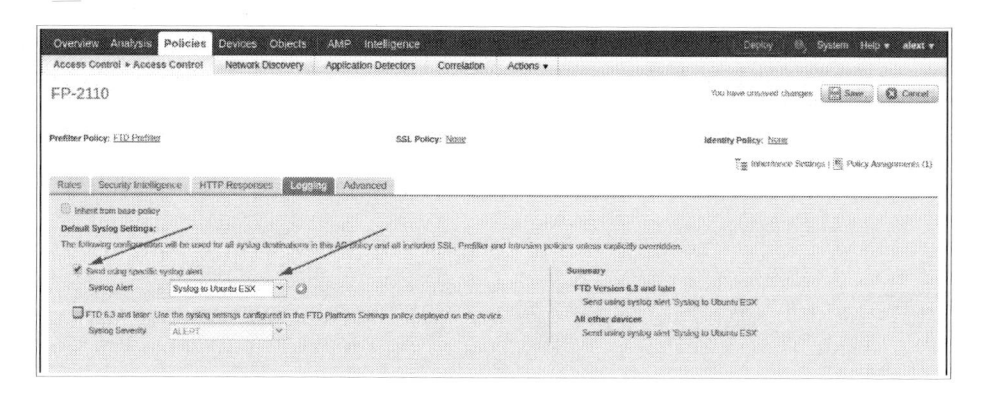

Then when you edit your rules, your logging tab would appear similar to the figure below.

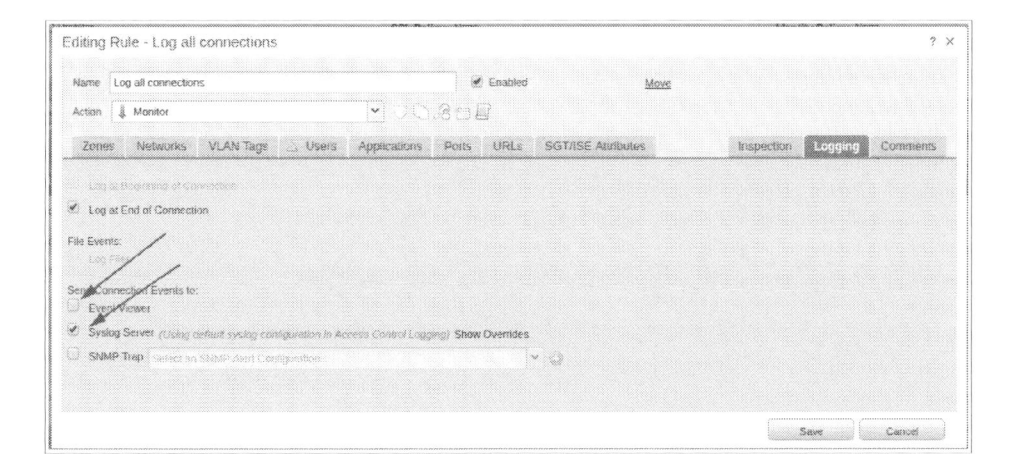

1. Check your logging preference (Beginning/End/both). In the example above the Monitor rule only allows logging at the end of the connection.
2. Uncheck **Event Viewer** as a logging destination. This means we won't send the connection event to the FMC.
3. Check **Syslog Server**, no need to select a server because we did that on the **Logging** tab.

Using this technique you can direct connection events to the FMC, the SIEM or both if desired.

One last comment to make sure there's no confusion. Any events sent to the FMC travel via the management tunnel on port 8305/tcp. In the example above, events are sent to the SIEM via syslog on 514/udp. This port can be customized in your alert configuration.

Trust/Fastpath/Bypass

We've discussed how to fastpath and trust traffic as well as using Intelligent Application Bypass (IAB) to bypass large flows. This section will be a summary of some thoughts on which technique is best depending on the type of traffic you want to pass through your devices.

How you bypass traffic depends on a few factors. One of these is the size of the flow (connection) itself. Is it a short-lived, low volume flow? Is it what we would call an "elephant" flow? Also, are you able to consistently identify this flow based on source/destination IP, port,

Essential Firepower

application, etc? How much effort do you want to expend to dig into your connection events and locate possible elephant flows? The table below takes these into consideration and makes some recommendations.

Flow size/duration	Easily identified in rules?	Recommended Method
Small/Short	Yes, by IP/port	Trust rule in AC policy
Small/Short	Yes, by application	Trust rule in AC policy
Large/Long	Yes, by IP/port	Fastpath rule in prefilter* policy or Trust rule in AC policy
Large/Long	Yes, by application	Trust rule in AC policy
Large/Long	No	Intelligent Application Bypass
Large/Long	Yes, but I don't have the time	Intelligent Application Bypass

* Flows bypassed in prefilter skip all inspection including Security Intelligence

As you can see, it's hard to go wrong using trust rules in your Access Control policy. However, these will require some work to identify the right rule parameters. If you simply need to bypass flows primarily based on their duration, speed, size and also take your device performance into account then IAB is a good one stop shop.

> Note: From a performance perspective, a flow needs to be longer than about 20 packets before you will see a performance benefit from Trust/Fastpath. You may want to bypass smaller flows to meet application requirements, but from a Firepower perspective there's no benefit to bypassing these short-lived connections.

The main thing you want to avoid is using prefilter fastpath rules to solve all your problems. Remember that they are promoted to hardware (depending on the device) quickly so they really should only be used for large flows you can identify easily. Also, anything fastpathed through prefilter skips all security checks including Security Intelligence lists - so you better be sure!

Admin Preferences

This is a quick tip about setting preferences for your FMC users. As you may know, you can set preferences for individual users on the FMC by going to **<username>** → **User Preferences** as shown below.

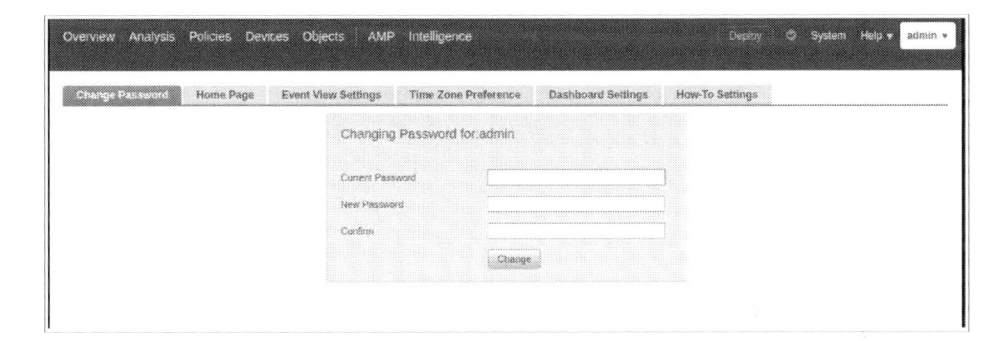

There you will find tabs such as **Change Password**, **Home Page**, **Event View Settings**, etc. I usually mention this to customers, especially when it comes to setting the **Time Zone Preference**. This adjusts the displayed event time stamps to match your selected time zone.

Other settings I like to mention are on the **Event View Settings** tab shown below.

Essential Firepower

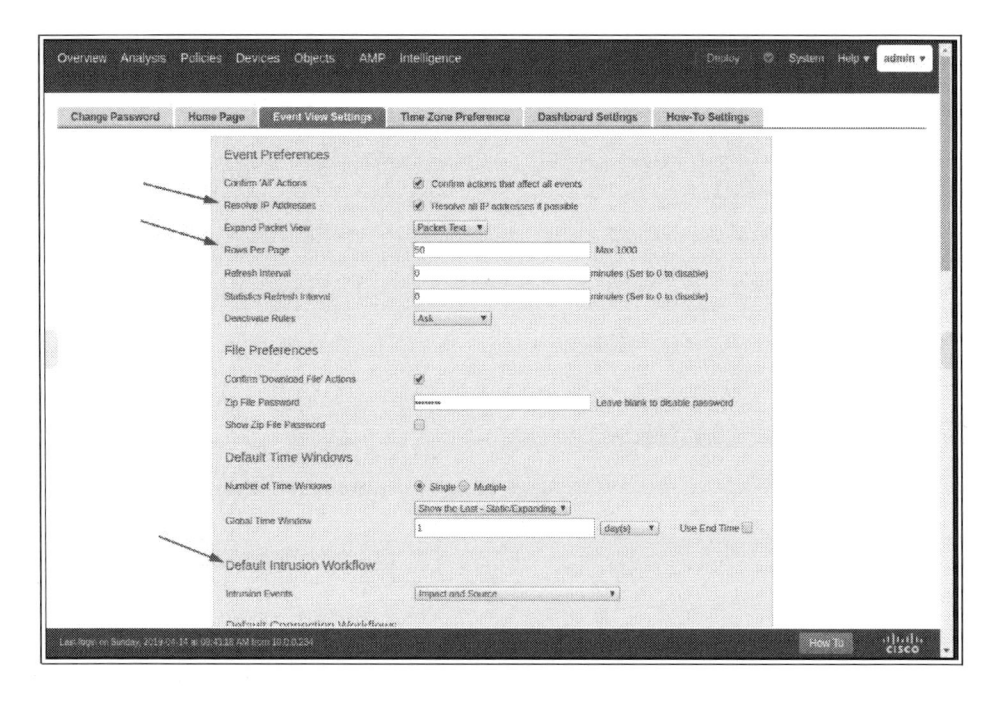

My favorites here are:

- **Resolve IP Addresses** – enabling this option causes the FMC to to a reverse DNS lookup on any IP addresses showing in the various event views. It will then display the hostname along with the IP address. This can be quite helpful when analyzing events. Keep in mind that it will cause quite a few DNS lookups as you navigate the various event pages. However, these lookups are cached so after the initial page load it's usually not too bad. Note however that if your DNS server is slow or misconfigured in the FMC settings this can cause event pages to load very slowly.
- **Rows per page** – this defaults to 25 but if you want to see events in larger chunks then increase this.
- **Default Intrusion Workflow** – Over the years, I have never been a fan of the Default Intrusion Workflow (Events by Priority and Classification). In short - I hate it. I've always hated it, I think there are much better workflows for displaying intrusion event data. Fortunately, I can come here and change the default workflow to any of the built-in selections or a custom workflow I have previously setup. I would encourage you to set the defaults for each workflow type here to your preferred selection. For intrusion events, take a look at any of the workflows with "impact" somewhere in the name.

15 – Misc. Tips and Tricks

Another not-so-commonly-known tidbit is that whatever settings you select here for the Admin account will be used for new account creation from that point forward. This means you can set defaults you think your administrators might appreciate. The biggest one is probably the time zone. If most of your folks are located in the same time zone you can save them all a step and set the time zone for the Admin account to your current location. Just remember this has to be done *before* you create the accounts. Once an account is created, preferences can only be changed when logged in as that user.

Hit Counts

One feature that I see requested often is the ability to see hit counts on Access Control rules. It's been requested often enough that it has been added to the Access Control policy in Firepower version 6.4 (see below). However, you have to have version 6.4 on your FMC and devices to take advantage of this.

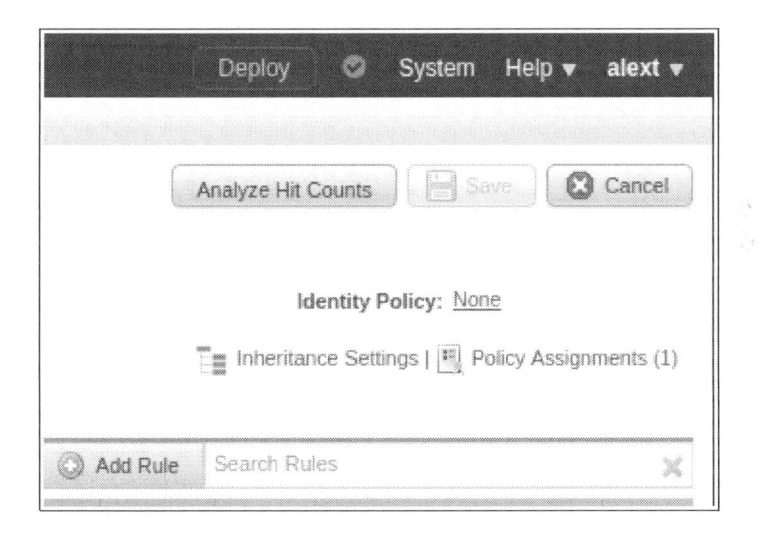

There are still many older Firepower installations where this feature is not available on the FMC. Because of that, I think it warrants some space in this book. This section applies to versions prior to 6.4.

Access Control rule hit counts can help to understand if there are rules in your policy which never match traffic. Let's face it, if a rule never processes traffic, you don't need it. Firewall access lists are notorious for continually growing. Administrators often don't want to

209

run the risk of removing firewall rules because they may be fulfilling some critical business need. The fact is, that firewall rules are seldom documented. This means that once a rule is added to the list, it is probably there for the long haul.

The method I'm going to describe here is to create a custom connection event workflow. This will show the number of connection events generated by each Access Control rule. It can definitely be helpful in determining which of your rules is processing the most traffic and which ones are being skipped altogether. There are a few caveats to this technique.

- The rule must log connection events to the FMC. Rules that don't log connection events or skip the FMC won't appear in this workflow. If you don't log connection events on some or all rules you can temporarily implement this by adding a Monitor rule to the top of your policy. This will log events for any successful connections (Allow, Trust). You will still need to ensure you have logging at the end of the connection enabled for any Block rules.
- Rules with zero hits will not appear in the list. The custom workflow we are going to create is for connection events. So, by definition, there has to be an event for it to show up in the list. If a rule has logging enabled and is not appearing in the workflow you can be pretty certain it's not processing any traffic.

While this method is not fool-proof it does provide some good insight into how your Access Control rules are processing traffic.

Before we get to the workflow itself there is another way you can see rule hit counts. This involves using SSH to connect to the management interface of your Firepower device (not your FMC). Once you connect, the command `show access-control-config` will spit out a summary of the rules and settings in the deployed Access Control policy. One of the pieces of data with each rule is the hit count. The screenshot below shows the command.

15 – Misc. Tips and Tricks

```
alextatistcheff@penguin:~$ ssh admin@10.0.0.29
Cisco FPR Series Security Appliance
admin@10.0.0.29's password:
Last login: Wed Apr 17 02:53:20 UTC 2019 from 10.0.0.234 on pts/0
Successful login attempts for user 'admin' : 3

Copyright 2004-2018, Cisco and/or its affiliates. All rights reserved.
Cisco is a registered trademark of Cisco Systems, Inc.
All other trademarks are property of their respective owners.

Cisco Fire Linux OS v6.3.0 (build 21)
Cisco Firepower 2110 Threat Defense v6.3.0.2 (build 67)

> show access-control-config
```

The command allows you to page through the policy and view each of the rules with their hit counts. Notice in the screenshot below shows two rules. The rule named "Allow WDEX2 Outbound" is processing traffic but my "Trust Mgmt" rule doesn't seem to be matching any connections. Either I haven't made any management connections recently or this traffic is hitting some other rule.

```
   Rule Hits                : 0
   Variable Set             : Default-Set

-----------[ Rule: Allow WDEX2 Outbound ]-----------
   Action                   : Allow
   Intrusion Policy         : Secure IPS
     ISE Metadata           :

   Source Networks          : WD-NAS (10.0.0.201)
   URLs
   Logging Configuration
   DC                       : Enabled
     Beginning              : Disabled
     End                    : Enabled
     Files                  : Disabled
   Safe Search              : No
   Rule Hits                : 2646
   Variable Set             : Default-Set

----------------[ Rule: Trust Mgmt ]----------------
   Action                   : Fast-path
     ISE Metadata           :

   Destination Networks     : ESXi-Mgmt (10.0.0.10)
   Destination Ports        : HTTPS (protocol 6, port 443)
   URLs
   Logging Configuration
   DC                       : Enabled
     Beginning              : Disabled
     End                    : Enabled
     Files                  : Disabled
   Safe Search              : No
   Rule Hits                : 0
   Variable Set             : Default-Set
```

Essential Firepower

Ok, so now that we've seen one way to view rule hits on the device itself, let's look at a custom workflow on the FMC to perform a similar task.

To create a custom workflow, the FMC navigation changed with version 6.3. If you are using a prior version, you'll find the page on the FMC at **Analysis → Custom → Custom Workflows**. However, in 6.3+ it is under **Analysis → Advanced → Custom Workflows.** Either way, once you are there click the **Create Custom Workflow** button in the upper right. At the next screen, give your workflow a name and select the connections database as shown below.

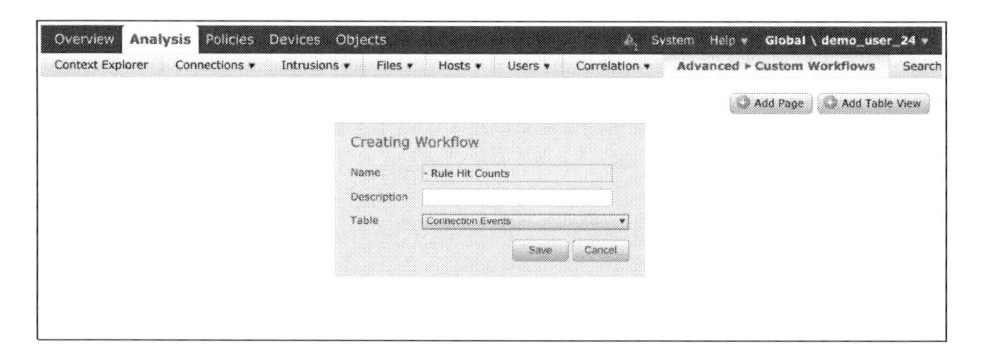

For the workflow name, notice in the example I named it **- Rule Hit Counts**. The important thing to note here is that the workflow name starts with a dash. This is a little trick I use to be able to quickly find my custom workflows.

As you will soon see, when selecting workflows from an event view, they are listed alphabetically. To ensure your workflows always float to the top of the list you can start them with a character like a dash. You'll see how cool that is shortly.

From this screen we're going to add a workflow page, click the **Add Page** button in the upper right. This will load a blank page where you can add columns to your workflow. This is shown below.

15 – Misc. Tips and Tricks

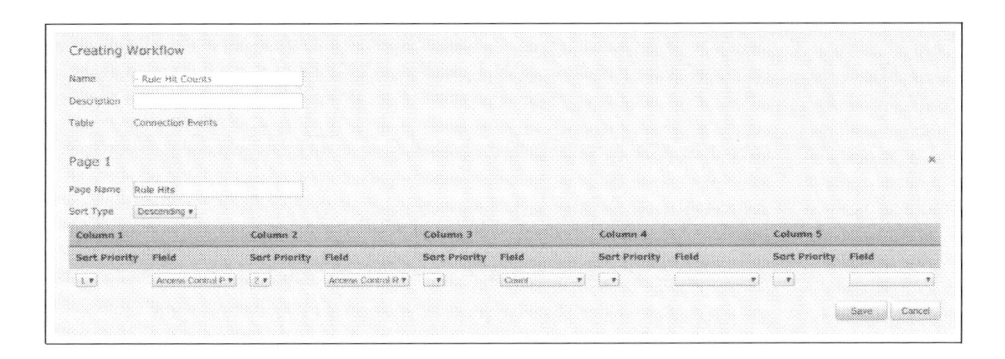

The figure is a little small so I'll describe the fields.

1. **Page Name** – enter something like "Rule Hits"
2. **Column 1 - Sort Priority** – 1
3. **Column 1 - Field** – Access Control Policy
4. **Column 2 - Sort Priority** – <blank>
5. **Column 2 - Field** – Access Control Rule
6. **Column 3 - Sort Priority** – <blank>
7. **Column 3 - Field** – Count

That's all we need for this workflow, now you can click the **Save** button.

To try the workflow out, navigate to **Analysis → Connections → Events**. You will start at the default workflow page. To load a different workflow click **(switch workflow)**. You'll find this just to the right of the current workflow name (probably called **Connection Events)** in red.

When you click **(switch workflow)** you'll see a pop-up list of all your connection workflows. If you named your custom workflow with a dash or other character to sort it to the top you will see your custom workflows first in the list as shown below.

213

Essential Firepower

Connection Events

- Global
- - Rule Hit Counts
- **Connection Events**
- Connections by Application
- Connections by Initiator
- Connections by Port
- Connections by Responder
- Connections over Time
- Traffic by Application
- Traffic by Initiator
- Traffic by Port
- Traffic by Responder
- Traffic over Time
- Unique Initiators by Responder
- Unique Responders by Initiator

If you had not started your workflow name with a dash it would be buried down in the menu and more difficult to find. But you did – you're so clever! Just click your custom workflow name and your rule hit count page should load looking something like the example below.

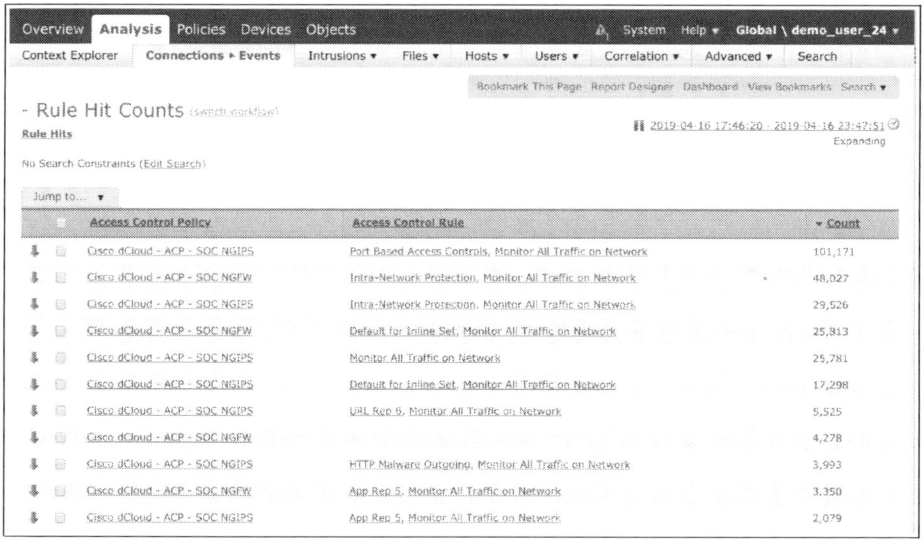
Overview
Analysis
Policies
Devices
Objects
System
Help
Global \ demo_user_24
Context Explorer
Connections ▸ Events
Intrusions
Files
Hosts
Users
Correlation
Advanced
Search
Rule Hit Counts
Rule Hits
No Search Constraints (Edit Search)
Jump to...
Access Control Policy
Access Control Rule
Count
Cisco dCloud - ACP - SOC NGIPS
Port Based Access Controls, Monitor All Traffic on Network
101,171
Cisco dCloud - ACP - SOC NGFW
Intra-Network Protection, Monitor All Traffic on Network
48,027
Cisco dCloud - ACP - SOC NGIPS
Intra-Network Protection, Monitor All Traffic on Network
29,526
Cisco dCloud - ACP - SOC NGFW
Default for Inline Set, Monitor All Traffic on Network
25,813
Cisco dCloud - ACP - SOC NGIPS
Monitor All Traffic on Network
25,781
Cisco dCloud - ACP - SOC NGIPS
Default for Inline Set, Monitor All Traffic on Network
17,298
Cisco dCloud - ACP - SOC NGIPS
URL Rep 6, Monitor All Traffic on Network
5,525
Cisco dCloud - ACP - SOC NGFW
4,278
Cisco dCloud - ACP - SOC NGIPS
HTTP Malware Outgoing, Monitor All Traffic on Network
3,993
Cisco dCloud - ACP - SOC NGFW
App Rep 5, Monitor All Traffic on Network
3,350
Cisco dCloud - ACP - SOC NGIPS
App Rep 5, Monitor All Traffic on Network
2,079

The example above is sorted by Count to show the highest to lowest. Remember, no zero hit rules will be here. To find zero hit rules you will have to compare this list to the rules in your policy to see if there are any that are not present.

Reduce Annoying Pop-up Notifications

You may have noticed that, by default, your system produces pop-up messages in the upper right corner for tasks and other notifications as shown below.

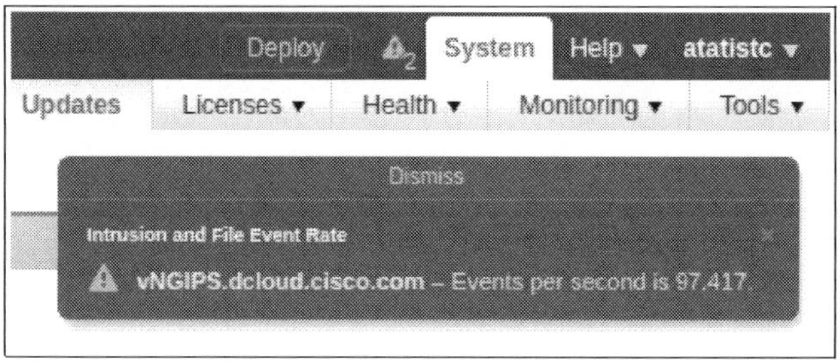
Deploy
System
Help
atatistc
Updates
Licenses
Health
Monitoring
Tools
Dismiss
Intrusion and File Event Rate
vNGIPS.dcloud.cisco.com – Events per second is 97.417.

This seems cool – at first. However, after a while it can get a little annoying. If you want, you can disable this pop-up behavior. To do so, click on the health status icon which is just to the right of the **Deploy** button in your top menu bar. See the screenshot below.

Essential Firepower

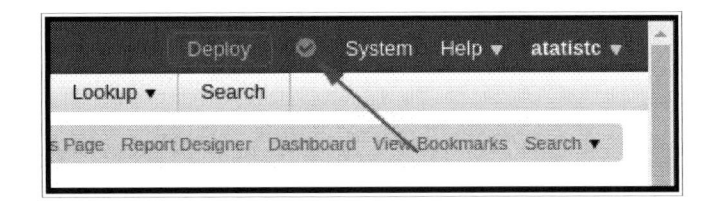

Once there you will see the familiar drop-down section below.

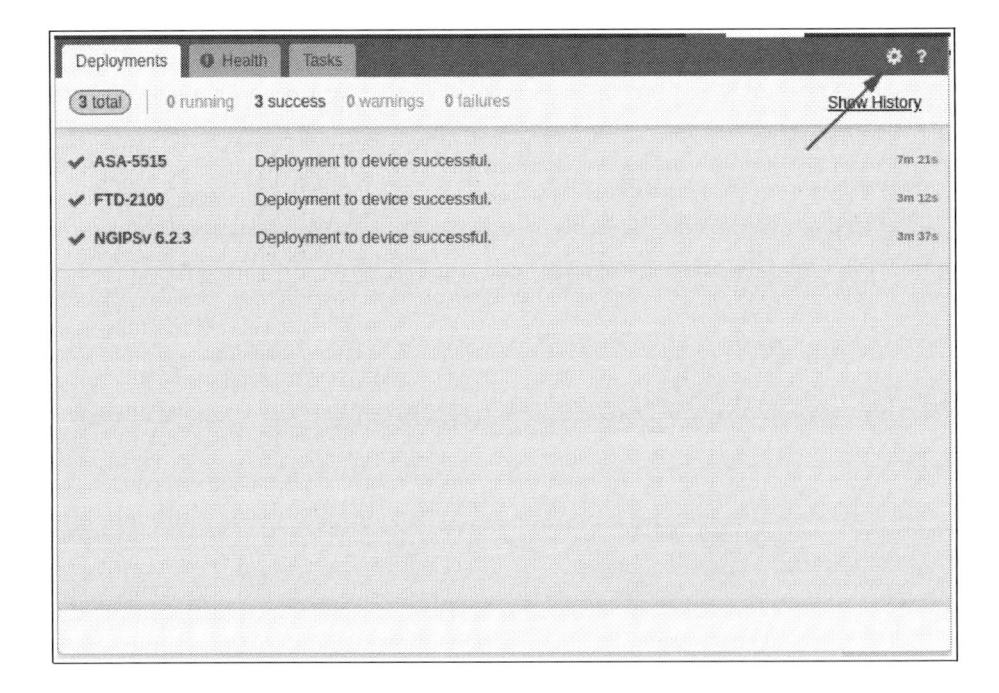

The arrow in the figure above is pointing to the gear icon. This controls these pop-up notifications. Click the gear and then click the switch to slide it to the off position as shown below.

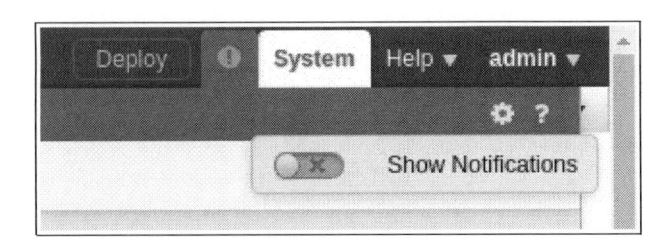

216

The notifications will now stay on their respective tabs (Deployments, Health, Tasks) instead of constantly monopolizing the right side of the screen.

Minimizing Network Impact

In this section I want to address some of the ways that Firepower can pass traffic to prevent impacting the network. What I mean by this is there are some cases where traffic can pass through a Firepower device with no inspection or reduced inspection. I already discussed methods for selectively bypassing flows based on trust or fast path rules. This section discusses traffic that passes through because of bandwidth or capacity issues on the device.

Allowing packets to pass without inspection is usually done in the interest of preventing the device from impacting legitimate business or user traffic. It's the trade-off between security and connectivity where – when push comes to shove – connectivity wins.

The methods discussed here include:
- Intelligent Application Bypass (IAB)
- Automatic Application Bypass (AAB)
- Packet Performance Monitoring (PPM)
- Rule Performance Profiling (also PPM)
- Snort busy/down

Intelligent Application Bypass (IAB)

We already discussed IAB in Chapter 14. It's included here in the interest of completeness. IAB is used to set thresholds for traffic flows which, if exceeded, allow the flow to pass at higher speed and without deep packet inspection. It is not enabled by default but you can enable and tune it so it only passes the flows you identify.

Automatic Application Bypass (AAB)

AAB has been around for quite a while. It is currently disabled by

Essential Firepower

default but in older versions this setting was enabled by default. To get there, navigate to **Devices → Device Management**, then click the edit pencil by a device. You can find this setting on your device's **Device** tab near the bottom in the **Advanced** section. (See the screenshot below)

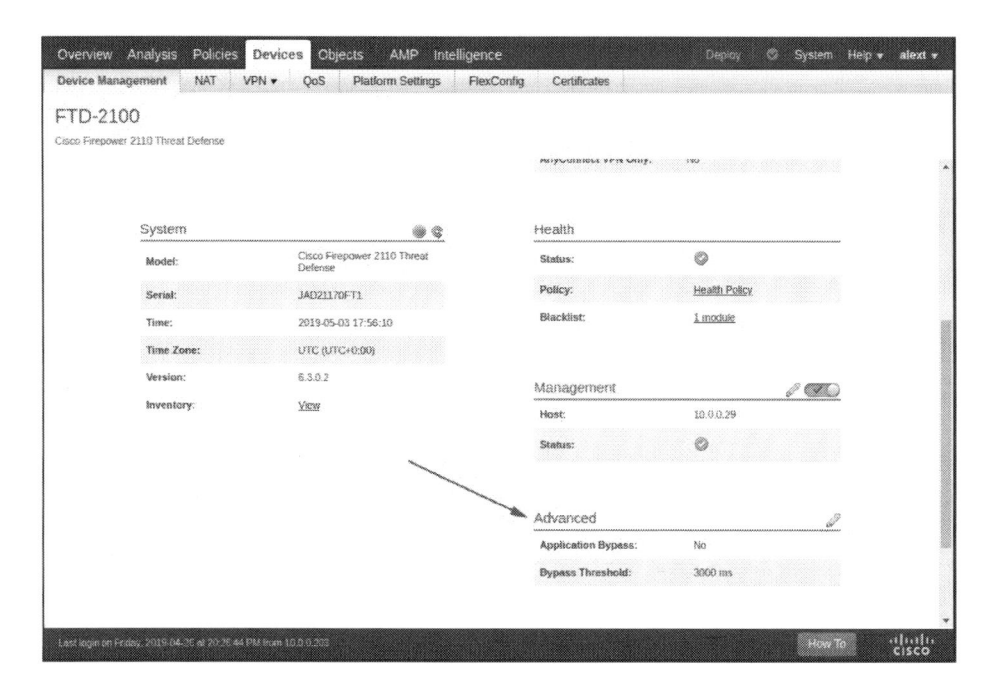

Clicking the edit pencil on this section brings up the dialog below.

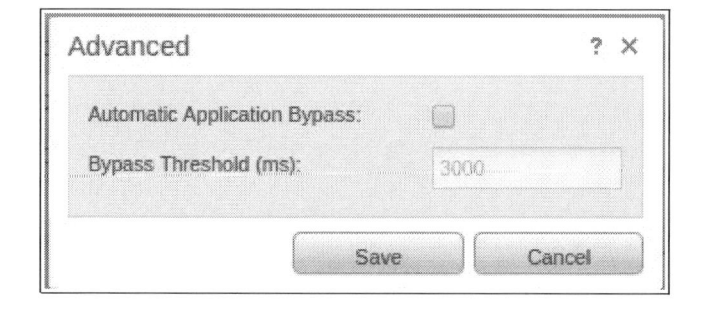

The default **Bypass Threshold** is 3000ms (3 seconds). This feature is designed to allow traffic to bypass Snort if something goes horribly wrong with the detection process. The help suggests this would be a misconfiguration or malfunction within Snort. Of course, anytime Snort hangs on to a packet for 3 seconds – something is wrong!

15 – Misc. Tips and Tricks

If this threshold is triggered, the device shuts down the Snort process and generates a memory core dump. You will find these core files on the device in **/ngfw/var/common** or **/var/common** depending on your Firepower/FTD version. Snort goes into software bypass and traffic flows through uninspected. Within 10 minutes a watchdog process will realize that Snort has stopped and restart the detection processes.

As you may have guessed, this is bad. It is not something you ever want to see happen on your device. You will get a health alert indicating it has occurred and you will want to call Cisco support and send them the core files for analysis. However, it's not as bad as stopping traffic completely which is why this feature exists.

When I explain this, I use the analogy of your hot water heater tank. Mine is in the garage. It has a safety valve on the top which is designed to release pressure if it gets too high. This is better than the tank exploding but the released steam and water will still make a mess. AAB is like that – better than stopping traffic but still kind if messy.

Packet Performance Monitoring (PPM)

PPM is another feature of Snort which provides a way to pass traffic before it starts to impact applications or users. It covers two specific areas:

1. Packet Latency
2. Rule Latency

Packet Latency

As each packet enters Snort a timer is started. It is then checked at various points throughout the inspection process. If the microsecond threshold set for this timer is exceeded then the packet is forwarded through the device. This prevents a single packet from gumming up the works and stopping other packets from being processed.

You can find this setting in the Access Control policy **Advanced** tab under **Latency-Based Performance Settings** as shown below.

Essential Firepower

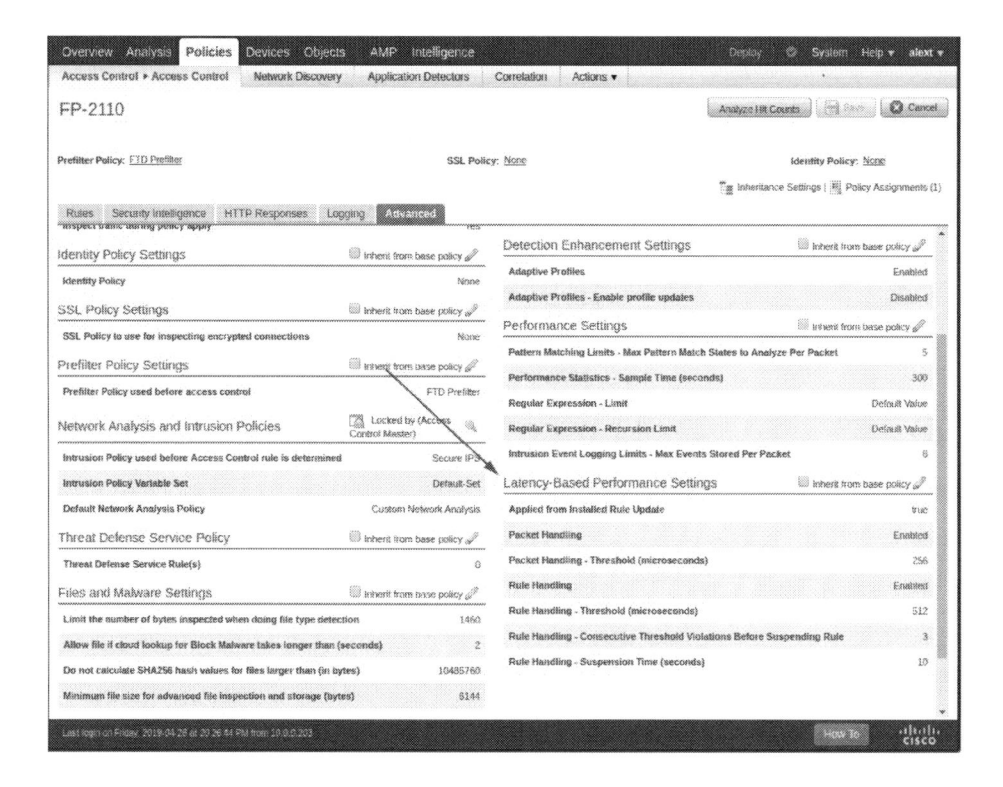

Clicking the pencil icon brings up the dialog below.

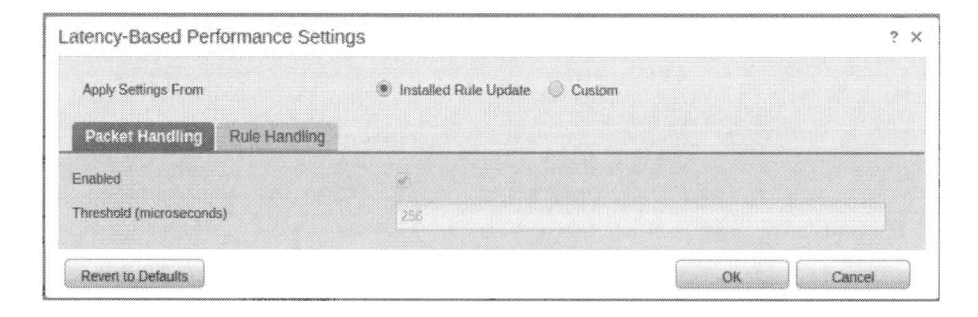

It may be hard to read because the value is greyed out but the default setting is 256 microseconds. This means that any time a packet exceeds this value during Snort processing it will be fast pathed.

This could be due to some kind of anomaly within the packet, it could be that there are too many Snort rules that are configured to inspect it, or it could be something else entirely. The process that Snort goes through to determine if it has to actually inspect a packet payload is quite complex and interesting but not one we have room for here. The bottom line is that something is causing the packet to take too long and so it is being forwarded without full inspection.

Rule Latency

Rule latency is another setting you'll see under **Latency-Based Performance Settings**. The figure below shows the dialog with the **Rule Handling** tab selected.

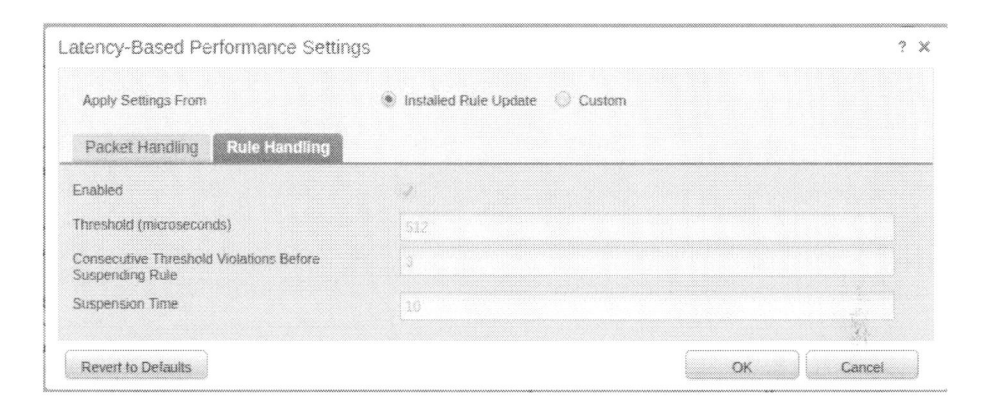

Again, the numbers are grey, so here are the values:

- **Threshold (microseconds)**: 512
- **Consecutive Threshold Violations Before Suspending Rule**: 3
- **Suspension Time**: 10 (seconds)

Similar to packet latency, there is a timer that is maintained every time a rule tree processes a packet. This keeps track of how rules are performing. The purpose of this setting is to identify rules that are performing poorly.

By default, if a rule exceeds the microsecond threshold (512 microseconds) for three consecutive packets, it is disabled for 10 seconds.

The idea is that the rule seems to be having a problem with the traffic it is currently inspecting. So, rather than slow down the entire flow, Snort will temporarily yank out the rule (actually rule tree but that's yet another story). Of course, this does impact detection because the rule no longer has the opportunity to detect or block. But again, the trade off here is security versus connectivity.

After the **Suspension Time** has elapsed, the rule is put back in play.

Snort Busy/Down

The last area I want to mention here is Snort Busy/Down. This is a setting that only applies when you use an Inline Set on a Firepower Threat Defense (FTD) device. To find this setting, navigate to **Devices → Device Management**. Then click the pencil icon by your device, then click the **Inline Sets** tab. On the Edit Inline Set dialog click the **Advanced** tab as shown below.

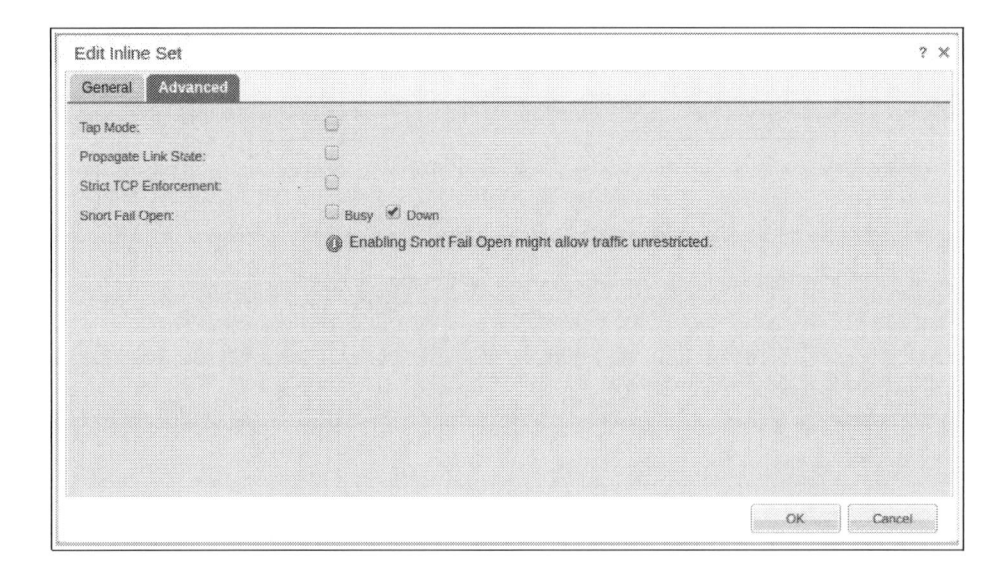

Under **Snort Fail Open:** there are two options:

1. **Busy** – Snort cannot process traffic because the buffers are full. This indicates there is more traffic than the device can handle.
2. **Down** – The Snort process is restarting because you deployed a policy that required a Snort restart.

Based on the advice I have been given from Cisco TAC, you probably do not want to select the **Busy** option. This has to do with how the Lina process hands off traffic to Snort and can result in Snort being bypassed even though it may not actually be very busy. Your mileage may vary, just be sure you understand the ramifications of enabling this setting.

By default only the **Down** option is enabled. This allows traffic to pass uninspected during Snort process restarts. The alternative is to uncheck this box which means there will be a slight pause (several seconds) in traffic passing through the device during a Snort restart.

Take Aways

Now that you know how these various features work, what are the key take aways?

The main thing to remember is that there are settings enabled by default which will kick in and prevent your Firepower device from killing network traffic. The defaults are set to provide inspection but also prevent your devices from slowing down traffic if there are transient network or Snort issues. There is more to say, but digging into Snort internals is beyond the scope of this particular guide. However, this is not off the table for the future!

Appendix A - Preprocessor Generator IDs

ID	Component	Description
1	Standard Text Rule	The event was generated when the packet triggered a standard text rule (Global domain or legacy GID).
2	Tagged Packets	The event was generated by the Tag generator, which generates packets from a tagged session. This occurs when the tag rule option is used.
3	Shared Object Rule	The event was generated when the packet triggered a shared object rule.
102	HTTP Decoder	The decoder engine decoded HTTP data within the packet.
105	Back Orifice Detector	The Back Orifice Detector identified a Back Orifice attack associated with the packet.
106	RPC Decoder	The RPC decoder decoded the packet.
116	Packet Decoder	The event was generated by the packet decoder.
119, 120	HTTP Inspect Preprocessor	The event was generated by the HTTP Inspect preprocessor. GID 120 rules relate to server-specific HTTP traffic.
122	Portscan Detector	The event was generated by the portscan flow detector.

ID	Component	Description
123	IP Defragmentor	The event was generated when a fragmented IP datagram could not be properly reassembled.
124	SMTP Decoder	The event was generated when the SMTP preprocessor detected an exploit against an SMTP verb.
125	FTP Decoder	The event was generated when the FTP/Telnet decoder detected an exploit within FTP traffic.
126	Telnet Decoder	The event was generated when the FTP/Telnet decoder detected an exploit within telnet traffic.
128	SSH Preprocessor	The event was generated when the SSH preprocessor detected an exploit within SSH traffic.
129	Stream Preprocessor	The event was generated during stream preprocessing by the stream preprocessor.
131	DNS Preprocessor	The event was generated by the DNS preprocessor.
133	DCE/RPC Preprocessor	The event was generated by the DCE/RPC preprocessor.
134	Rule Latency Packet Latency	The event was generated when rule latency suspended (134:1) or re-enabled (134:2) a group of intrusion rules, or when the system stopped inspecting a packet because the packet latency threshold was exceeded (134:3).
135	Rate-Based Attack Detector	The event was generated when a rate-based attack detector identified excessive connections to hosts on the network.
137	SSL Preprocessor	The event was generated by the SSL preprocessor.

Essential Firepower

ID	Component	Description
138, 139	Sensitive Data Preprocessor	The event was generated by the sensitive data preprocessor.
140	SIP Preprocessor	The event was generated by the SIP preprocessor.
141	IMAP Preprocessor	The event was generated by the IMAP preprocessor.
142	POP Preprocessor	The event was generated by the POP preprocessor.
143	GTP Preprocessor	The event was generated by the GTP preprocessor.
144	Modbus Preprocessor	The event was generated by the Modbus SCADA preprocessor.
145	DNP3 Preprocessor	The event was generated by the DNP3 SCADA preprocessor.
1000 - 2000	Standard Text Rule	The event was generated when the packet triggered a standard text rule (descendant domains).

Appendix B – Talos Intrusion Policy Criteria

Policy	CVSS Score	Vulnerability Age
Connectivity over Security	10	Current year, plus 2 prior years
Balanced Security and Connectivity	9+	Current year, plus 2 prior years **Rule categories:** Malware-CNC, Blacklist, SQL Injection, Exploit Kit
Security over Connectivity	8+	Current year, plus 3 prior years **Rule categories:** Malware-CNC, Blacklist, SQL Injection, Exploit Kit, App-Detect
Maximum Detection	7.5+	2005 and later **Rule categories:** Malware-CNC, Exploit Kit

Appendix C – Security Intelligence Categories

Security Intelligence Category	Description
Attacker	Active scanners and blacklisted hosts known for outbound malicious activity
Bogon	Bogon networks and unallocated IP addresses
Bots	Sites that host binary malware droppers
CnC	Sites that host command-and-control servers for botnets
Cryptomining	Sites used by cryptomining malware
Dga	Malware algorithms used to generate a large number of domain names acting as rendezvous points with their command-and-control servers
Exploitkit	Software kits designed to identify software vulnerabilities in clients
Malware	Sites that host malware binaries or exploit kits
OpenProxy	Open proxies that allow anonymous web browsing
OpenRelay	Open mail relays that are known to be used for spam
Phishing	Sites that host phishing pages
Response	IP addresses and URLs that are actively participating in malicious or suspicious activity

Security Intelligence Category	Description
Spam	Mail hosts that are known for sending spam
Suspicious	Files that appear to be suspicious and have characteristics that resemble known malware
TorExitNode	Tor exit nodes

Printed in Great Britain
by Amazon